Death 28 10

MW00683070

Cal 28.10   Death

James Clarke

A Mourner's Kaddish

Suicide and the Rediscovery of Hope

A Mourner's Kaddish
Suicide and the Rediscovery of Hope

James Clarke

NOVALIS

© 2006 Novalis, Saint Paul University, Ottawa, Canada

Cover design and layout: Audrey Wells

Business Office:
Novalis
10 Lower Spadina Avenue
4th Floor
Toronto, ON
M5V 2Z2

Phone: 1-800-387-7164
Fax: 1-800-204-4140
E-mail: cservice@novalis-inc.com
www.novalis.ca

Library and Archives Canada Cataloguing in Publication

Clarke, James
    A mourner's Kaddish : suicide and the rediscovery of hope / James Clarke.

ISBN 2-89507-693-6

    1. Clarke, James–Diaries. 2. Suicide–Psychological aspects. 3. Suicide
victims–Family relationships. 4. Bereavement–Psychological aspects.
5. Loss (Psychology). I. Title.

BF575.G7C53 2006   155.9'37   C2005-907572-4

Printed in Canada.

Poetry by James Clarke is reprinted by permission of Exile Editions, Toronto, Canada.
Selections from "Hogg, The Seven Last Words" by Barry Callaghan are reprinted by
permission of Barry Callaghan.

We acknowledge the financial support of the Government of Canada through the Book
Publishing Industry Development Program (BPIDP) for our publishing activities.

5 4 3 2 1   10 09 08 07 06

I dedicate this book to my wife,
Mary Elizabeth Clarke
(March 5, 1938 – April 8, 1990),
my children,
Adele, Paul, Marilyn, Mira, Ruth and Joy,
and my nephew Stephen

Hope

Death
like the night
only
darkens
the
door
of
day
at dawn
long
enough
to
disappear

Barry Callaghan
"Hogg, The Seven Last Words"

Contents

Foreword

By Barry Callaghan

Suicide is an end for the person who has jumped to her death, but it is a beginning for those left behind. It is a terrible beginning because – as Plato said somewhere – staring at death, staring into the black hole of nothing – is the beginning of philosophy. Since we can know nothing about being dead, we can only try to know something about being alive.

To know the play of perspectives, the play of possibilities: Life as a cankered rose, or life as a rose in a canker.

But suicide is the utter and complete rejection of perspective and possibilities. The suicide is a killer.

Unlike any other killer, the suicide gets away with murder while the lovers left behind get punished for the crime.

Since suicide is an act that is inexplicable – that is, the killing of one's self – the achieved dead-end ends up as beginnings: –

The beginning of horror, of guilt, of remorse, of mourning, of blame, of tenderness, of renewed love but a love to be forever unrequited, of resentment, of anger – unrelenting anger, at oneself, at the suicide, at God – the interminable questioning of God while resurrecting past joys, past passions, past affections, followed by repeated penances, and perhaps most painful of all, the silences – the silence of the suicide, the silence of God.

In other words, suicide is the beginning of a consuming obsession – the hour by hour, day by day asking of the question: Why?

And so, suicide, for all its seeming surrender to death, is a defiant, angry act against the living.

This is what James Clarke's book is about.

Clarke has tried, as a judge, poet, loving husband, lover of God – to not only defend life but to affirm life, to redeem life, to redeem even God.

He's done this by turning to all any of us have, memory. Out of memory he has made anecdotes and stories, and out of anecdotes and stories he has made prayers – prayers for his wife, of course, but prayers mostly for the living. Those prayers have often become poems. Songs. He has tried his best to sing life. To celebrate life.

But he is not just a singer.

He is a judge and that has complicated matters for him.

He is in the habit of passing judgment.

He has, of course, done so in the most expected of ways – he has passed judgment on himself.

The loved one blames himself, convicts himself of a crime he did not commit, shows a mercy to the murderer that he does not show to himself...is even ready to forgive – but then, he can't quite do that. He knows that to forgive there must not only be a crime, but an acknowledged crime.

And who is the criminal? His beloved wife.

It has to be said: The loving judge has to judge her of a crime against that which he loves most, life.

He has to, among all his prayers, turn judgment into a prayer, but before he can do that he has to convict her.

Her, not himself.

And so, here is the revelation in this book: whether life is a cankered rose or a rose in a canker, the great mystery at the heart of Christian experience is being played out. In the end is the beginning – and perverse as it may seem – the closer James Clarke comes to that moment when the unforgivable is to be forgiven, the more everything about life seems to come alive for him. Through her death and his loss – a death and a loss he would have done anything to prevent – not just his love of life, his love of her, and his readiness to love anew, but even his faith in God is refreshed, is renewed, and is begun again.

Preface

SEVERAL MONTHS AFTER MY WIFE'S SUICIDE ON APRIL 8, 1990, I BEGAN THIS journal as a way to cope with overwhelming grief. Intermittently over the next two or three years I sat down in the early morning at the computer and allowed my thoughts, feelings and pain to pour out in uncensored, free-association journalling. Healing, not publication, was my goal. At the time I'd read Rabbi Harold Kushner's *When Bad Things Happen to Good People*, a book that crystallized for me some of the anguish I felt over Mary's death. In Kushner's moving account of the death of his son, I encountered for the first time the Jewish prayer for the dead known as Kaddish. In the Jewish tradition this special prayer recited by mourners is not about death, but about life. It praises God for having created a basically good and liveable world. By reciting the prayer the mourner is reminded of all that is good and worth living for. Without denying the tragedy, it insists that everything is for the best and sees the tragedy in the context of a whole life, keeping your eye and mind on what has enriched you and not only on what has been lost. The life-affirming character of the prayer drew me strongly and I adopted the name (I hope not presumptuously) for these journal entries. As Frederick Buechner says, God makes himself known to us powerfully and personally through our stories: trusting each other with our secrets enough to share them with each other has much to do with the secret of what it means to be human. While it may be true, as Oscar Wilde said, that memory is the diary we carry with us, it is also true that it is a frail and fallible instrument. Much has changed since these words were written but they remain my story, warts and all, not my children's or anyone else's, set down in the fire of the moment, a slice of life that doesn't pretend to be objective history or a definitive analysis. Doubtless the story could have been told from many different perspectives. While there has been some editing, the journal is presented largely as it was written. In deciding to share these kaddishes with the public after the passage of so many years, it is my hope that they will be as life-affirming for others as Rabbi Kushner's account was for me. I wish to thank my children for allowing me to tell my story, which is partially their story, too. I am greatly indebted to my editor, Kevin Burns, for his invaluable assistance in bringing form and order to my sometimes chaotic outpourings. The reader should know that these kaddishes have been sequenced thematically, not chronologically, and a few names altered to protect privacy. In referring to the law, I've taken the liberty of changing certain details from the mosaic of cases I've heard over 23 years on the bench. I would be remiss if I didn't also express my gratitude to Anne Louise Mahoney for her help in editing the manuscript. Finally, I thank my friends, mentors and fellow wayfarers Barry Callaghan, Susan Musgrave, John B. Lee, Susan McCaslin, George Whipple and Clair Crowley for their unfailing wisdom and encouragement.

James Clarke
October 2005

A Mourner's Kaddish

⅋

Now that Holy Week's rolled round again I think of you, fallen eleven storeys over Niagara Falls, lying in some deep cavern of silence with the diamond I gave you for our 25th still on your long bony finger, sad because we couldn't hold you, failed to make you feel how deeply madly truly we loved you, stop you from being sucked into the black hole. Sad because I will never hold you again in my arms, kiss your lips or see the goodness shining from your grey-blue eyes; sad, too, because of the gaping wound in our children's hearts. Today in church Ruth broke down sobbing and couldn't be consoled because she doesn't understand why God would allow this to happen to you. Sorrow presses down on all our heads, an unbearable weight, unrelenting and unexplainable, a sorrow that never goes away.

Dream

I swim in the cold grotto of memory,
Past the flotsam, the wavering eel grass,
The silver schools of mackerel, my eyes
A pair of phosphorescent fish, starlight
Thrumming off my shiny scales, thinking
Of you, searching for your hiding place
In the shadowy weeds.

CR

Last night I slept on your side of the bed, the cold moonglare on your pillow, and imagined my body filled the cavity where you used to sleep. I wanted to inhabit your space, feel close to you again. Unlike me you were a sound sleeper and found it trying getting used to my twisting and turning during the night, especially when the nails of my wiggly toes scratched your legs. Sometimes in exasperation you'd grab your pillow and find another bed.

I dreamt I was presiding over a jury trial in Guelph. The case was scheduled
to start at 10 a.m., but for some inexplicable reason I noticed the clock said
3 p.m. and I still hadn't opened court, nor was I even robed. I rushed into my
chambers, where I was shocked to find my robes neatly laid out on a table and
myself lying in them, stone-still, a corpse. In my confusion I couldn't find my
socks and began to fumble around like a drunk when Bourke appeared and
offered help. "Bourke, I'm afraid I'm losing it," I told him. A female juror
stomped by, threw me a dirty look. When I glanced at the clock, it was now
4 p.m. and I still hadn't opened court. Panic gripped me, but just as I was
wondering if this bumbling spelled the end to my career on the bench I woke
up and realized with a huge sigh of relief that it was only a dream. Wow!
What did the dream mean? Maybe all this dwelling on death is affecting my
mind, making me morbid. Sometimes I'm not only badgered by anxieties,
but feel I'm hacking through a thicket of undigested experience. Lately I've
been getting stomach spasms and since you left I've noticed my zest for life
has diminished. In court today I found myself in the middle of a family
war over custody of a young boy and division of matrimonial assets – you
know how wrenching I found these cases. The faces of the man and woman
had put on the sour, purse-mouthed masks of grim litigants; they were even
bickering over ownership of the family pet, a plug named Lucifer. I knew they
couldn't afford costly litigation and urged them and their lawyers – pleaded
would be more accurate – to settle, but no luck; they wanted to fight. I
came home emotionally and physically drained. Later, my good friend Dave
Stewart dropped in and we watched a TV documentary entitled *Fame* together
and it was like entering a time warp, for there they all were, the icons of our
times, like old friends visiting from a far country: Senator McCarthy, Bishop
Sheen, Ed Sullivan, the bobby soxers, Doris Day, Yuri Gagarin, the Beatles,
Marilyn Monroe, James Dean, Brando, Judy Garland, Martin Luther King,
the civil rights marchers, Neil Armstrong and the landing on the moon, Bob
Dylan, the hippies, the savage footage from Vietnam, Bobby and President
Kennedy, etc., etc., etc., and it was as though you and I were together back
again in the cozy den on College Street watching it all for the first time.

When they showed Lee Harvey Oswald being marched through the basement of the Dallas Police Headquarters and Jack Ruby slithering out of the crowd I shouted, "Come here quickly, Mary, someone's going to kill Oswald!" just as I did in 1963 when you rushed out of the kitchen just in time to see my grisly prediction come true. Before he left Dave said I'll have to end these kaddishes sometime and, being the generous-hearted man he is, offered to accompany me to the Falls if I ever decide to go; I thanked him for his offer and told him my healing couldn't be forced, but would be finished in its own good time – that is, if I live long enough. It's a short life.

CR

FOR MONTHS AFTER YOU LEFT US, GRIEF HELD THE BLACK GUN OF despondency to my head. I felt numb and breathless, on the verge of keeling over, as though I'd been punched in the solar plexus, but underneath the numbness I was angry. As the consolations of the memorial service and friends faded and the stark reality of your absence sank in, I had more and more trouble controlling my emotions. Though I tried to stay calm for the sake of the children my nerves were raw, tears never far from my eyes. When the teller at the bank refused to transfer our joint account into my name – Letters-Probate were necessary, she claimed – I blew my stack. "Are you telling me, a judge, what is legally required?" I bellowed, and the manager had to be called over to straighten it out. I seem to recall customers standing about, jaws agape, staring at me as if I were a wild man. Later that same day at the license bureau, where I'd gone to transfer the ownership of the New Yorker to my name and explained to the woman at the counter – I remember she was wearing chunky coral earrings – that I'd recently lost you (did my voice betray self-pity, I wonder?) her cold face showed no reaction. She continued to chew gum and shoved a form across the counter at me. "Sign here," she snapped, as though my personal woes were of no concern to her. I concluded that the living have too many problems of their own to waste time on the bereavement of others, and I had no choice but to place the lingering rawness of my grief in the mouth of language, let this journal grieve for me, but at the time I was angry at the world and anger is a surly, disagreeable fellow no one likes to have around.

CR

COOL DAY; LONG RIFTS OF LIGHT RIPPLED ACROSS THE CLOUDS BRIGHTENING the sky; Highway 401 was full of bumps and cracks, scars of winter I hadn't noticed before. Yesterday in court I heard the case of a widow who was being sued for a rebate because she'd sold a lot 150 feet deep, which a subsequent survey revealed to be 7 feet short. I knew she couldn't afford a three-day trial so I called a last-minute settlement meeting in my chambers. When I heard the widow explain, "I didn't try to cheat anyone," I knew immediately that it wasn't the rebate that was sticking in her craw, but the stigma of having done something dishonourable and deceitful. After I assured her that she had made an honest mistake, that there had been nothing morally reprehensible in her conduct, a settlement was quickly reached. Litigation isn't always about greed. How do you cope with a banged-up heart? Immersing myself in the law every day has proved a blessing, a saving routine that keeps the furies at bay. I'm amazed how the left brain can continue to function despite the presence of the Black Dog. Depression does not stop me from dancing with my skeletons in this journal, nor impair my judgment in court. But today when a sad-eyed widow – a star of David on her lapel – took the witness stand and mentioned that her late husband had hanged himself from a beam in the basement of their home, my grief surged back, and when tears began to well I called a recess and stayed in my chambers until I'd recovered my composure. But it isn't always like this. Often you'll slip into my thoughts on tiptoe, linger a few moments and just as quietly leave.

Rain

Listening
to the expert drone on
the judge scarcely heard the drumming
on the courthouse roof
as he drifted away to
another time,

where huddled under the Norman Tower,
they gazed at dark clouds
over the Cliffs of Moher
and listened to the crashing
surf.

"You died, I was alone," she said.
He touched her hand, kissed her brow,
told her it was only a dream, but
her tears fell like rain,
as the witness, nodding
to the ceiling, said,
"Quite a storm."

CR

THE DAY OF YOUR SUICIDE THE CHILDREN AND I WERE IN A TRANCE, DRIFTED
around the house like zombies, our swollen faces reflecting the red hot pain
folded inside us, our brokenness. Sobs and moans replaced speech. That first
night no one wanted to sleep alone; instinctively everyone gathered in our
bedroom as though the solidarity of being together could lighten the crushing
weight of our sorrow. I slept on the old mahogany bed, Mira and Joy cradled

in my arms while the others stretched out on the carpet. All night I listened to their groans and sobs, too stricken and powerless to lift a finger.

Yes, I uttered the stock platitudes: how you were happy with the Father in Heaven, that you wanted everyone to be brave, etc., but my words came back to mock me, broke like frail sticks in my mouth. The transcendent little bird of hope, Dickinson's "thing with wings," had flown from our life. But somehow we got through the night; huddled together with the children on our common bed of pain made me feel our family was still alive and intact.

The Caterpillar

You spotted the caterpillar
on the road,
green glass inching along
in the noon sun
on nubby pairs of feet.

And when you held her
in your palm
the caterpillar spun
into a ball
of jade.

After the police left that evening
the children came to our bed;
somehow it felt safer there,
coiled,
soft as broken wings.

CR

DEAR GOD, WHERE HAVE YOU BEEN HIDING? I FEEL SOMETIMES LIKE NORMAN Beale in the movie *Network* and I want to scream, "I'm sick and tired and am not taking it anymore!" In court this afternoon a young woman pleaded guilty to impaired driving causing death; she had changed lanes on a busy street and ploughed her luxury car into the back of a Pony that had stopped for a pedestrian on the crosswalk.

The force of the collision was so powerful it hurled the Pony sideways into a concrete telephone pole and cleaved it in two. The driver of the Pony, a middle-aged man, was crushed behind the wheel and died in hospital ten days later. At the scene the woman appeared glassy-eyed and unsteady, the officer testified, kept insisting in a slurred voice that she'd done nothing wrong, that it was the other driver's fault.

As the crown recited the facts, the woman slumped in the accused's box, face downcast, chewed her lower lip and now and then dabbed Kleenex on her wet cheeks. At the time of the accident the victim, a long-time volunteer with the disabled, was on his way to Kelso ski hill to teach downhill skiing to disabled children. Two victims here: a husband with a wife and two children, and a young woman who would have to live the rest of her days with the knowledge of having snuffed out the life of a good man. Sometimes being a judge and sitting in judgment of others seems unnatural, even frightening. Yes, I know I represent Justice, and as society's surrogate part of my job is to absolve the innocent and punish the guilty. Yet I, too, feel helpless before the reality of death and sorrow and guilt; I, too, am wounded and in need of healing, a victim carrying a load of guilt over your death and no silk robe or red sash to hide my nakedness.

CR

LAST EVENING ON TV, MARGARET LAURENCE SAID THAT FEW SERIOUS writers write for immortality; they write because they have to or to put bread on the table. There is a counterforce not to write. Instead of sitting down to write we prefer to sharpen pencils or pick lint off the carpet. Sometimes it takes a jolt like your suicide to crack the shell around the heart, set the words in motion. Your suicide up-ended my applecart, scattered all my precious apples on the ground. Before I put them back I want to examine them carefully, know the load I will be carrying, the direction of the market. I desire to bite into the apples and savour their tart sweetness before I die. But nature can be gracious. Something unexpected always bursts forth to counter my gloomy thoughts and lighten my path. Like listening to Bach's "Magnificat" on the CBC this morning. Choral singing stirs me deeply. It hints at a harmony and unity I've always longed for, a prefiguration of a more perfect society, far removed from the fractious and smudgy laundry of the law. Today on the 401: the white circle of sun surrounded by a pink haze fading into pure blue followed me like a celestial searchlight all the way to the courthouse – a good omen. A beautiful spring day that lifted my spirits and gave me a stab of joy, a feeling I haven't had much in my life lately. Is joy a sign of God in us?

Unexpected Gift

After dismissing the sexual
assault charge because the Crown
had failed to prove its case
beyond a reasonable doubt

the judge observed the accused,
a free man now, smirk
as he shook the hand
of counsel.

Entering his chambers, the judge
met the interrogating
eyes of his five daughters on
his desk (how can you ever

explain that probable guilt
is never enough?)
and his spirit began to sink
in the spongy bog

of an imperfect justice system,
till he heard someone
outside his window
in the April sunshine, whistling,

the kind of tuneless
whistling you do when Spring
unfurls its new flags, trembles
with green mercy.

CR

YOUR SUICIDE WAS LIKE A FIST IN THE TEETH; I WAS KNOCKED REELING AND
confused. Hundreds of friends, acquaintances and family packed St. Joseph's
church in Guelph for the memorial service – a busload even drove in from
Cobourg – and the church overflowed, many standing outside in the spring
sunshine, the only tangible evidence of you a blown-up colour photograph at
the altar. Our faith is not for getting around grief, but for getting us through
it; not for denying bodily mortality (the body seen only as spiritual shell), but
for confronting its reality. The absence of your body cast an air of unreality
over the memorial service, made closure more elusive. You were a people
person and touched many in your short life. The kids and I were surprised
and amused by the number of your women friends who confided you were
their best friend. Everyone tried to be helpful and consoling but they were
as perplexed by your death as we were and, not knowing what to say, some
fell back on the usual clichés: "You can be certain she's with the Father in

Heaven," "God sends suffering on those he loves most," "God gives us the strength to carry our cross," and so on – bromides that perhaps work better for those who are sure of their spirituality or who consider themselves saved, but didn't work for us. Faith doesn't wrap you in a bubble. As someone said, the opposite of faith is not doubt, but certainty. In the face of the mystery of your death, was everyone just whistling in the dark, I reflected afterwards, for it seemed as though we'd all lost our water wings, didn't know how to tread water in the dark whirlpool you created.

Proper Burial

We must give them a proper burial
the poet from Jamaica said
of the 25,000 slaves
destined for the islands
pitched into a watery grave.

O how we tried to give you a proper burial
that sunny afternoon in Easter week,
while your portrait gazed at us
from the sanctuary,

sprinkling you with holy water,
robing you with incense,
singing till we could no longer hear
your unquiet spirit. And still

at Eastertide I sometimes hear
lilies weeping in the sun, your voice
like Niagara, roaring in the night.

Since your death I've become even more acutely sensitive to injustice.

In court today a bank sought judgment on a promissory note against a woman with three small children whose husband had abandoned her. The husband, who had pressured her into co-signing the note, squandered the funds on gambling and booze and later defaulted on the debt. His whereabouts was unknown. The woman lived in a dingy apartment and was struggling to raise the family on $25,000 a year as a clerk in a department store, with no support and no savings. I asked the bank's dapper Bay Street lawyer if he wanted to pursue the lawsuit.

"Of course," he answered, in a tone that suggested he was offended by my suggestion. "She co-signed the note."

"But you can't get blood from a stone?"

"The law's the law," he said testily, and I could feel my blood begin to boil.

A judge is sworn to render justice according to the law, not his private conscience, I knew, but I also knew the law could sometimes be an ass. Though the lawyer made a strong case I ruled against the bank, citing "duress and coercion" in the co-signing of the note. The lawyer immediately shot to his feet, ramrod straight.

"But, your Honour," he protested, but I cut him off.

"That's my decision," I said. "If you don't like it, appeal," and left the courtroom.

Back in chambers I began to wonder if your suicide wasn't influencing my judgment. Was I starting to play God, I asked myself, compensating for his/her failure to save you from the Black Dog, to stop you falling into the narrow house of death?

"O Lord, send my roots rain."

Dream

We're driving across the Arizona desert.
Suddenly a storm blows up, sticks, sand, tumbleweeds bounce across the
pavement, a tumbleweed snags the bumper like a burr. We decide to stop
the van, wait out the storm. I want to have sex but she isn't interested.
Now the wind picks up, leans on the van, shakes it like a toy. Outside
everything is bathed in eerie, yellow light, a nether world between life
and death.

∝

YOUR SUICIDE MADE ME MORE SENSITIVE TO THE FALLOUT FROM ADULT
behaviour on children. Contrary to popular belief, it's family cases, not
criminal cases, that most judges find distressing. Nothing is more heart-
rending for a judge than to see children caught in the murderous crossfire of
a headbanging couple duelling in the name of love, especially where the desire
to win at all costs, grind the other into the dust, fuels the litigation. Children
rarely come out winners.

Today in court, during a bitter custody battle over two young twin girls,
I was aghast to learn that the parties, both high-school teachers, had spent
all their equity from the sale of the matrimonial home on legal fees – almost
$150,000. "You've shot yourselves in the foot," I told them as their lawyers
nodded in agreement. "The money should have gone to your children, not
your lawyers' pockets." If the strength of a legal system is its ability to be
accessible to all, then we've failed. Justice has become too expensive for the
majority of the middle class. The question "How much justice can you
afford?" is no joke. The much-touted phrase "access to justice" may suggest
the power to transform, but in reality justice favours the rich. For a long time
after your suicide, I was immobilized by a feeling of unfairness; you didn't

deserve to die this way. The question "Why do bad things happen to good people?" skewered my thinking. How easy to slip into self-pity, the "poor me" syndrome. Was it self-pity or mental paralysis that blinded me to the reality that unfairness runs through all of life like a fault line?

In the War Zone

of family court everyone
        is always racing somewhere:
spouses race to make war,
        judges and lawyers race
to make words,
        write dispatches and
children race to make trenches,
        cover their faces,
listen to the distant artillery fire.

ભ

DRIVING TO EAST SIDE MARIO'S FOR DINNER, JOY SAID THAT WHEN WE DIE we slip into a dreamless sleep, like the void before birth, and never wake up. Some people believe that, I told her, but as a Christian I didn't. I was putting on a brave front for her sake, for although I cling to belief in an afterlife – the thought of never seeing you again is unbearable – I'm often racked with doubt, with fear that life is random and meaningless and that God is more an earthquake than a nice uncle. Remember how upset and frustrated I'd get when I took Paul to hockey and a referee would turn his back and do nothing when Paul was unfairly bodychecked or tripped? Sometimes I think of God as a blind referee who lets the game go on without penalties. Though I want to believe, as a judge I find it how hard to credit this feckless God-referee. In *When Bad Things Happen to Good People*, Rabbi Kushner postulates a God who doesn't will evil – even weeps with us – but is impotent to stop it; yet this same God, despite his/her impotence, widens our hearts, gives us the strength to go on. Leon Bloy said, "There are places in the human heart that do not yet exist and into them enters suffering so that they may have existence." When Doris and Norm, our neighbours at the lake, came to our rescue and took charge of meals, the laundry, and the million other practicalities of daily living, they had no inkling that within a month of your death Norm's only daughter and son-in-law would be incinerated in a freak accident on the 401. I vividly remember the morning Doris came over to our cottage with the news, asked me to come over, and how I found everyone sitting around with a beer, dry-eyed and stoical, discussing the accident as if it had happened to strangers. Still raw and bleeding inside, I went into an emotional meltdown and began to bawl like a baby, and though I felt like an idiot, wrapped my arm around Norm's shoulder, kissed him on the cheek and led him into a bedroom where he was able to drop the mask and let the tears unabashedly flow, at first fitfully, then in torrents, from the deepest core of his being. I couldn't have done that before your suicide.

CR

WHY AM I WRITING THESE KADDISHES? MEMORY IS THE SENSE OF LOSS, AND loss pulls us after it. Writing these kaddishes is a raid on the inarticulate, a way of ensnaring the past in a web of words, enfleshing memory so that it can fulfill itself. There's nothing extraordinary about what happened to you: suicide's an old sad story everyone's heard a thousand times. But I read somewhere that though the story remains the same, the individual experience makes it unique, that it's not the song but the singer that counts. In reflecting upon your death I've sometimes felt that I was being self-indulgent and narcissistic. With millions all over the globe perishing each day from wars, genocides, AIDS, tsunamis, famines and other calamities, how significant is one life? History could make a stone weep. And yet all tragedy and sorrow ultimately reduces itself to a single face. The Talmud says to save one life is to save the world. Though the mind boggles before the immensity of suffering, the heart is stirred most deeply by the loss of a loved one.

In the Jewish tradition, a kaddish is not about death, but a prayer about life; there's a crucial difference between denying the tragedy and seeing it in the context of a whole life, keeping your eye and mind on what has blessed you and not only what you have lost. In his book *The Clown in the Belfry*, Frederick Buechner quotes a definition of writing by Red Smith: "Writing is really quiet simple; all you have to do is sit down at your typewriter and open a vein" – a definition that seems to define the bloodletting of these kaddishes. In baring my soul about you and the things that touched me to the quick I'm not trying so much to catch the eye of the world as to come to terms with the demons of being human, save my life. Maybe if I write passionately and truthfully enough others will be touched. At least, this is my hope.

The Present Folds into the Past

☙

DO YOU REMEMBER THE FIRST TIME WE MET? I WAS IN SECOND-YEAR LAW school and had gone home for the weekend. I'd arrived back at Union Station in Toronto and was walking to my room on Spadina Avenue along Prince Arthur Street when I heard music. I stopped, glanced around. The music was coming from the Newman Centre, a gathering place for Catholic students, where I knew they held a dance every Sunday evening. Curiosity piqued, I decided to drop in for a few minutes.

I set down my small black cardboard suitcase, which also doubled as my briefcase (the ugly one with floral interior I'd bought at Zellers that you thought was so hideous), in the vestibule and looked around. Subdued light flickered on floor, ceiling and walls.

A large crowd, all strangers to me, milled about in small groups; a few couples were dancing to the current hits, which the young disc jockey was playing with plenty of teasing advice from a bevy of females. My eye caught you on the perimeter of the dance floor talking a blue streak (did you ever talk any other way?) with another young woman. I recall you were dressed in a light blue crinoline dress and had your dark brown hair in an upsweep that accented your long neck and made you look tall and elegant. I glimpsed too your narrow waist and large grey-blue eyes, which sparkled with laughter. I finally screwed up enough courage to ask you for a dance, sidled over and tapped you on the shoulder. Later you told me that you'd seen me first, a dishevelled figure in a ratty tweed jacket with cracked leather patches on the elbows which, when I later discovered how observant you were, didn't surprise me.

From the first dance our personalities meshed. I was shy and hadn't dated much but you were a good dancer and your questions made me feel attractive and special. Even then you wore a mask, for I found out later that you were there on the rebound, feeling in the dumps, having just broken up with someone you liked who'd stood you up. I think we danced every number and talked about everything: our families, our careers, the law, art, what we wanted out of life (as if we knew). Art had always fascinated me and I peppered you with questions about the Ontario College of Art, your chosen field as a fashion illustrator, your theories of art, etc., and as we talked

I noticed your eyes glowed and your words became passionate. Art was your life. By the end of the evening we were spilling our guts to each other like two soulmates. Your mom told me later that I was the only one of your boyfriends who ever showed an interest in your art. I had a large box of Smarties in my trouser pocket that evening, remember, and as we swirled around the floor the Smarties kept trickling out and bouncing around the polished hardwood. I tried to retrieve them but there were too many and I soon gave up. I put the box in another pocket and while other dancers gaped and laughed the spillage continued. All my pockets, it turned out, were ripped at the seams. I felt like a klutz but it struck you funny. After the dance we went to a restaurant nearby and I treated you to lemon meringue pie and a glass of milk (all I could afford) and we continued our breathless conversation. When I complimented you on your strong artistic hands I recall how ill at ease you were and how quickly you changed the subject. And when I learned you were only eighteen, still a teenager, my jaw dropped. (I was an ancient 23 at the time.) "Why, you're younger than my kid sister!" I exclaimed. I offered to take you home and you told me you lived at the end of the Bloor streetcar run, that it was too far, but I insisted. We made a date on your front porch for a movie the following Saturday and I left. No kisses that evening, just a polite and tremulous handshake. But when I got back to my room, I knew a rich new vista had opened up in my life.

CR

FOR MONTHS AFTER YOUR SUICIDE, WHEN PERIODICALLY THE NUMBNESS would wear away and my boundless sense of loss would break through like a clearing in a fog, I'd feel overwhelmed and physically weak, almost to the point of vertigo. The reality was too much for my puny mind to take in and there were moments I entertained the fantasy that perhaps a mistake had occurred, that maybe you'd faked your death to get away, or run off with a lover and were living in some quiet trailer park in Florida, and that eventually you'd come to your senses and return. Many nights I'd awaken with a start, believing you were still beside me in the bed and all I had to do was reach over to touch your warm flesh again.

Revenant

Woke up suddenly – a nightshift
of crickets outside our bedroom
window, thinking
– only for the briefest moment –
you were there beside me on the bed and
I could breathe your breath in the blue night
air, deeply, slowly,

reached across the sheets to touch
your cheek – stopped, remembered;
the moonlight on your pillow cold.

CR

IN TALKING ABOUT YOUR DEATH, OUR FRIEND BILL CLARKE S.J. USED AN expression that startled me at first: he said you'd gone "home." But on reflection I thought how appropriate, for all your life you were quintessentially a homemaker, one who created roots for me, the children and others, a place where we could feel connected and secure. Even Simcoe Street, my precarious foothold in a sometimes cold and hostile world for the first eighteen years of my life, had hints of that other place, the secret garden, the lost Eden. As a boy I had a powerful urge to locate myself, affirm my place in the universe. All my schoolbooks bore the same inscription:

JAMES HENRY CLARKE
249 SIMCOE STREET,
PETERBOROUGH,
ONTARIO,
CANADA,
NORTH AMERICA,
THE SOLAR SYSTEM,
THE UNIVERSE.

The Canadian National Railway tracks ran along Bethune Street only a few feet from our front door. The train would start up at the old station a block away and rumble past our intersection clanging and belching. The exotic markings on the boxcars spoke to me of faraway places and adventure. I loved to stand beside the tracks and let the big tents of acrid-smelling steam envelop me, lost in clouds of whiteness, powerful and invisible like my hero The Shadow. In the middle of the night the thunder of the passing freight cars rattled the walls of the tenement, rocked my bed; I could feel its vibrations in my mattress and chest. Hitching rides on the side ladders became a dangerous hobby. Home was a two-storey rundown red-brick terrace, divided into three tenements, ours in the middle. Dad considered our home a palace, but Mom called it a dump and always dreamed that one day she would own a little bungalow of her own. Built before Confederation, the house's window frames were askew and fissures gaped between the flaking brickwork. A narrow strip of beaten earth separated the front from the sidewalk. Mom often tried to plant flowers but next day they and the low green wire fence she erected to protect them would be trampled flat. Simcoe Street was cruel to beauty. Each tenement had a rusty shed and a small dandelion-choked backyard enclosed by a dilapidated board fence. One scrawny maple cast a bit of shade, a convenient meeting place for a host of nattering sparrows in the summer. Before the York Trading Company bought the land beyond the fence it belonged to a coal and lumber company, and the air reeked of coal dust. In winter the stacked logs along the fence became snow-clad mountain ranges that I loved to climb and explore. Once I lost my footing, fell to the ground, scraping both knees badly, and Mom made me promise never to climb the woodpiles again. "You could kill yourself," she said. Though I wasn't sure what "kill" meant exactly, her worried look and cross voice conveyed that it was bad.

The upper half of the front door had two narrow vertical windows and, just below, a brass letter slot where my sisters and I spied on the world. On rainy days we'd peer through the opening at the pedestrians sloshing past on the sidewalks, umbrellas raised, heads bent, trying to avoid the newly created puddles. The splashing raindrops made tiny upside-down bells on the pavement, and when it poured the gutter frothed and gurgled like a small stream. Sometimes the manhole clogged, creating an instant lake, and my sisters and I would race outside in our bathing suits and jubilantly splash through it in bare feet. The front door opened into a dark hallway with a kitchen at the end. On the left as you entered, thirteen steep steps led upstairs to three bedrooms and a bathroom the size of a cubbyhole. Off the hallway near the kitchen was Mom and Dad's bedroom, and there was a small parlour to the right as you entered the front door. There was also an unheated room off the kitchen with an unpainted splintery wood floor (which everyone called the summer kitchen) where Mom kept her washing machine, empty preserve jars and dirty laundry. In the middle of the floor a trap door led to a cellar with an earthen floor. The cellar always smelled sour and humid, and once Mom trapped a rat as big as a rabbit at the open sewer pipe near the front wall. The tenement had no furnace, just a wood stove in the kitchen and a potbelly coal stove in the parlour that was connected to stovepipes suspended by wires that ran upstairs through a hole in the ceiling. On freezing winter mornings my breath appeared in puffs of white vapour and I'd snuggle under the warm blankets till Mom or Dad lit the fires. I'd marvel at the intricate lacework on the frosted windowpane and though it shot shivers through my body I'd scratch my name with my fingernail across the exotic ferns and flowers. When I finally gathered enough courage I'd haul myself out of bed and sprint downstairs, the icy floors pricking my bare feet, to the warm kitchen.

Across the street from the tenement was Moldaver's scrapyard piled high with used car parts, twisted pipes, rusty girders, old boilers, and mountains of old magazines and newspapers that always smelled of decay and damp. The slow-moving jaws of the giant metal cutter held me in awe. Not even the strongest metal could withstand its powerful bite. Simcoe Street offered other delights for an imaginative boy. Every Sunday evening, the Salvation Army band would congregate outside the Temple up the street and the sound of bassoons, cymbals, tambourines, horns, drums and trombones reverberated in the golden dusk. And nearby was the fire hall with its square brick tower where the firemen dangled the wet hoses like spaghetti to dry. Evenings I could hear the clang of horseshoes and see the firemen's cigarettes glowing in the soft twilight. But what I remember most vividly is the halo of neon that lit the downtown skyline at night, the darkness alive with the honk and hum of cars, snatches of laughter and words carried on the breeze, and occasionally the bark of a dog or the flaring of a siren, but most memorable of all, the *pee-ent, pee-ent* of the nightjars in the inky sky. My bedroom window overlooked the rusty shed, and the shadowy limbs of the maple wove scary and mysterious patterns on the bedroom wall, stars glittered through the leaves, and sometimes a fat moon, big as a plate, washed the bedroom with a delicate creamy light. I'd hide under the covers and listen to the thump, thump, thump of my heartbeat, a beat so relentless I imagined I was being stalked by a stranger and knew that if the stranger ever caught me my heart would stop forever.

The tenement is still, my mom, dad, sisters asleep, fled from the tumult of living into the holy world of dreams. Someone stirs, a bedspring creaks, I can hear the soft snoring of my dad. Night rocks the tenement like a shaman; I can feel his cool fingers on my brow. Somewhere in the countryside beyond Jackson's Park I hear the sound of a train whistle, imagine I can see the orange glow from the furnace on the sweaty faces of the coalmen. Who travels through the star-ringed night while all the world sleeps, I wonder. Is the train, like me, my dad, my mom, my sisters, born to the light, but destined to journey blindly into the enfolding dark? Where is the train going and why?

❦

TODAY AT CHURCH WHEN THE PRIEST RECITED PSALM 23 AND TALKED ABOUT
the Good Shepherd it was too much. I got up and left. Where was the Good
Shepherd when the Black Dog cornered you? Did the Good Shepherd make
you lie down in green pastures beside still waters? Did he anoint your head
with oil? Did he clasp your hand as you stood on the parapet? A medieval
writer described life as a bird entering an open window of a lighted castle
only to flit through the room and out the other side back into the night
– a brief interlude between two darknesses. Lately, a chorus of demonic
voices has been howling in my ear: your existence is but a brief crack of light
between two eternities of darkness, your belief in an afterlife an illusion born
of your fear of pure extinction, they mock; you will never see Mary or any of
your loved ones again; a black calamity awaits us all. At least the pure atheist
doesn't delude himself, they insinuate, because the desire to die is the desire
to be elsewhere, and he knows all such longings are false because there is no
elsewhere. Maybe the ancient Greeks had it right after all, we're all snared
in the delusional web of believing we're masters of our destinies whereas all
along, each life has been laid out as in an acorn and our fate is in the lap of
the gods.

Years ago my buddy Clair and I walked in Victoria Park late one summer's
evening, talking about life in the earnest and intense way teenagers sometimes
do. The night was still and balmy, I remember, a field of molten stars overhead.
Like a bolt out of nowhere I was zapped with an overwhelming feeling of
God's presence, a feeling so powerful and preternatural it impelled me to
run to the nearest maple and wrap my arms around its trunk as though the
tree was a tangible incarnation of divine energy. I desired to cling to this
ecstatic moment of wholeness forever, never let it go. In a stuporous voice I
whispered, "Did you feel what I felt, Clair?"

"Yes. The presence of God."

"You, too!" I couldn't believe we'd had the same epiphany, a shining of the brightest brightness at the same time. Accompanying this epiphany was a sensation of lightness, as though a great weight had been lifted from my soul, the same feeling I often got after confession of being scrubbed clean and free of sinful grime, floating on pure air. This certitude of the presence of God – what some psychiatrists today might call a peak experience – was so shattering and profound that for months Clair and I talked of nothing else and even today, more than 50 years later, we still talk about the God-tree. Though such experiences must be extremely rare, I read that the poet W.H. Auden had a similar epiphany. One summer evening in 1933 he was sitting on a lawn after dinner with three colleagues, two women and a man (like Clair and I they'd had no alcohol to drink), chatting about nothing in particular when he was suddenly and unexpectedly invaded by a power that convinced him his colleagues had infinite value, and he was also certain (one of them later confirmed it) they'd had the same experience. The intensity of that moment marked Auden so deeply that it stayed with him the rest of his life and was one of the factors, he says, that led him a few years later to embrace Christianity. Why has even this feeling now deserted me? Why do I feel that nothing is possible that might give meaning to my flat and colourless world, that all my longings for God and the afterlife are vain strivings? In the aftershock of your suicide I find it hard to shuck off these black thoughts, fear my faith could snap like a thread anytime. Pray for me.

ʘʀ

As a boy the fire hall played a big role in my life. The red brick hall with its square tower where the firemen strung up the long grey hoses by the neck to dry (I loved to rub my hand along their rough cool skins) was only a stone's throw from the tenement. The dripping hoses formed large puddles on the cement floor and the tower always smelled damp. When I was four

I got written up in *The Peterborough Examiner* for reporting a "timney fire" in our tenement, became a local hero. After that I hung out at the hall so much the chief finally decided to appoint me fire mascot, outfitted me with a pint-sized waterproof turnout coat and a British army helmet painted red, with "Deputy Chief PFD" in white letters on the front. I still have a black-and-white photo taken of me at six or seven in full regalia behind the wooden wheel of old yellow pumper no. 7, a proud, solemn expression on my face, my feet dangling above the floor pedals, with the chief in his navy-blue overcoat standing beside me, gazing benignly on. Images of the firemen polishing brass and nickel fittings on the pumpers, waxing the dark oak hardwood floors till they gleamed, still linger in my mind. Except when an alarm sounded, triggering a flurry of activity, life in the hall appeared relaxed and happy, with the firemen lounging about in their peaked caps, blue shirts, and navy-blue trousers (many wore small black leather bow ties) or playing horseshoes. To this day the clang, ping, clang of the shoes resounding against the steel posts rings in my memory. Was it boredom that drove some of them to sneak out on warm summer evenings to the parked cars for a nip from the flat brown bottles of rye they'd hidden in glove compartments or under a seat? The old chief, who had a shock of snow-white hair, commissioned me to stash his liquor in the tower. Whenever he needed to quench his thirst he'd give me a prearranged signal (sometimes it was just a wink) and I would scoot upstairs, open the small wooden door to the tower and fetch him the bottle. After the chief took a good pull and smacked his lips it was my job to return the bottle to its hiding place carefully wrapped in a towel.

Many of the other firemen availed themselves of my covert operations and I became very skilled at finding new nooks and crannies in that monstrous old building to hide the booty. Other sights and sounds, random and unbidden, crowd to mind: the men sliding down the brass poles from the dorm upstairs, half dressed, the clack-clack-clack of the old-fashioned alarm system in the coop, myself leg and arm clamped in the fireman's hold being carried up and down a ladder on the firemen's backs, the feeling of being suspended in mid-air and the thrill of jumping off the back roof, free-falling through space, knowing they were waiting below to catch me in their round canvas net. But mostly it's the quieter moments I recall best: the men, in the cool of the evening, shirt sleeves rolled up, digging in the flower garden they'd made behind the hall, moving nimbly between the rows of asters, carnations, cosmos and tulips or relaxing on the bench in front after a game of horseshoes, almost invisible in their blue uniforms in the ebbing twilight, chattering and smoking into the still night. In the winter the firemen created huge snow banks in the yard where we'd hollow out elaborate tunnels with small candlelit rooms that the girls were forbidden to enter. In the months before Christmas they would be busy at the long table in the basement repairing and painting wagons, dolls, sleighs, carts, scooters, hook-and-ladder fire trucks, tin dump trucks, wind-up climbing tanks, self-reversing wind-up tractors, Spitfire automatic cap guns, sparking pop guns, jack-in-the-boxes, trains sets, etc., which they'd collected to distribute to poor families (like ours) at Christmas, and sometimes they'd let me help. To this day I can still smell the paint and turpentine of those dark winter evenings. And then there was Jack, the bodybuilder who had real weights and bars and pumped iron most evenings in the basement, till his hard, sinewy legs and muscular torso glistened with sweat, small in stature but to me a hero like Charles Atlas. And when death intruded on this enchanted world and four of the men I knew and loved were overcome with smoke and suffocated to death in the big Woollen Mill fire I was struck dumb, just as I was struck dumb by your suicide. I recall the day after the fire, sitting and gazing at the still smouldering ruin — the stench of bales of yellow wool like burnt flesh in my nostrils, transfixed and mystified by the mystery of death, and just as now any waterfall reminds me of you, so too death is forever associated in my mind with burnt wool.

Seven Years Old

Snow fell all night.
The Snowman filled the fire hall
with hills of white.

Next morning I tunnelled through
        my palace,
frolicked in its fleecy cave

        till
my sister Babe came by and
I persuaded her to dive headlong
from the firehall roof,

        watched
her nearly drown below, red
knit leggings waving in the air,
buried to the waist in snow.

ଔ

WHY AM I WRITING THESE KADDISHES? THE QUESTION MERITS AN HONEST response, but a simple clear answer eludes me. Sometimes the furies assail me: unpacking your heart with words, circling the hard rock of your wife's suicide with pious longings is just a vain attempt to find comfort, create a facsimile meaning where no meaning exists, they taunt. Perhaps the answer is still hidden from me, only to be brought forth in pain and labour like a woman giving birth to a child. Why do I write? For the applause of others? What befell me and my children is hardly novel or unique; much worse happens in different ways to countless others each day all over the globe. Death wears many disguises but leaves the same mark. Your suicide thrust me, the children, your friends into deep shock. Taking your own life was so out of character, a repudiation of your deepest values, the life-affirming way you lived your life, that it became a defeat for us all.

Every day I sit in judgment of my brothers and sisters and dispense justice according to the dictates of the law. There is a split between judging and compassion that is sometimes hard to bridge. In judging we put a distance between ourselves and others, ignore the trail of our own sins and shortcomings behind us. In compassion (or love) we become one with the person we love, which involves a kind of death of our own self, our separateness. Is this why my role as judge sometimes sits uneasily on me? But despite these misgivings I try to be a good judge and honour the law, conscious of the trust society has conferred on me. I don't believe in cynicism, try to keep its talons from clawing my soul. I remember my own childhood and the poor bastards who lived under the curse of the bottle and try to exercise compassion as much as I can. But your suicide forced me to my knees. Why do I write? Because I've been burned badly and wish to convey what that experience means to me and my family? Because I desire to arouse the dormant compassion of others (and myself) so that we can better cherish the fragile gift of existence? Because I want to leave a memorial to the vibrant, unrepeatable person you were, mother of our children, my lover, my friend, so that after we're all dust, you'll be saved from the great indifference of things, your presence remembered? Why do I write? To objectify what's happened, tame it and pour balm on my own wounds, make them more bearable? To make friends with the ghosts that have bedevilled me since childhood, find my own long-lost father? Your death opened the trap door to the dungeon where those ghosts have nested all these years, unacknowledged and friendless.

Why do I write?

To express the inchoate longings of the heart and bear witness to the joy and sorrow of what it's like being alive, a solitary pilgrim in our time on this blue whirling planet? To affirm my passage through the beyond-the-mind galaxies, to sign the guest book of life, scribble "Jim was here"? For, dammit, I am Kilroy, Everyman, and I want the silence to hear my voice just once before I go.

Lord, I ask you to teach me, your dull-witted and error-prone creation, the art of love, that life and suffering go hand in hand and that love is not a luxury but our beginning, our middle and our end, mercy within mercy within mercy.

⳼

AFTER YOUR SUICIDE MY SUNNY BELIEF IN A MELLOW AND BENEVOLENT GOD was shaken. Yet faith, however shaken, was all I had to cling to. Driving to court in the blue-black dawn the other day I noticed a blind man on the sidewalk in a blue windbreaker, dark pants and socks that showed white at the ankles above his black Adidas – a dim figure on a shadowy street. His cane, a white antenna, probed the sidewalk ahead of him for cracks and obstructions and I felt as he must feel, benighted and insecure. I clasped my faith like the blind man's white cane, my only guide through the murkiness that encircled me. To fortify myself I drew up a list of beliefs on a yellow card and placed it on my desk – a mantra of consolations I could recite each day to keep the Black Dog at bay.

MARY IS IN HEAVEN, PERFECTLY HAPPY WITH GOD.

I had to believe this, otherwise the apparent meaninglessness of your death would have driven me to despair, and goodness knows what might have happened. It was bad enough that God – what worn coinage to describe the ineffable – had cold-cocked me with your suicide, but to believe he'd let you free-fall into a black bottomless hole without a net would make Him a sadist; I want to believe that he was with you from the moment you stepped into the New Yorker, held your hand all the way to the Falls and leapt with you into the rushing waters. Gaby, who took care of my sisters and me during the war, was a good cook, a meticulous housecleaner, and made sure we were always well fed, our homework done and out to school on time. But she also had a sadistic streak, devised cruel and ingenious ways to punish us when her rules were not obeyed to the letter. When my sister Babe began to wet her bed, Gaby would lock her in the cellar and terrorize her by saying the rats would eat her. I still remember my sister's screams.

On fudge night, Tiny, Gaby's dog, got first dibs, and only when he'd had his fill were we given a square. Threats of reprisal guaranteed our silence, stopped us from revealing anything to Mom. But when Mom came home from work one bitter winter evening near the end of the war and discovered my back covered with purplish welts – I'd peed my pants at school and Gaby had beaten me with a leather belt – Gaby's days with us were numbered. After Mom confronted her she fled outside in her thin cotton housecoat, Tiny clutched in her arms, and threw herself into a snowdrift where she sat, blue and shivering, teeth chattering for the longest time before Mom finally persuaded her she'd catch pneumonia if she didn't come in. I don't believe God, like Gaby, is a tyrant. But oh, how I wish he'd make his ways clearer; sometimes I feel so abandoned that I'd like to grab a giant megaphone, climb to the top of the CN Tower and shout, "Where the hell are you, God, when we most need you?" And yet I don't believe that a good person like yourself can fly away, forgotten as in a dream, and I cannot conceive of a God worthy of belief who would not welcome you into paradise with open arms.

IN THIS LIFE MARY LOVED AND KNEW SHE WAS LOVED.

"Be a friend, make a friend," was your motto. The crowd at your memorial service and the hundreds of letters and cards we got attest to the uncommon way you touched the lives of others. The children and I tried to love you back to life but sometimes love is not enough. Because you believed that your continued existence meant your loved ones would suffer – in the hospital the week before you died you confided to Marilyn that you thought you'd harmed the children by shoving religion down their throats – you saw your death as a necessary sacrifice. In other words, an act of love.

MARY'S EXAMPLE OF STRETCHING FOR OTHERS AND HER SPIRITUAL PRESENCE LIVE ON TO HELP US BE MORE LOVING PEOPLE.

It's here that God never fails me. Driving home from Milton two evenings ago fog shrouded the 401, a fog so dense it was almost impossible to see more than 30 feet ahead. The naked eyes of oncoming headlights converged out of nowhere, vehicles and people invisible, but still I trusted the highway would see me home. Faith for me is like that. We're like Blondin at the Falls; we dare not look down from our tightrope lest we fall. I trust God has a plan and all will be well, that you, by some mystery of grace, found your way home. I can't believe that the desire for permanence is fool's gold, that our unfinished symphonies in this life will never be completed. Your suicide was a wake-up call to live our lives fully in love.

MARY BELIEVED HER DEATH WAS NECESSARY IN ORDER THAT HER FAMILY COULD LIVE FULLY; HER DEATH WAS CONSISTENT WITH THE WAY SHE LIVED, A PERSON FOR OTHERS.

At first blush what a bizarre, even scandalous statement, to elevate the life-denying act of suicide into an act of love. Your life was a celebration of love and some took advantage of your good intentions. Like the woman at the drop-in centre who persuaded you she needed rent money but insisted you give her cash because all along it transpired she only wanted to buy more booze. You sacrificed a promising artistic career as a fashion illustrator for the sake of your family and paid the price, for no gifts are denied with impunity. You thought your death would lead to our freedom; instead, you sealed each of us in a dark box of sorrow.

THE PAIN OF OUR LOSS MUST BE BORNE AND LOVING WAYS FOUND TO CUSHION THE BLOW. BUT WE MUST NOT DWELL ON YOUR SUFFERING, BLAME OURSELVES OR LANGUISH OVER REGRETS.

Your suicide has been a "hard rain a-fallin'," a steel shower that lacerates every day and never seems to end. I've doubled, tripled my efforts to be both mother and father to the children, but I've fallen short, as these kaddishes demonstrate. I have to constantly remind myself that I'm not responsible for the happiness of others, even those I love most. Millions of others like me have had to look into the bottomless well of unmerited bad luck, so I'm not alone. Salvation, like creation, is a continuum. As Augustine said, we have to start our relationship with God all over from the beginning of every day. Faith is a leap in the dark, with no assurance that we won't find utter darkness, yet we leap and leap every day, suspended above our doubts in order to breathe deeply and feel the air in our lungs. Your death did not destroy my faith, just changed it; I've learned to live creatively with the unanswered questions, to be humbler (I hope), more aware of my flaws and contradictions. I don't want to become a psychological cripple and flounder in guilt the rest of my life. I pray to you and God to help me finish the journey.

WE MUST SEARCH TO DO GOD'S WILL, PRAY FOR DISCERNMENT AND BE AWARE OF THE NEED FOR HIS GRACE, KEEPING IN MIND THAT OUR LIVES ARE ONLY SPARKS IN THE GRASS AND THAT SOON OR LATE WE WILL JOIN MARY AND ALL OUR OTHER LOVED ONES. THEREFORE WE SHOULD RANSOM THE TIME AND MAKE ROOM FOR GOD IN OUR HEARTS.

Oh, what a bold declaration in the teeth of God's silence and seeming indifference. And how do I know God's will? As I approach my 60th birthday, the sheer lunacy of life shouts in my face, makes it hard to believe, like Augustine, that the Lord loves each of us like an only child. I am like the blind man; all I hear is the rattle of my cane on the hard pavement. As I ponder the alphabet of my days I wait with empty heart for the whisperings of the Spirit, find the way to inner peace so that I can radiate God's love to others.

WE MUST PRAY FOR THE GRACE OF THE PRESENT MOMENT AND ACCEPT OUR SUFFERINGS WITH JOY.

With joy? What does that mean? I find it impossible to accept your suicide with joy, but I can learn to accept it with resignation, believing that Niagara is not the end of the story, that out of the wreckage of your death, good will somehow come.

A pipe dream? Maybe. But it's my only hope.

> I shall rise from the dead, from the prostration, from the prostration of death, and never miss the sun, which shall be put out, for I shall see the son of God, the sun of Glory, and shine myself as the sun shines. I shall rise from the grave, and never miss this city, which shall be nowhere, for I shall see the city of God, the New Jerusalem. I shall look up and never wonder when I shall be nowhere. And I shall see and see cheerfully that last day of judgment, which shall have no night, never end. And be united to the ancient of days, to God Himself, who had no morning, never began.

—John Donne

Sister Bernadette stands at the front of the class, reading. Sister has big green eyes, pale oval face and soft musical voice. Dink Hotts glares at me across the aisle, wrinkles his nose. I adore Sister Bernadette, but I'm too shy to raise my hand. Sister slowly edges down the aisle, long pauses punctuate her words. She stops beside my desk and bends down; her crisp white veil grazes my forehead. I feel her warm breath, taste the peachy fragrance of her cheeks. I'm positive she can hear the hammering of my heart. "Do you have to go somewhere, Jim?" she whispers. I glance around: thirty pair of mocking eyes are staring at me. Cheeks aflame, eyeballs erupting tears, I bolt from my desk, race out of the school, legs pumping as hard as they can, my red-faced shadow chasing me all the way home.

இ

HOW TORTUROUS TO TROLL THROUGH THE WATERS OF YOUR SUICIDE, DREDGE up these memories! Why am I doing it? Palm Sunday, the beginning of Holy Week, is forever associated in my mind with your death as though like Jesus you'd picked the hour of your destiny. Why was I blindsided, why did I fail to see it coming? The cues were there: you whispering to me in the hospital that last week that the friendly Italian woman in the next bed was spying on you, reporting your secrets to the police; you instructing me at the Chinese restaurant Friday evening after they'd let you out of the hospital to select your dishes for you, something you, a picky eater with a fastidious palate, normally never did; later, in bed you turned to me, an enigmatic smile on your wan face and suggested we "boff" – an expression I'd never heard you use before, and I had to gently put you off because it didn't seem right; and the next day, Saturday, you urging me to slip away for a day or two to visit friends in Port Hope, "You need a break," you said, assured me you'd be fine till I got back, that you needed a little time to yourself, a bit of rest, that's all. Were your plans already made? Adele told me that you confided in her two weeks before you took your life that you intended to leave me, start a new independent life. "But of course she couldn't do it," said Adele. "She chose Niagara instead." How I reproach myself that I didn't stay, but would it have made any difference? I know now that people determined to kill themselves usually find a way to foil their rescuers. And although misgivings still lurked at the back of my mind – your woebegone look as you groaned in bed, complaining about the back that had always given you trouble, your grey-blue eyes cold and detached as if outside your body watching a play in which all of us were playing out our scripts – I ignored the signs and left anyway. And then the next day the call from Joy informing me you'd dropped her off for Mass and hadn't come home, the mounting terror as I sped back to Guelph on the 401, numb and sick inside. And waiting in the parking lot of St. John's Church, my heart sinking lower and lower by the minute, until the last parishioners had dispersed and I knew you were not there, and coming home to find the unmarked police cruiser across the street, collapsing into the arms of the young blond detective in the middle of the roadway, clinging to him for dear life, as if somehow by holding him I could stave off the black news, and the screams of our daughter Ruth ringing in my ears, catching the words "Niagara" and "the New Yorker" and knowing without further explanation (you'd once told me on a visit to Niagara that drowning was the sweetest death) that the unthinkable had happened, that you'd thrown yourself into the death-dealing waters. That Palm Sunday was a day of sunshine and warmth, but it will always remain for me a day of cold and dark. In days that followed, our friends rallied round the family, hugged and comforted the children and me as we sleepwalked through our imploded lives, my sorrow magnified by the pain I observed on the children's faces; and always the cold assassin of regret: why, why didn't I read the signs that tried to tell me you were withdrawing from us, sinking back into the womb of your ancestors? Why so blind? Oh, the sorrow of being human and weak and blind and hurting each other by our lack of wakefulness; I pray that I will never be so asleep again.

CR

FROM THE START OF OUR MARRIAGE YOU WERE THE STALWART CATHOLIC in the family. Missing Mass on Sunday was a no-no, a principle instilled in you by your pious mother Teetaw, and one of the children would have had to break a leg to stop us from going. You inherited the full panoply of Irish Catholicism: daily Mass with your mother, prayers before meals and bedtime, litanies and novenas, first Fridays of the month, etc. Remember at the cottage, the time we couldn't get to church because a can of gasoline had spilt in the back of the station wagon (gas fumes always made you nauseous) and it took two hours of soap, ventilation and hard scrubbing to get most of the smell out; even then we weren't off the hook until we'd recited a decade of the rosary before the shrine of the white-and-blue plaster Virgin Mary you'd rigged up in a corner of the cottage. For years we'd trek to Mass every Sunday to Bancroft, an 80-mile round trip, to listen to the stained-glass voice of the pious but old-fashioned pastor who didn't appear comfortable with the reforms of Vatican II. How the children bridled at leaving the cottage for three hours while their friends slept in or swam in the lake. Though they never refused to go (which wouldn't have been tolerated in any event), their surly, resigned expressions betrayed their true feelings. Then we discovered St. Bernadette's, the pioneer church on the Old Hastings Road at Ormsby, and our travelling was cut in half. Remember the opaque glass of the church windows, how they reflected the cedars, and when people moved outside – the church couldn't hold everyone in the summer and many had to sit on the grass – it appeared like they were swimming in greenness and the liquid notes of birdsong.

And the time Father asked me to be extraordinary minister of the sacrament and distribute the Eucharist to those outside and I stepped on a wasp's nest and they swarmed my ankles, the stings so excruciating I started to whirl about in a dervish frenzy trying to shake them off and finally in desperation hopped up the hillock behind the church, hoping to escape, the chalice clutched in both hands and someone shouted "Don't drop the hosts!" Afterwards, back at the cottage, you swabbed my red swollen ankles with calamine lotion and we both had a good chuckle when you told me my suffering was the price I had to pay for serving God.

After a row the evening before, how often just hearing the word of God in that little church would soften our hearts, give us the grace to ask mutual forgiveness, and when we reconciled and embraced the faces of the children lit up, for they loved to see us happy and in love again. My upbringing was different from yours; Mom was French Canadian, brought up to believe Protestants were doomed to eternal hellfire, while Dad – an Ulster Protestant "black Irishman," Mom called him, who was taught that Rome was Babylon and the pope the anti-Christ – never lost an opportunity to crack jokes about the Pope's nose. Though believers, neither was pious in the traditional sense, and they rarely attended church. Religious patriotism, not piety, fuelled their attitudes. When they married in the rectory of St. Peter's Cathedral in 1932 (in those days "mixed marriages" were frowned on by the Church) Dad had to sign a solemn promise that any children of the marriage would be raised in the "one true faith." But later, when I came along, he had a change of heart and one day announced without prior consultation that he'd made arrangements for my baptism in St. John's Anglican Church the following Sunday. "There'll be no Fenians in my family," he'd declared, and nothing Mom could say, she told me, could make him change his mind. In desperation Mom threw on her wool winter coat and galoshes, ran to the rectory and told the old monsignor in charge what had happened, how Dad had reneged on his word. The old monsignor thought for a long while before speaking. "The last thing you want is a fight in your home, Flo," he said. "Bring Jim to the church Friday evening and we'll baptize him properly. Sam needn't know."

That's how it came about that I was baptized twice in one week in two separate Christian communions and peace was restored. Today some of your children have turned their backs on the institutional church; they're angry at a so-called loving God who would allow you, their mother, to fall into a bottomless pit, and blame you, too, because they've come to believe that your unquestioning adherence to the Church's teaching, especially in matters of sexual morality, contributed to your sickness. Time alone will heal.

CR

Been having crazy dreams and wild fantasies lately. I feel convinced that stream-of-consciousness journalling flattens the silt of convention that impedes the free flow from the deeper mind. Did you die? Or like the mad honeymooner are you ensconced on a ledge in some secret cave behind the Falls, listening to the singsong of water, contemplating the newlyweds who gaze blindly at your awesome white curtain? Yes, water is everywhere, even in my dreams. Last night I dreamt Mira and I were in a skyscraper and a river ran through it; we were fearful that someone would push the red hydraulic button that would dam the river and drown us both, but when we tried to escape it was too late: someone had already pressed the button and the waters had begun to shoot skyward like a mighty reverse Falls and we had to scramble up the fire stairs to keep ahead of the water, hoping to find safety in your cave. By good fortune we reached the top of the skyscraper and the vast river flowed harmlessly past.

But then a sergeant came along and put me in charge of the Falls. "You're our man," he said, pointing his long bony finger at me. My friend Gord Kelly materialized out of nowhere. "It's crazy, you can't put that man in charge," he protested, "he's no soldier," but the sergeant was adamant: "He's clearly army material," he said, "and will do just fine." I knew then I was done for, that I'd be the button pusher at the Falls for the rest of my life. What a bizarre country, I thought, but on reflection I realized it wasn't any crazier than you fooling everyone and hiding in the cave: are you watching my dream now and secretly laughing?

> Are you having fun now love
> ensconced in your dark cave
> beneath the Falls
> squinting at newlyweds
>   with Corso
> the Mad Honeymooner
>   through
> the pulsing glass curtain,

trying to imagine
confetti and clanky cans and shoes,
their trance-like faces
streaming into cozy hotels
past the knowing clerk,
the whistling elevator boy,
                    the winking bellhop –
all rosy with the same fever,

you and Corso
                    devising ways
to catch the wild promises
                    living will not let them keep.

CR

ALTHOUGH YOU RARELY TALKED ABOUT IT, THAT YOU WERE AN ADOPTED
child never seemed to bother you. Even in the 1960s and '70s when it became
common and fashionable for adopted children to write articles or appear
on TV to talk about identity crisis and the search for roots you remained
relatively indifferent. As a long as your beloved Teetaw was alive, you promised
yourself that you would never delve into your background. To seek out your
biological parents would have been seen by you as an act of treason to the
mother who adopted you, gave you a name, a home, a family and showered
you with attention and love. Secure in your faith that you were a child of God,
the existential question "Who am I?" never vexed you unduly, at least until
your last illness. You were always grateful to your birth mother for the gift
of life. "Oh, isn't it great to be alive," was one of your favourite expressions.
After your birth you were in a foster home for three months – family gossip
has it that your putative father paid the costs – until Teetaw, who longed for
a child, came along, accompanied by a nursing friend, and found you. "There

were several babies in the home," Teetaw told you. "I chose you because you were the only one who smiled at me." In the late 1930s, adoption was relatively uncommon, still viewed in some quarters as socially unacceptable, and initially your dad, Mac, and grandmother, after whom you were named, were unenthusiastic about Teetaw's decision. But after your arrival you quickly melted their hearts and became the darling of the family.

John Newlove, a poet, has written somewhere that remembrance is a two-headed snake, biting in all directions. Once, when I was a boy Mom drew me aside to inform me, in a hushed tone as though she was imparting some dark and dangerous secret, that one of my school chums was adopted, that his mother and father whom I'd met, were not his real parents. "But you must never, never tell anyone," she made me promise. The revelation knocked me for a loop, for the idea of such a possibility had never crossed my mind and I felt as though I'd just been handed some forbidden fruit from the tree of life. Oh, the intoxicating feeling of power that knowledge imparted! Every time I played with my friend or went to his house I thought of my deep dark secret and the cloud that hung unbeknownst to him over his head, secure in the knowledge that I wasn't like him – Mom had assured me I was her natural child, not adopted, an assurance that made me feel normal and blessed. Although my friend and I by times bickered, and there were occasions when I wanted to hurt him, I kept my lips sealed for I believed that if my secret had ever leaked out it would have made a ruin and desolation of his life. Your mom, who was progressive for her time, proclaimed to family and friends that you were adopted and made you feel extra special because she'd personally chosen you. After our own children grew up you'd sometimes speculate about your birth mother, how she fared in life, her health, if she was still alive, had other children, etc., but your curiosity never escalated into an obsession. After Teetaw's death you entered your name in the provincial registry the government had set up for natural parents and adopted children who wanted to make contact, but nothing came of it. Adopting Joy and taking Stephen into our home were your way of saying thank you and doing for others what Teetaw had done for you.

CR

STRANGE DREAM LAST NIGHT. I SAW A RED ROSE ON YOUR BEDROOM DOOR THAT was turning black. The dream didn't frighten me or seem ghoulish. I sensed you were inside the bedroom at peace, and after I woke the peaceful feeling lingered. These dreams that speak to me of the kingdom of the dead make you more alive, more real than flesh and blood. At the judges' conference at the Four Seasons Hotel in Toronto last weekend I looked out the window of my room at the Victorian terrace on Yorkville Avenue where I roomed in the '50s during my last year of law school. The morning sun cast long blue shadows from the eleven third-floor dormers that jutted from the roof. I lived in one of those garrets (which one I couldn't recall, for they all looked alike) for a year, remember. Most mornings two grungy pigeons, one white, the other dark grey, small orange buttons for eyes, would strut behind me along the sidewalk on tiny pink feet. Except for the gingerbread and the two narrow garret windows, the facades were totally altered. Instead of decaying dark-green verandahs, flaky red brickwork and cracked walkways, the terrace was now a trendy row of modern bistros, boutiques and restaurants. I remember we could barely stop our sides from splitting when the kind-hearted widowed landlady (who used to serve me tea in the kitchen) told us she intended to sell the place soon for $20,000, a fabulous sum to us in those days; we thought the poor woman deluded and her expectations ridiculous. Little did we know! In contrast to the luxurious hotel room with its queen-size bed, TV, mini bar and slick paintings, my attic bedroom was a cramped space that you reached by climbing a vertical ladder through a trap door and had only the barest furnishings: a cot, a desk and a small lamp. The room was unheated and I had to leave the trap open to allow in heat from below or I would have frozen. In the winter the floorboards creaked, my breath came out in frost angels and ice feathered the windows. But under the thick comforter I felt cozy and warm, and what beautiful dreamless sleeps. For $14 weekly I couldn't complain. Yes, those days in Toronto bring back fond memories. We'd often meet after your work (you were a part-time filing clerk in a collection agency at the time) at the corner of Bathurst and Bloor and wind our way to Chinatown, where I'd order dinner in my faux-Chinese accent which for some reason tickled your funny bone (in retrospect I realize it wasn't funny, in fact downright gauche) and afterwards we'd amble north to Bloor Street, laughing and kibitzing all the way and I would throw snowballs and do entrechats and pirouettes which you also found comic, and then the long ride west on Bloor on the wobbly streetcar all the way to your house at 11 Traymore Crescent, where we'd park ourselves on your mom's big Barrymore sofa and cuddle and smooch into the small hours of the morning, your mom meanwhile upstairs wide awake (you found out later) strangling the rosary pooled on her lap, praying to the Virgin that you wouldn't lose your virginity before you were married, and though we came close you never did.

CR

THERE WAS A RED FIRE HYDRANT ON THE NARROW EARTH BOULEVARD OPPOSITE the front door on Simcoe Street that the firemen used on summer evenings to test their hoses, a great boon for my sisters and me, who would put on our bathing suits and get them to spray us with jets of cold water. After a rain, the dreary tin fence that enclosed Moldaver's scrapyard across the street took on a red sheen, and in the yard behind we played cops and robbers, hide-and-seek and war games among the mountains of scrap, yellowing newspapers and magazines. On warm summer evenings I'd sit under the big elm at the corner of Aylmer and Simcoe to watch the cars whiz by, listen to the hum of their tires on the hot asphalt. In winter, car chains crackled on the icy pavement. We didn't own a car — no one even had a license and a car ride was always a thrilling adventure. When Hubert, Dad's drinking crony, dropped by for a visit he'd station his rattletrap blue Chevy at the curb at the front of the house and I'd mount the running board and imagine I was a G-man, Tommy gun blazing, chasing Al Capone. Sometimes Hubert would allow me to sit behind the wheel and I'd pretend to drive. The stiff grey upholstery gave off a mouldy odour and prickled the skin. The gearshift, a stick in the floor, had a blue knob at the end that felt smooth and cool in my hand, and a vertical chrome strip bisected the windscreen. Occasionally, if we badgered Hubert enough, he'd give in and take us for a spin around the block. The ride, a major event in our lives, got us so excited that we'd rush into the house afterwards yelling our heads off and for days brag to friends about our adventure. Once Hubert took us fishing to his cottage on Rice Lake and I caught a sunfish; watching Hubert clean the fish made me bring up and I vowed never to fish again.

From the moment I first laid eyes on your house on Traymore I was impressed. None of my friends lived in detached brick homes on cool elm-shaded streets lush with front lawns and a rose garden at the back with fountain and pool shimmering with goldfish in summer. No house of anyone I knew boasted hardwood floors or sandalwood fireplaces. But most of all I was impressed by your dad's Ford sedan in the driveway (Ford the only make of car he ever bought) and my first sight of him bent over the engine, screwdriver in his big hairy fist, greasy baggy pants, wide red suspenders and a blue beret askew his head. Tools, samples, notebooks, old newspapers and the other paraphernalia of the packrat plugged up the interior to the height of the windows, and your mom, I recall, refused to enter the car unless he first tidied it up. And she wouldn't let him back into the house until he scrubbed the grease from his hands and changed his soiled T-shirt. When we first dated you and he had a love/hate relationship. You admired his honesty but were embarrassed by his drinking and outspokenness. Like the time at Sunday Mass when the parish priest pronounced from the pulpit that any Catholic who sent their child to a public school was committing a mortal sin and in grave danger of losing his immortal soul and your dad sprang up from the pew like a jack-in-the-box, bristling and outraged, shouted at the top of his lungs in his big bass voice, "Like hell, he is," and then stomped out of the church. Or the evening you had me over for Sunday dinner and he began to badmouth French Canadians and you could tell by my wounded silence that he'd tapped a sensitive nerve and after he dropped me off at Union Station (I was catching a train back to Peterborough that weekend) you and your mom became so furious you tonguelashed him all the way home. And when he went on a binge you and your mom would conspire together to give him the cold silent treatment. Despite his bluntness and prejudices your dad and I got along well. I liked his unconventionality and integrity and after you moved to Cobourg you began to better appreciate his many good qualities, too, and regretted your occasional outbursts and harsh words. You always claimed I helped you restrain your quicksilver temper, accept him the way he was, and I'm happy for that.

Sunfish

When I remember
              her slim brown legs
gold cascading hair
              strange wild feeling
    surging in my loins,
              I see the sunfish;
eye,
              amber button
black marble locked inside
              glint of silver
in Hubert's hairy hand
              silken entrails
gushing out,
              but most of all
tiny bright-red heart
              throbbing
on the plank,
              my shout:
"She's still alive,"
              the look
on her face.

CR

HOW SWIFTLY THE PRESENT FOLDS INTO THE PAST AND EVERYONE'S FORGOTTEN. None of your grandchildren were born when you took your life. When the children and I are gone, who will be left to remember your living presence? The other day I discovered a cardboard box of your mom's memorabilia in the basement. Most of the photos are black and white and have been long neglected, crumbled, creased or stuck together. There is one of Teetaw's parents and her siblings taken on the verandah of the big house on Maynard Avenue. It's a summer evening and the sun casts a large band of light across everyone, seated or stretched out on an old striped mattress. Your mom's lying down, chin cupped under both hands, elbows propped on the mattress, grinning as though someone had just cracked a joke. Your grandfather, who wears a dark suit and fedora and has a walrus moustache, squints directly at the camera – the story is he'd lost not only his hotel but also his mind by this decade – his right arm wrapped around the waist of your beautiful dark-haired grandmother. Arthur, your uncle (who died at 37 from emphysema), the clown of the family, has closed his right eye against the glare and is also grinning. Your four aunts, two in white bonnets, look sedate and composed and you can see the shadow of the photographer's elongated head cast by the sun – it must be Ralph for he's not in the group – all of these faces now gone forever. I found a photo of your dad in his salad days sitting on a stump, both hands over the end of a canoe paddle. He's dark haired and slim – so different from the portly senior I knew who always had his nose stuck in the pages of the *Star* or *Saturday Evening Post* – and sports a striped summer jacket and light flannels, in the background a lone spruce, a lake and what looks like a small treed island. There's also a picture of him and your mom in their courting days standing in a field between two Lombardy poplars as though the unknown photographer was striving for some sort of artistic symmetry. Both are wearing old-fashioned black bathing suits – the ones that look like oversized sweatshirts and reach to the thighs, and your mom's at attention, her matchstick legs and knobby knees touching, a white belt around her waist while your dad – already beginning to bald (he married your mom at 42) and wearing the Clark Gable moustache I always remember him by – strikes a casual pose with right arm folded behind his back, left hand at chest level, a cigarette dangling between his fingers. And here's a couple of you, one when you're about two in a light suit and bonnet frowning out the window of your dad's 1940 Ford as though you didn't trust what you saw. The car has big round fenders and chrome that runs along the hood and up the middle of the windscreen; in the other you're standing at the front door of 11 Traymore, three or four years old, a mirror image of your granddaughter Mira, smiling while Rags your favourite dog, looks up at you with beseeching eyes. A pencil note scribbled on the back says May 1941, and the sun catches you and Rags full face and dapples the brick wall behind and a moment of suntime – for all our moments are suntime – in transition, is captured forever. There are some snaps of your mom, too, from Chicago and California, where she'd gone to work as a nurse in the late '20s, gussied up like a flapper with cloche hats, and one old photo of 11 Traymore with the big elm (now gone) looking straight and healthy and sun spots splashed against the brick verandah in the background. The box is full of other memorabilia, too: old letters, Christmas cards, school reports, thank-you notes, prayer bouquets, class photos, Mass cards, death notices, etc.

When Rose was gardening this week she asked me to pick up some manure, and when I asked the attendant at Kmart if cow manure was better than sheep he said he didn't know, and an old man in white Adidas, grey slacks and a blue peaked cap broke into our discussion, said he'd been a farmer all his life and recommended sheep manure. I thanked him and asked if he still kept a garden. "Not since I got cancer a year ago," he replied, then added, "but it's no use complainin', I've had a dandy life." Not long ago Nicole and I visited Little Lake cemetery to look for Dad's grave, but I was unsuccessful. I don't want you to be consigned to the dustbin of history, a disembodied memory tucked away in a cardboard box in the corner of a dank basement with a pile of family relics, faded and forgotten like my father's gravesite. Live fully and authentically in the present moment, these old photos say, confident that ultimately no one's unremembered, that though we now see through a glass darkly, as St. Paul said, someday we will see face to face. I pray for that day.

Searching for Father

I drove through the iron gate, told
Nicole to wait, I'd soon be back.

I remembered you weren't far away,
near the shore, close to a maple,

but I'd only been there once before
and all the maples looked the same

to me. Up and down the shore I paced
looking for your Irish face

(once I thought I saw you peek
behind a stone). I panicked, grew dizzy

in the head, cupped my hands, shouted
out your name — the old couple

with pink carnations must have thought
I'd gone insane. Later I leaned

against the van and explained
(she wondered why I'd been gone so long)

that you'd been cunningly mislaid.
Next time I'll bring a map, I said.

CR

You always said I possessed a vivid imagination. The remembering heart is a river with no banks. Memories of childhood and sunken psychic wounds rise up and are borne along on the flood of grief. Puberty dropped on me like a bombshell. My voice deepened and almost overnight I was catapulted from a clear-skinned, nimble boy into a pimply-faced awkward teenager. Acne blazed a scarlet trail across my face and I became morbidly self-conscious and shy, would even cross the street to avoid the scrutiny of girls. I swallowed handfuls of foul-tasting yeast (someone had told me yeast was good for acne) and spent hours before the bathroom mirror attacking every white-tipped eruption. "Stop picking your zits," Mom harped. I began to mimic the lopsided grin of my favourite actor, Glen Ford, which provoked Dad to comment, "What's that stupid grin on his face for?" Life frightened me and my adolescence became a cover-up and pretence, a flight from reality. Ronnie Colson, my new friend whose English parents had just immigrated to Canada, lived in a tenement on Louis Street, not far from our place. One day he invited me to the Odeon to see *Great Expectations* (he'd been bragging ad nauseam about the superiority of British films); until then I'd gorged on Hollywood fare (cowboy and Indian, Abbott and Costello, propaganda war flicks, etc.) and I remember how I almost jumped out of my skin during the opening graveyard scene. It was like a religious conversion; I was smitten and soon became a regular at the Odeon. Olivier, Mills, Guinness, Richardson, Gielgud became my new cinematic idols; though I kept the grin even Glen Ford began to lose some of his lustre for me. The truth is I didn't like myself, was ashamed of my impoverished home and undistinguished parents and had set out to reinvent myself.

One Saturday afternoon I overheard Dad asking Mom in the kitchen. "Is there something wrong with that lad?"

"What do you mean?"

"That bloomin' English accent is what I meant!"

"Why don't you lay off the boy," I heard her reply. Mom was always coming to my defense.

But Dad was right. Consciously or unconsciously I'd adopted an English accent – a hybrid of Alec Guinness and Michael Wilding. The transformation had happened almost overnight: one day I was Jim Clarke, a poor kid from the wrong side of the tracks; the next, a sophisticated Englishman of the world. British expressions like "jolly good," "crashing bore," and "bloody" crept into my vocabulary. My friends were disgusted, thought I was losing it. "Got the flu or something?" one of them mocked.

At school I fancied that the girls found me charming and irresistible. Whenever I came near they'd stop what they were doing and gape. Soon after I acquired the accent Sister Clothilde, my history teacher, decided the time was ripe for a symposium on the newly formed United Nations and asked me, her star student, to participate. The Cold War was just beginning, people were terrified at the possibility of nuclear war, and the UN offered a ray of hope. The symposium was scheduled to be heard in the auditorium before the entire school. For my part of the program Sister had asked me to explain the differences between the new body and the old League of Nations. I researched for days and honed my delivery in the bathroom. My diligent efforts paid off in soaring confidence. After one of my bathroom rehearsals I overheard Dad again:

"Somethin's got be done about that lad, Florie," he was saying. "The Limey accent is getting on my nerves."

When the day of the assembly arrived and my name was called (I was the last speaker), I bounded to the podium, Ford's lopsided grin still plastered on my face. "Thank you for the jolly good introduction," I began, referring to my friend Jonesy, who'd introduced me. From the start of my speech I had the feeling my voice belonged to a stranger. No longer Jim Clarke, I was Alec Guinness and Michael Wilding rolled into one, and their dulcet accent was music in my ears. The silence in the auditorium became almost palpable and I had the euphoric feeling that I held the audience in the palm of my hand, spellbound. Out of the corner of my eye, I caught Sister Clothilde's broad freckled face frowning in the sea of blurred faces. My friends slumped in their seats, ducked their heads, and the nuns in the front row fidgeted with their beads. A scattering of applause, a few titters, but mostly silence greeted me when I finished; the audience seemed frozen in their seats, but I wasn't the least fazed. I attributed the reaction to my stunning performance. The next day Sister Clothilde asked me to stay after class, said she had something important to discuss.

"That was quite a speech you gave yesterday," she started. "Congratulations."

"Thank you, Sister," I replied, trying to sound casual, but inside secretly glowing.

A compliment from Sister Clothilde, the best teacher in the school, meant something.

We chatted for a while about schoolwork and then she went on, "If you don't mind me asking, Jim, is your father English?"

"No, Sister, he's Irish."

"And your mother, then?"

"She's French Canadian."

"French Canadian," she repeated pensively, and gazed out the window. There was a long pause before she turned and smiled.

"Well, you must have spent time in England, then," she said, as though she'd finally solved the puzzle.

"No, Sister," I said. "I've never been out of Canada."

"But of course then you've got an English nanny at home?"

"No, Sister."

"No English nanny?" She looked bemused.

I shook my head.

Then Sister fixed me with a steely look.

"I'm confused, Jim," she said. "Then where did you pick up the English accent?"

The directness of her question threw me off balance and I felt blood rushing to my head. I started to fidget, fell mute. Sister's intense blue gaze burned through me, reducing my carefully constructed alter ego to ashes. The silence seemed to go on forever. I could feel a gnawing, burning pain in the pit of my stomach, my eyes beginning to tear up.

"That's fine, Jim," she finally said. "I was just curious, that's all."

"One last thing, Jim," she said softly as I hastened to leave. "Keep your own accent, it's good enough."

One day soon after my talk with Sister I was walking home from school with my friend Colson. "Jim, what happened?" he asked. "Where's your English accent?"

"Oh, shut up, Colson," I snapped.

My English phase came and went like a fever. I was soon back to my old self, Jim Clarke, only son of Flo and Sam, a poor kid from the wrong side of the tracks who wasn't English and never had an English nanny. I would have to find some other way to reinvent myself.

Stigma

In those days drugs and nostrums didn't exist.
No one had money for doctors. Squeezing,

Ivory soap and warm water, Noxema, baker's
yeast swallowed by the handful, fruit diets,

nothing worked. You felt like a leper, hugged
the shadows, crossed the street too shy

to look any girl in the face. When you tried
to hide your shame with talc, friends jeered,

called you queer. Acne became a state of mind,
an unwashable stain leaking through eyes

onto skin, clothing and grass, until the whole
world became one big, crimson sore. Acne was

the curse of Cain, a public confession
of self-abuse, a sin so heinous it dyed

the soul black, merited the unquenchable
ovens of hell forever and ever.

CR

GRIEF, THE TIME OF ASHES, SAYS ROBERT BLY IN IRON JOHN, IS THE
door to feeling. The volcanic ash from your suicide pelted me with images
and feelings from my childhood on Simcoe Street. Memories of Dad,
the unfinished business between fathers and sons, thrust themselves into
consciousness. I vaguely recall the day he came home from work – it was June
26, 1940 – face flushed and a little unsteady, to announce he'd joined the
army. "It's my duty," he declared. "The country needs me." And all Mom's
tearful pleading couldn't make him change his mind. At 31, with a wife
and three small children, he could have sat out the war with honour, Mom
later told me. "He didn't like the responsibility of married life, wanted to
get away, that's all." Is this where my own restlessness comes from? It was
about this time, too, that Mom hired Gaby, a young woman from Quebec,
as housekeeper.

I still have a black-and-white photo of him in Central Park taken shortly
after he signed up; he's wearing a white shirt, dark suspenders and a pith
helmet and doesn't look military at all as he grins for the camera, but that
was soon to change. In another photo he's marching down George Street in
full battledress – the last parade before transfer to Nova Scotia, rifle at the
slope, arm swinging in unison with the rest of the platoon, the unswerving
determination of a patriot on his face. Despite his instructions to me not to
follow, the temptation was too great. The whirling kilts, sound of bagpipes
and rhythmic stamp of big black boots on the pavement drew me like a

magnet. I dodged in and out of the onlookers all the way to Exhibition Park far from home, trying to catch a glimpse of his face. Only when the sky behind the big drill hall turned red and purple did I remember his warning and race home, late for supper. Gaby met me at the door, ordered me to my bedroom. "Wait till your dad hears of this," she said. My head was still throbbing with the excitement of the day when the door opened and she brought me an egg salad sandwich and glass of milk. She didn't say anything. She mustn't have told Dad, either, for I never heard of the incident again. After Dad's regiment was shipped overseas in 1941 the war became an invisible but glamorous backdrop to my life. Ration books were a constant reminder that a bitter struggle was taking place across the sea against an evil foe, and I was proud Dad was part of it. On Saturday matinees at the New Centre theatre, newsreels showed footage of the war, planes tracing deadly arabesques over the blue summer skies of London and the peaceful English countryside. The black specks looked more like lazy bees than war machines. Occasionally a newsreel displayed twisted and smoking wreckage, invariably a swastika on its side. Instead of cowboys and Indians my chums and I chose sides and played war. We charged up snowbanks and lobbed snowball grenades at each other. We bought helmets and goggles at Millard's Sporting Goods and morphed into Spitfires and Messerschmitts. Arms extended, school bags on our backs for parachutes we flew through snowy streets and backyards, tongues rattling as we raked our make-believe skies with lethal fire.

I kept a secret projector in my head. Before falling asleep I'd become the hero of daring feats, rescuing people behind enemy lines, just like Dad, exploits that went on and on every night just like the Hopalong Cassidy serials at the Regent, and uncannily I never lost the thread of the story, could pick it up precisely where I'd left off the evening before. Compared to my nocturnal life, school was flat and boring. Yet despite my fantasies the war never became real until that Saturday morning in the York Trading yard when I heard the high-pitched voice of Billy Foster, my friend: "Hurry! Enemy at nine o'clock!" I craned my head, spotted him on the highest platform of the York Trading fire escape, hands shading his eyes, staring into the clear blue morning sky. I heard a faint rumble, scrambled up the staircase, the rumble now a deafening roar, but I still couldn't see the enemy until Billy shouted, "Messerschmitts, nine o'clock!" and pointed to the sky over Albert's junkyard. Five mustard-coloured planes in single-line formation, so low they seemed to skim the roofs of houses, shot into view, heading straight towards us. "Man the ack-acks!" Billy shouted. As the giant yellow birds thundered over our heads, the pulsing air drowned out the rat-a-tat-tats of our guns and I thought I glimpsed one of the pilots in his cockpit with goggles and leather helmet, but wasn't sure. In an instant the planes had turned into black specks on the horizon and disappeared and our first encounter with the enemy was over. The war became a deeply ingrained metaphor for my generation of boys, and you, who always discouraged the children from watching violence of any ilk, could never understand (or approve) my fondness for war movies.

Dad became a prolific letter writer. Once a week the thin blue envelopes dropped through the mail slot in the front door, scrawny blue birds exhausted from their long sea voyage, scattering like pale blue feathers on the old linoleum. The letters, postmarked "somewhere in Britain," had an aura of mystery. Mine were invariably addressed "Master James Clarke" and I never understood the "master" part. The letters took on a life of their own and littered the floor of the summer kitchen, where my sisters and I spent hours poring over them. Those to Mom always began "My Dearest Darling" and were chock full of endearments (not all of which we understood), how much he loved her, promises to reform his ways, give up the bottle, be a good father and husband. "You'll see, darling I've changed." Invariably he'd end with the pledge that his gratuity would go to the new house Mom always dreamt about. Mom and Gaby spent hours in the kitchen packing cigarettes and other treats into cardboard boxes to send overseas, tying the boxes with butcher string. Before bedtime Mom would croon "The White Cliffs of Dover" in her soft melodious voice and tears would appear, especially at the part my name was mentioned. And when she talked about the end of the war her face took on a glow of wistfulness and anticipation.

July 1944, a warm august morning and I'm playing baseball cards in the kitchen. The front doorbell rings and the long gaunt mien of Canon Robertson appears. He puts an arm around Mom's shoulders and leads her into the front parlour. Soon we hear Mom's sobbing. After the Canon leaves we join her in the parlour. Her face is splotchy and red; she's dabbing a white handkerchief on her eyes.

"Your dad's been wounded," she tells us in a broken snuffling voice.

"You mean he's dead?" I say.

"How could you say such a thing?" says Gaby, clicking her tongue. "No, of course he's not dead."

"He's just wounded," Mom adds gently, but she doesn't seem convinced. My sisters are crying, but I haven't shed a tear. I feel guilty, wonder if there's something wrong with me.

A few days later Dad's picture appeared on the front page of the newspaper. "City man wounded at Caen," the caption read. Dad instantly became a local hero and my lack of tears didn't stop me from bragging to friends. "The bullet went through here," I'd say, pointing to my right temple as they listened bug-eyed in silence. I felt more elated than sad.

Early Sunday morning, a few weeks before Christmas 1945. I hear voices in the kitchen. I slip out of bed, peer through the chimney hole in the cold linoleum floor. Mom is pacing back and forth, fists at her waist.

"How could you have?" she's saying.

Dad doesn't answer, gets up abruptly, knocking over his chair, and stomps into the bedroom, slamming the door. For a long while Mom leans against the kitchen sink, head bowed. Then she picks up the toppled chair, sits and lays her head on her folded arms on the table and begins to cry. I climb back into bed, gaze at the grainy light in the window. The morning cold and Mom's weeping seems to seep into every corner of the desolate tenement. For the first time in my life I feel the fire of impotent rage.

Yellow Flypaper

It would start in the kitchen
on hot summer evenings,
pleasant enough at first,
but after a few drinks
her eyes would narrow,
her mouth twist,
and I'd turn away,
stare at the squirming flies
on the yellow flypaper
near the stove,
for I knew what was coming next —

how he'd broken his promise,
blown his gratuity, $1453.21
— five years of hope —
enough for a downpayment
on a good house
in one night of poker,
and now "we're stuck in this goddam
hole," she'd say,
which was his signal
to grab the bottle and leave,

but not before he'd slammed
the kitchen door so hard
I thought the flies would
shudder loose,
but they never did.

CR

WOULD IT HAVE MADE ANY DIFFERENCE IF I'D STAYED HOME THAT PALM Sunday? I don't know. All I know is that my absence that Sunday stirred recollections of other times I was absent when it most counted. I loved my father but we were never close. We were like two strangers calling to each other across a wide canyon, our voices lost in the wind. His drinking dropped a curtain over the inner man; I rarely saw him sober and to this day have trouble imagining him as my father. I had a dream the other night. I was in a roomful of people and everyone was talking about his saintly death. "He died with such dignity," a woman said, eyes aglow with admiration and the others nodded in agreement. Their admiration made me reconsider my opinion, view him in a different light. And then I woke and remembered the old gypsy saying: "You have to dig deep to bury a father." Once when I was still in high school Mom dispatched me to the Johnson House, a popular watering hole in the city. "Hurry, Jim," she told me, "the bartender says he's in bad shape." When I got there the dark cavernous beverage room was almost deserted; the stench of stale beer made me nauseous. "Looking for your father, son?" the bartender said, pointing to a corner of the room. "He's over there." Slumped at a table, staring at the floor, chin propped on his thick chest, Dad was muttering to himself, his breath shallow, skin yellowish even in the dim light. I tapped him on the shoulder.

"Dad, it's me, Jim. Time to come home," I said. He raised his glazed eyes, tried to focus. "Oh, Jim, it's you," was all he said. The next day his doctor warned that he'd have to stop drinking or he'd be a dead man in two years, but Dad fooled everyone; he never stopped and lived a dozen or so more years, proud of his indestructibility. "We Irishmen are tough," he'd brag, quoting Marshall Foch: "Give me a thousand Irishmen and I'll lick the world." Jean Vanier said we're all looking for spiritual fathers, someone to guide us through the maze of life. Dad had no gift for fatherhood, was incapable of opening up even to those he loved most, and was like a phantom in my life. In his last few years you and I could see he was losing the battle, that the jaundice was slowing destroying his once robust body. I found it painful to watch his decline; he'd boxed in the army and according to family lore held the heavyweight championship of his division and I always considered him unbreakable, a force of nature. He was husky and well muscled, and his head seemed fused to broad shoulders like a ball, giving the impression he had no neck. When he arm-wrestled with cronies at the kitchen table (few could beat him), his short powerful arm reminded me of a sturdy piece of oak. After a while he began to lose his appetite but he never showed fear – the word was not in his vocabulary. The last year of his life he did something unusual, at least for him: he reduced his consumption of alcohol to two beers a day. When you and I visited him in those last few months, mostly Saturday mornings, he'd be sitting at the kitchen table reading the sports page of the local paper and when he'd see us he'd rise to offer you his chair. "Your dad's such a gentleman when he's sober," you'd always comment. All his life he hated gardening but in that last spring he planted a bed of red and yellow tulips along the verandah at the front of the house. Even when the jaundice ravaged his body so badly he could hardly get out of bed in the morning he watered the tulips faithfully. One Saturday when I dropped by alone he insisted I see them. Outside we discovered a small spotted black-and-white mongrel rooting in the flowers.

"Get outta there," Dad yelled, clapping his hands. The dog stared at us boldly, then trotted down the sidewalk as though insulted. Then Dad's brown eyes brightened and he pointed at the tulips. "Beautiful, eh?" he said, "and next year they'll be even better."

That warm afternoon in July 1968 when Mom rang to say he was very sick and needed to go into hospital right away, I sensed urgency in her tone. "Hurry, Jim, it's bad," she said, voice quaking. When I got to the house Dad was in bed upstairs lying in the fetal position, his left eye glistening and unblinking like a stricken animal, skin ochre, belly distended. He looked awful. "Florie, take care of the tulips," were his parting words as we drove off. At the hospital I found a wheelchair and wheeled him into the reception area. After a short time I said goodbye, shook his thick rough hand. "See you soon, Dad," I said. Then, duty done, with no kiss, no embrace, no "I love you," just a brief handshake, I made a hurried getaway. Why are my partings always such disasters? That same day I left for a short holiday in the Laurentians. I had just arrived at my Aunt Palma's when the phone rang. It was Mom. "Your dad's dying," she said. "You'd better hurry back if you ever want to see him alive again." All the way back I felt terrible that I wasn't there with Mom and my sisters, the people I loved, during Dad's last hours. And when I finally got to the hospital and saw Mom standing in the corridor, bleary-faced with grief, I knew I was too late. "Your dad passed away fifteen minutes ago," she said. I held her for a long while and then went into his room alone, the venetian blinds half-closed, the room eerily quiet. A beige plastic curtain encircled the bed and I paused to wipe the sweat from my brow with my coat sleeve. As powerful feelings of regret and guilt roiled inside me, I could feel my heart thumping, but mostly it was anger I felt: anger at myself, the nurses, and especially Dad.

All my life I'd been cheated of a father and now I'd been cheated by death. Who would I find behind the curtain? I tried to pray but couldn't. Then I took a deep breath and yanked open the curtain. Yes, it was Dad, smaller, thinner, his face bonier than I'd ever remembered him. His swollen belly had shrunk and I could see the outline of his skull under the grey skin. His lips were partly open and a drop of moisture clung to the side of his long patrician nose, which appeared longer and sharper than when he was alive. I touched his hands; they were still warm but the flesh had already begun to stiffen. I gazed for a long time at this passionate Irishman who was my father, no longer flesh and blood, now an icon of clay, and I felt a deep sadness for all of us – my mother, my sisters and especially for him and me and the deep gulf we were never able to bridge.

The Visit

"We never knew him," my sister said,
and so I told her about my trek
to Sunnybrook
the year before he died,

the time they operated on his hand,
carpal tunnel syndrome,
the doctor called it,

shocked to find
not the quarry
I'd hunted all those years, but
a stranger
calm and sober.

And while he fed an old comrade
who'd lost both arms in Normandy,
he asked about the law,
my wife,
    the kids,
        our plans,
and for the first time in my life
listened to me talk.

I told her about my trek
that year before he died.
I didn't tell her
I overstayed my time.

CR

ON THE WAY TO COURT THIS MORNING I NOTICED A MOBILE YELLOW SIGN IN front of a house on Kortright. "You can still be productive after 50" it announced as a good wish to a birthday someone. As though the criterion for successful living is productivity! Today a legal ruling confronted me I didn't want to make. The plaintiff, who received a blow to the head in a rear-end collision, claimed it triggered grand mal seizures. She called as her first witness her doctor, a gentle woman with strong convictions about holistic medicine. Counsel for the defence sought leave to cross-examine the doctor about the recent death of her own fourteen-year-old daughter, citing an autopsy report that suggested she'd failed to come to her daughter's aid the night she died from a severe asthma condition. The lawyer tried to justify the line of questioning on the grounds that it went to the competence of the witness as a medical practitioner. "How could you?" the woman cried. Great sobs racked her, her face took on a ghostly pallor and she had to be assisted from the witness box. During the recess my court officer told me she was still in the washroom, sobbing. After court finally reconvened I breathed a big sigh of relief when the lawyer announced he'd decided to drop the line of questioning. Since your suicide I easily slip into the shoes of people like the doctor suffering pangs of guilt. In the presence of the children I'm always conscious of their pain, try to steer the conversation away from their tender and live spots.

At the start of our marriage you and Mom didn't get along. My sister insists to this day that I was Mom's favourite and at the beginning of our married life you labelled me "momma's boy," remember? When she entered the hospital that last time for what was supposed to be a routine check-up and my sister phoned to say her condition had turned grave, I was thrown into deep shock. At the hospital the young doctor gave us a stark choice: "Do you want to let her go or do you want us to do everything to save her?" he asked.

As she'd always been a fighter we agreed on the spot to pull out all the stops. Little did I know what the word "everything" implied, the torture we were about to visit on her. Immediately they wheeled her into Intensive Care, strapped her into a teeter-totter gurney (she'd picked up pneumonia in the hospital and had trouble breathing), rammed a fat white plastic tube down her throat, rendering her totally immobile, unable to talk or move. Eventually the tube rubbed her lips raw and they began to swell and bleed. Her frantic eyes begged us to put an end to her ordeal, but we persisted, convinced that doctor knew best, that it was her only hope. But after ten days even the doctor must have given up for they finally removed the tube, unstrapped her and put her back in a regular room. We salved her lips, whispered in her ear how much we loved her, but we could see it was too late. The tremendous vitality that had kept her fighting for so many years against great odds was slipping away, and along with it the will to live. And later when I got my sister's call in my chamber to come, that Mom was leaving us, I dropped everything and rushed to the hospital – for I didn't want to be absent for her death as I'd been for my father's (and as I was to be for yours) – to find her still breathing, eyes sunk inward, dull blue stones, hands already cold as marble and I knew she was far away, back in the sunlit blueberry fields of her Quebec childhood where she'd been so happy growing up. A few minutes later (I'd left the room momentarily) my sister emerged, tears in her eyes and said, "She's gone, Jim," and I knew another part of me had died.

CR

WRITING ABOUT YOUR SUICIDE AND MY INVISIBLE WOUNDS IN THESE kaddishes scrapes my soul raw, but Carl Rogers says sharing what is personal and unique in our life, even when it makes us feel exposed and vulnerable, finds resonance in others and speaks to them deeply. We grow a skin over our wounds by finding words for them. Your suicide was not my first experience of abandonment. The most traumatic episodes of my childhood occurred when Mom periodically took to the bottle and abdicated responsibility for running the household; her defection represented a loss of control and total breakdown of security in our lives. We had learned to navigate around Dad's tippling by distancing ourselves from it, carrying on as though he didn't exist. As long as Mom was in command our family could fly on one engine, just like the bombers in the war movies, and we knew we were safe, but when the other engine conked out we knew a crash was inevitable. To use a nautical metaphor, our home became a ship without compass and keel, drifting towards the shoals. Oh, the crushing feeling of helplessness and panic! To watch Mom waft woozily around the house, slack-jawed, in a soiled white slip, head encircled by a haze of blue smoke, hair mussed, eyes bleary, eyelids puffy, shook us to the core. In the miasma created by drink Mom would turn her guns on Dad, recite her litany of grievances, fleshing out in lurid detail his infidelities and thereby enlisting my two sisters and me, wittingly or unwittingly, as allies in her ongoing war. When the cupboards were bare she'd slip us a few dollars, dispatch us to the Chinese restaurant on Charlotte Street, where for 75 cents you could get a three-course supper. After we'd get home I'd sneak upstairs and ensconce myself in the airless cubbyhole of my closet, which I'd rigged up with lamp and table as a study.

Monday mornings there was always a big hangover; her body quaked, hands shook, and often she'd dispatch one of us to the Empress with a note saying she had the flu and couldn't come in to work that day, the same flimsy excuse each time. And then with gritted teeth she'd begin the gruelling uphill climb back to sobriety, groaning and sometimes bringing up, nibbling a little, all the while feeling increasingly guilty and contrite because she'd let us down. We were so happy to see her on the road to recovery, returning to her old responsible self, that her growing shame didn't register on us.

In hindsight I marvel at her resilience and indomitable spirit, for though often down she never gave up and always bounced back. You knew she'd won when she began to issue orders, tell us to tidy our rooms and start to clean up the house, bathe, wash, starch and iron her white uniform, girding herself for her next battle with the unforgiving and harsh reality of her life.

Adrift

The dingy pushes off from the shore. It's early evening,
the sun is hiding behind stone blind clouds. As the man
rows towards the middle of the lake, oars rock in their

sockets, fog swirls off the waters in ghostly pockets.
But the man and woman don't notice; they're too busy
taking turns swigging from a bottle, having fun.

Soon the banter changes, old hurts break the surface
like famished fish, their words begin to snare. The
children, who've heard it all before, shut their eyes,

cup their ears. Abruptly the man stands up, declares
he won't take it anymore, plunges into the lake. The
woman is furious, shouts for him to stop, but he won't listen,

thrashes like a rogue wave towards the invisible shore.
Quickly, she undresses down to her panties, exposing
small white breasts. She tells the children she's going

to find their daddy, not to fret, she'll soon be back. Then
she too dives into the grey-brown mist. As the sound
of her splashes fades in the distance, silence

descends over the boat, fog thickens, night closes in.
The cries of the children are swallowed by the dark
mouth of the lake. The battered shell begins to drift.

CR

LAST EVENING I PONDERED AGAIN THE GIFT OF FAITH, CONCLUDED IT WASN'T
so much a question of taking solace in divine certitudes as a way of seeing the
world – a kind of double vision whereby we read the flinty sobering events of
our lives (and the happy ones, too) against the backdrop of eternity and the
infinite. Some skeptics argue that "soul," "spirit" and even "consciousness"

are an exclusive by-product of the brain or bodily functioning, yet quantum physics has enshrined the "uncertainty principle" at the heart of the universe. Put differently, ultimate reality is much more unknowable and immeasurable than previously believed, is more akin to a "great thought" than a clockwork machine. In the eyes of faith, as Ronald Rolheiser says, there are no conspiracies or accidents, only the loving arms of Providence.

As a Christian I was taught that God so loved the world that he gave his only-begotten son to suffer and die for us, and that to suffer with him is to participate in God's plan and to become partners in the work of redemption – a belief anathema to the modern mind, which sees all suffering as useless, the enemy of humankind, to be eradicated at all costs. Throughout history, paradoxically, Christians have been in the forefront of the battle to alleviate pain and suffering. Was redemptive suffering the theological underpinning to your desire to please, to put the needs of others ahead of your own? Or was it something more mundane, like desire for social acceptance, a way to buttress low self-esteem? Sometimes I think we're all conscripted co-partners and that God's got us all twisting on the head of a pin. In his memoir *Now and Then*, Frederick Buechner recounts the impact of the departure of his daughters for boarding school, how it felt like kissing them goodbye forever, that their Vermont home would never be their home again and how fearful he was for their future, the "cruel and hurtful" things the world would do to them. When I left home for McGill University in 1953, Mom went through a similar experience. One day she was cleaning my room and in the closet came upon my old Daisy air rifle (which she'd smashed to pieces years earlier in reprisal for my shooting birds), and the sight of the broken parts unleashed a flood of tears that lasted for days, she said. In contrast to Christianity, Buddhism teaches Upekkha – a state of detachment that breaks all fetters, including love, that bind humans to the wheel of rebirth, a necessary stage on the road to Nirvana. Since your suicide I've felt the "cruel and hurtful" things that happen to our children, including your death, sometimes more sharply than my own pain and have been helpless to stop them. Why didn't someone warn me a parent's heart is permanently wired for pain?

Buechner thinks Buddhism has something to teach us about standing back from, leaving space for others and letting go. He concluded that his involvement in the lives of his daughters through loving and needing – "co-dependency" is the buzzword today – ran the risk of crippling both him and the children. "They have the power to destroy us," he wrote, and therefore a detachment must be kept not just from them, but from anyone we love. The image of the Buddha under his Botree, eyes closed upon an inner peace that he would not permit even his great compassion to disturb, is emblematic. Though we can't stop the bleeding – the price of loving – we must not become "bleeding hearts."

A hard truth, something I've yet to learn.

CR

YOUR SUICIDE UPROOTED ME, THRUST ME INTO LIMINAL SPACE, NAKED and alone, like entering the womb again, a period of gestation, waiting for something new to be born. Sometimes I feel as detached and isolated as the white rind of the moon in the sky this morning; it's as though I'm living under a bubble of glass that separates me from the world and others. But the firewall of the mind can't stop the flood of unleashed memories.

After four years of courtship you finally cornered me one evening on the porch of 11 Traymore: "What are your intentions?" you said. "I need to know." Your bluntness caught me off guard. "Marry you, of course," I blurted and thus the train of our marriage was set in motion, only to be detoured for one brief period just a few weeks before my final Christmas law exams when you got cold feet and called off the wedding. I was devastated. I walked around in a trance, your decision glued to my heart like heavy plaster, and flipped through my law school notes mindlessly for days, unable to concentrate and already blaming you for what appeared like my impending failure. I needn't have worried; we reconciled a few days before the start of exams and despite my emotional and mental befuddlement I managed to do very well on the exams (two A's and two B's, as I recall) — much better, in fact, than my Cassandra-like friends who'd been predicting my academic demise ever since you dropped your bomb. The year before our marriage (before the move to Cobourg) I'd worked in Peterborough and saved the princely sum in those days of $1500, which we'd decided to spend on an exotic honeymoon (how thrilled we were) in the Bahamas. The honeymoon got off to a rocky start, remember? Our flight to Nassau got sidetracked in New York (an overbooked connection) and we were forced to spend a night in a seedy downtown hotel. The prospect of our first nuptial night together unnerved me so much (despite guzzling most of a bottle of bootleg Jack Daniels to fortify myself) that I was incapable of consummating the marriage. When we got to the Montague Beach Hotel in Nassau — will you ever forget the turquoise colour, the flaking paint on the damp bedroom walls and the enormous black cockroaches skittering across the shower room floor and up the walls that made you scream? — my flagging manhood showed no signs of improvement. After two or three days of frenetic and fruitless efforts my sexual libido looked like it had permanently surrendered the ghost and you grew worried — so worried, in fact, you began to surmise I was a closeted gay and the marriage a colossal mistake. You buried your head in the pillow and sobbed, remember, all your romantic dreams blown to bits. Attributing my lack of performance to "iron-poor blood" I glugged several bottles of evil-tasting Geritol at the dock, but instead of helping it only gave me a sore tummy. Then to cap off our misery I made the ill-advised decision to rent an open convertible to tool around the island in the blazing sun till our skins were puffed crimson and agony to the touch. That spelled the demise of our abortive lovemaking. But when we got back to Canada this interlude of defeat changed; my nervousness gradually dissipated and our lovemaking took on fresh life, so much so, remember, that the embarrassing episode eventually slipped into history and we began to look back on it with amusement. And over the years (despite your fear of pregnancy) there were moments when the "little deaths" of our couplings dissolved egos and we experienced a sense of at-onement, two souls enfleshed in one body, swept up in a wave of unity with the universe as though God had slipped between the tangled bedsheets and was part of our lovemaking. But those moments were rare and fleeting; despite our God-intoxication we eventually bumped into our limits, knew there was something missing in our brave new world of the heart, some distance between us we could never fully bridge no matter how often or how smoothly we rubbed against each other. We came to realize that our hearts were too wide, our longings too deep, our craving for the infinite too powerful, for each of us to fulfill the other, and the best we could do was to console the other for our inability to totally meet each other's expectations. As Ronald Rolheiser put it, in the end we sleep alone.

CR

OUR FIRST HOME AS A MARRIED COUPLE WAS A RENTED BUNGALOW ON Cedarmere Avenue in Cobourg, which had a creek at the back fringed with weeping willows and cattails and a few hundred feet away the shining platter of Lake Ontario. Traditionalists that we were I carried you across the threshold (one of the neighbours told me later she found it sooo romantic) and plunked you down on the sofa in the front room. From the kitchen window we could see the grey-blue waters of the lake, hear the rasping of the surf on the pebbly beach. To celebrate our arrival you decided on a special dinner of French crêpes (the favourite recipe of a friend) in the front room before the fireplace; we wheeled in the antique green tea wagon we'd purchased for a song at the Salvation Army, laid a fresh white tablecloth and, sipping good French wine in the soft glow of candlelight, accompanied by the crackle of the flames, we gazed into each other's eyes, the movie theatre of our dreams, completely immersed in the magic of the moment – until, that is, I leaned forward on the leaf of the tea wagon and a loud metal snap resounded in our ears and your special crêpes together with our burgeoning romance came crashing down on the carpet. We collapsed in a heap of laughter at the trick the rusty springs of reality had played on us.

It was on Cedarmere that the first faint rifts appeared on our marital horizon. After a quarrel I sometimes ran off to Peterborough (my pretext was always the same: I had to visit my mother) and left you behind seething with resentment and when I returned you'd be there at the door to greet me with cold eye and biting tongue. "Did momma take good care of her little boy?" you'd ask sarcastically. Do you remember the occasion we invited our neighbours, the retired Major and his wife, for a spaghetti supper in the garden? We were outside and you were just about to serve when I said something about the sauce being a little spicy (in hindsight I surmise there must have been a more substantial reason for your reaction) and you exploded, threw a plateful of spaghetti at me that missed (at the last second I ducked) and hit Bonzo, the neighbours' prize Boxer, who was just sitting there minding his own business, square on the snout; the dog couldn't believe his luck, let out a grateful woof and proceeded to lap up the spaghetti like caviar and then had the unmitigated gall to hike his leg and piss on your garden chair.

"I taught him that," quipped the unflappable Major, a comment we found so hilarious we immediately forgot our spat and made up. And remember Sambo, our black-and-tan mongrel, police dog and God-knows-what-else, we couldn't control? He was always roaming the neighbourhood, contrary to the town's animal control bylaw that I'd been instrumental as a newly elected town councillor in getting passed. We got an irate phone call from another neighbour, a breeder of purebred hounds, early one Sunday morning. "Your goddam mutt was over to our property again in contravention of *your* goddam bylaw," he spluttered, "and worse, he's got one of my bitches pregnant." He demanded to know what I intended to do about it, but assuming the legalistic stance that was my professional persona in those days I coolly rejoined, "Can you prove it?" which only infuriated him more and made him slam down the receiver. But it was the strolls on the beach on early summer evenings when the setting sun daubed the scattered clouds with gold leaf, holding hands and listening to the hiss of the receding surf on the shore, gazing at the colourful shark fins of sailboats on the horizon and those lovely salmon-pink and scarlet sunsets that bathed our world with dreams and the promise of tomorrow that I remember most poignantly. And it was on Cedarmere that we made our first lifelong friends in the town that was to be our home for the next 23 years of our life.

CR

NOT TOO LONG AFTER OUR MARRIAGE YOU LOANED ME YOUR BRUSHES AND paint box and I began to dabble in art. Art fascinated me and I was always in awe of your skills as an artist. Do you remember my first oil (a windy lake, gun-metal-grey sky and a pine island, all dark greens and blues), which you diplomatically said wasn't that bad for a beginner's, how elated I got? I was always a messy painter and to your chagrin would come home after an outing with face, hands, clothing smeared in paint. And you'd have a conniption every time I failed (which was often) to screw the caps back on the tubes. In the next few years my interest evolved into an obsession and I'd steal away from the office every opportunity I found (I always kept easel and paint box in the trunk of the car) to paint, fancying myself a second Van Gogh. After I switched mainly to watercolours and would do a batch at one sitting (I was prodigal and slapdash, letting the watercolours do the work for me, which on lucky days they did), I'd rush home to display my efforts around the front room and insist you drop everything for a few minutes to critique them. I considered you the artist in the family and me the dilettante, and your approval even of a single sketch would make my day. How galling it must have been for you, the frustrated artist saddled with children and large household, to watch as I, *puer* – the eternal boy – free as a bird, winged all over the countryside to sketch, my only talent, a little art in my soul and the derring-do of ignorance. I was encroaching on your sacred space and making a nuisance of myself to boot. And then I made the egregious error of suggesting we paint together.

Remember that sunny summer afternoon we set up easels side by side in an cow pasture north of Cobourg, the foaming greenness of the countryside all around us, to paint the same scene, a sylvan panorama of stream and woods and both of us reached for the yellow ochre at the same time, gripping an end of the tube and shouting at each other, neither willing to let go. You and I were never ones to hide our rows behind lace curtains; nor did we believe in the old Irish adage "Whatever you say, say nothing." After that you vowed you'd never paint with me again and you never did. And the noon hour I phoned all excited about an old house on College Street that had just come on the market and you rushed over and were enchanted by what you saw: the lush garden with the catalpa in the middle, polished hardwood floors, wide oak staircase and bevelled windows, three fireplaces and a wide verandah with a screen of Dutchman's Pipe on the street side and the ivy-covered wall of our neighbours on the other that made you feel you were cocooned in a green, cool underworld – a solid home in a good neighbourhood, a firm foundation on which to raise a family.

Home

Not anymore the steep edge
of the field, the wet sedge,

not anymore the pins of light in
polar night;

I have fitted my hand to the latch,
the sloping roof, found

that haven in the mind where
kisses, bread, talk

are cradled, the gravity of the
world lifted,

a place to hold onto against
the long hours of emptiness,

the irremediable cold.

CR

You were fond of saying our marriage was made in heaven and
that raising a family and being a full-time mother was a vocation. You and I
belonged to Father Peyton's rosary generation of the '50s: "The family that
prays together, stays together." In the office I have the last family portrait
I took in the old house on College Street before our move to Guelph, the
family intact, including Steve and Belle, all the girls still virgins, the boys too,
everyone smiling, a portrait of the happy Christian family firmly anchored
in the Church and the old values. Life then seemed clear, straightforward,
simple. How difficult it must have been for you to see many of the old verities
crumble in the aftermath of Vatican II, and divorce, abortion, premarital sex,
gay rights, euthanasia, etc., gain acceptance in society. And as if that wasn't
destabilizing enough, to have some of your own children rebel against the
Church's teachings. Do you remember how upset you were when Marilyn,
your redhead, started to date John, a man twelve years older and divorced?
He didn't fit your concept of the ideal Christian suitor. Only near the end
did you begin to appreciate his good character, commitment and deep love
for your daughter. If only you had lived to see them today and little Mira,
the fruit of their strong love, you would have realized how baseless your fears
were. The other day I found two of your old Cursillo retreat notes from the
'70s in the drawer of the bedroom night table and marvelled again at your
beautifully scripted and confident handwriting – so big and clear and easy to
read and such a contrast to the way I remember you at Homewood, shuffling
along the corridors, slippers rasping on the polished floors, the shuffle of an

old woman afraid of her next step. The children and I mimicked your baby steps (our imitation made you laugh, remember) but it really wasn't funny and had we not laughed we would have wept. At the end you were worn out and discouraged and none of your friends were there to buoy you up and your children were doing their own thing and you were unable to get back into your art and I was emotionally absent and I could go on and on but what's the use: you gave up and left us to pick up the pieces. For women of your generation the role of wife and mother was a virtuous enterprise abetted by both Church and culture. Driven by clocks and calendars women like you, in your quest to become the perfect nurturer, sliced and diced yourselves into such tiny morsels that you often lost track of who you were or where you were going and (I've come to believe) buried important parts of yourself, lost touch with your own inner vitality. In this post-Christian age there is no such thing as a hand-me-down faith and the Church as spiritual bomb shelter no longer exists, but love and goodness live on and each of us has to find our own way in fear and trembling. I wish you'd stayed to see the changes, to learn that God is really in charge, not us, and that we don't have to carry the weight of everyone's spiritual destiny on our backs alone.

As I sit at this computer in my chambers, an overcast but warm spring afternoon, and gaze at the lime-green buds in the maple outside the window I feel sad. A slow soft silvery rain is moving across the landscape. Am I running out of steam? How hard to be human, still the chattering monkeys, extinguish the carnal fires. How hard to dismantle the overlays of armour around the heart. In following the lodestar of memory and mourning you, my companion of 29 years, the mother of my children, I'm not only trying to capture the past, encapsulate the present and make sense of being alive but also grieving for myself and everyone.

Give my tongue wings, Lord.

☙

IN COURT TODAY I LISTENED TO THE DISHEARTENING STORY OF A MARRIED couple living under the same roof for the past two years – he in the basement, she upstairs – who never speak to each other. To minimize contact they'd worked out a rigid schedule to share bathroom and kitchen; if communication becomes absolutely necessary they write what they have to say in a journal they keep on the dining room table. Two solitudes under a single roof. Why is intimacy so difficult?

Is there a Californian fault line running through our hearts, a gap often too wide to bridge? Gut-level communication is always difficult, particularly if we ignore our shadow side, fail to deal with unmetabolized grief, remove our masks: sometimes I think we are lost in our solitudes like people in an asylum trying to communicate in half sentences, asides, silences. Is communication even possible? In the aftermath of your suicide there was so much unspoken grief, breast beating and Monday morning quarterbacking (not to mention anger and guilt) in the family that communication (especially between me and the children) became tricky, at times almost impossible, but I'm glad to report we're maturing and the scapegoating is getting less. Since your death I find jests about suicide sickening and offensive. Last evening I saw the movie *Peter's Friends* at the Bookshelf cinema: it irked me (no, that's not the right word – revolted me) when one of the characters joked about her ex-boyfriend (portrayed as a loser in the film) who threw himself off a three-storey building and almost botched his death but for a car that chanced along and finished him off. Trying to keep up with the everyday needs of the children frays my nerves; something unexpected is always cropping up, like Ruth's call today for information concerning her new driver's license, which I promised to look into for her; she'll phone back Sunday to find out what I've learned. Poor communication troubled our marriage, too. I was preoccupied with career and you were always embattled trying to keep up a busy and boisterous household; finding time together was never easy. Even our cocktail hour which we squeezed in most evenings, was often a hurried affair. After our Marriage Encounter retreat, remember, we exchanged letters about our feelings, a strategy the course suggested, and it helped for a while until we gradually went back into our old routines and our good resolutions petered out. One of the enduring regrets of my life, as you know, was my relationship with my father, our inability to talk. All my life he remained a remote, alien figure. What's that expression about two ships in the night? Jung calls dreams the royal road to the unconscious. Since your death I've kept a dream book to track my Doppelganger or "boss of my dreams," as Anne Sexton describes the stranger travelling the dark canals of my heart who wants to break out; dreams help me glimpse the fire storms raging inside – analogous, I suppose, to the giant telescopes used to detect the flare-ups of incandescent gas on the rim of the sun. It's hard to pause, look and listen; sometimes I feel trapped in the middle of a forest fire and want to flee.

My Father Never Swam for Me

My father swam in a frozen sea,
His hands were cold as snow.
My father never swam for me.

I often climbed a lonely tree
To glimpse him drifting to and fro.
My father swam in a frozen sea.

He never rocked me on his knee
Or told me how the dolphins grow.
My father never swam for me.

He longed to frolic always free
And go where silver waters flow.
My father swam in a frozen sea.

He had no time or gift to be
The kind of dad a son could know.
My father never swam for me.

There was no boat that I could row
To reach him on his truant floe.
My father swam in a frozen sea,
My father never swam for me.

CR

IN THE EARLY DAYS OF OUR MARRIAGE LIFE SEEMED TO OFFER UNLIMITED
possibilities. You were proud of your brood and because faith to you was
God's most precious gift, you wanted the children raised good Christians;
when they were small you'd often drag them to weekday Mass at St. Michael's
a couple of blocks away, the whole operation usually a last-minute blitz.
Grace before meals (Bless us, O Lord, and these thy gifts, etc.) was mandatory
and during Advent we'd light the wreath and recite special prayers from the
Advent card. "God's blessed us so much, Jim," you'd often exclaim.

Before bedtime we'd all gather at the white wood shrine you'd rigged
up on the radiator in the upstairs foyer and say a decade or two of the
rosary on our knees before the blue-and-white Virgin flanked by red votive
candles. Oh, how the hardwood floor tested our patience! The children were
restless, anxious to escape, with excuses about homework or the need to visit
friends, and it was always a battle of wills to get through the prayers, but
you persisted, coaxing special petitions, often perfunctory and half-hearted,
from each of them. I was as guilty as the children, for I always had a book
on the go, a favourite TV show or a client to meet. How you drilled into us
the importance of kindness, leading by example with myriad small acts of
thoughtfulness: visits to the sick, cookies and cakes for the bereaved, little
notes of encouragement for the downhearted. Your 110 per cent effort made
me feel like a slacker. Yes, they were mostly happy days for you on College
Street when the children were young and the house overflowed with love and
laughter. Remember the Simon and Garfunkel evenings when we danced and

cavorted in the front parlour, scandalizing the prim mainline neighbours, who must have thought we were a bit crazy with our peals of laughter and wild antics. Life seemed innocent and bright in those days before the children grew up and started to think for themselves. Many years later, when Adele taught in Mexico and was involved in a turbulent relationship (her first real love), you talked with her for hours remember, in the hotel room at Bari de Navidad, listening to her argue that the Church was sexist and virginity a farce. It was Easter Week and the Mexicans were in a festive mood, children and adults playing and frolicking on the beach outside our hotel room, the air redolent with the smell of frying shrimp. Later I awoke to find Adele snoring in bed and you still awake, pacing the tiny hotel room, fretting about her. The following evening, the singing of Mexican men, women and children drifted up from the beach, the voices so moving and melodious I opened the door to let the quiet way of song pour over us – a welcome contrast after the tumult of the day. When we made Marriage Encounter retreat many years later I had a strong premonition (it came out of the blue) that you would die before me and it disturbed me so much I began to weep because I loved you so much and the thought of you dying was unbearable; you tried to comfort me, remember? "Where did you get such a foolish idea?" you said, but the intuition was so visceral and powerful I couldn't stop; I just felt it would happen and it did.

CR

TIME WAS YOUR NEMESIS. TEETAW TOLD ME HOW SHE AND MAC NEVER understood why you always got behind in your art assignments. Fortified with coffee you'd begin your projects at the last second and work into the night well after they'd gone to bed. Often she'd get up in the wee hours, Teetaw told me, to beg you to go to bed, but you'd brush aside her entreaties and sunrise would find you still at the drawing board. Your nemesis tracked you into our marriage. Sundays, you'd rush out the door breathless, shouting, "Hurry or we'll be late for Mass!" Rounding up the children and packing the station wagon Fridays evenings for weekends at the cottage became a tug of war, with me prodding everyone to get the lead out of their asses and you snapping back, "Hold your horses" or "Go fly a kite." Sometimes you'd say you couldn't take it anymore and vow to sell the cottage unless I stopped hectoring, and I'd have no choice but to back off and sit, arms folded, in the station wagon and wait. Whether you were preparing your face for a dinner party, scrambling about the kitchen preparing dinner and muttering under your breath "I hate cooking" (which wasn't true), racing out the door with a shopping list crumpled in your fist or making a dress for the girls – you let them choose the design and material, taught them to sew – you were always in a big hurry, behind schedule. And your problems with time were complicated by your perfectionism. Unlike me, you never did anything slapdash.

In the concentration camp that was our home on Simcoe Street during the war, Gaby was the camp commander and my sisters and I the prisoners. A martinet for order and punctuality, her word was law and the kitchen Westclox, which she often carried around with her, the sole arbiter of time. Her obsession with punctuality, which she pumped into us every day, was a facet of her need to control every part of our lives. Being late, even one minute, was a serious crime (the true time didn't matter, only what her clock decreed) and meant punishment. During our one hour of liberty in the evening before bedtime, my sisters and I got into the habit of pestering passersby for the time, for we dreaded the consequences of being even one minute late. Often we'd rush home at the last moment only to have the front door fly open and find Gaby waiting, a scowl on her face, maple switch in her fist and Tiny, her dog, like a dutiful sergeant, yapping at her feet. "You're late," she'd announce, a malicious glint in her brown eyes, and begin to flail our bare legs. Or sometimes she'd lock the door, draw the curtain and yelp (Gaby had Tourette's syndrome and made strange sounds and involuntary twitches) for us to go to the back door, which we'd find was also locked, and so we'd have to trudge back and forth between the front and back until her lust for punishment was sated and she'd finally relent and let us in. Other times, if the whim overtook her, she'd hide behind the door as we entered and splash our faces with icy water. Another variation in her repertoire of punishments we dubbed "the treadmill." Instead of the back door / front door shuttle she'd plunk herself on a kitchen chair at the foot of the stairs, Tiny on her lap, the switch by her side, and force my sisters and me to march up and down the thirteen steps while she read her comics and fed Tiny morsels of fudge. We crawled up and down the stairs so often our thighs began to ache and we could barely pull each heavy leg up. If anyone faltered or complained she'd slash the back of our bare legs and bark: "Keep going till I tell you to stop." Only when we were totally exhausted and breathless, our calves often crisscrossed with faint red marks, would the punishment cease. Then Gaby would quickly whisk us off to bed before Mom got home. Small wonder you and I sometimes clashed over management of time. Even to this day a tiny dread jumps up inside me whenever I'm late for anything.

Fudge Night

After dishes Gaby orders us to wash up and get
into pajamas. She inspects outstretched hands.
Gaby has a fetish about hands; she oils her bony fingers
with Jergen's Lotion, paints her nails bright red.
She peers into ears, makes us open wide our mouths.
Failure to pass inspection means no fudge.

Tonight the dishes are stacked, the linoleum gleams.
Gaby polishes the woodstove with a wad of bread
wrapper. Wax sizzles on the hot plates, the surface
shines. Already the fragrance of maple
fills the kitchen. My mouth waters, I can almost taste
the creamy sweetness

on my tongue. Now we are seated at the table.
Gaby sits near the stove, Tiny across her lap.
Snow scratches on the window. The kitchen
is warm and cozy. Gaby wears a pink kimono,
white furry slippers. Her thick, black hair
falls in waves below the shoulders. The single over-

head bulb casts shadows on her face, makes her bright
lips glisten. Her brown eyes are fastened on the latest
Captain Marvel, her tic barely noticeable tonight.
Without raising her eyes she dips her hand
into the pan of fudge and slips a square into her mouth,
but not before giving a morsel to Tiny.

My sisters and I watch in silence as Tiny nibbles
the fudge, licks his lips with small, pink tongue.
Gaby loosens her kimono, leans forward in her chair,
the signal for me to get behind. Her thighs
feel warm against my legs. I rub her back, careful
not to touch the straps of her brassiere. As I push

my hands up and down her nobby spine the skin rolls
ahead soft and oily. Gaby moans and sighs, orders me
to use my fingernails. I notice faint red trails
where my nails have been. "Okay, enough," she says.
I scramble from behind, wait for my reward.
Gaby puts two small squares in my palm,

Tiny and my sisters get one each also. Soon
it's time for bed. I lie awake – why
am I so afraid? Gaby keeps us
clean, feeds us, helps us with our homework.
Sometimes she gives us fudge, lets us read her comics.

CR

RECENTLY I'VE HAD TWO DREAMS ABOUT SIMCOE STREET. IN THE FIRST, developers had ripped open the tenement, exposing its dark entrails to the light. But instead of a dank cellar with crumbling stone walls and the rat's hole of an open sewer pipe at one end was a magnificent wall composed of hewn granite blocks, the size of doors; the wall appeared to be part of an ancient monastery or castle and made me think of the Western wall of Jerusalem, and the sinister rat's hole had vanished. When I asked a workman the age of the tenement he answered, "Ancient." A sense of the sacred suffused the place and I felt a deep peace inside. In the second dream I was a boy living there again; the tenement was draughty, desolate and dilapidated, almost uninhabitable, and the wind sifted through the thin walls of my bedroom, ruffling the loose floral wallpaper. I took refuge in the closet, where I discovered a secret door and a steep winding staircase leading to another door. When I pushed it open I found myself outside in a beautiful tropical garden filled with the fragrance of jasmine and bougainvillea, a sickle moon on the pale blue morning horizon. It was like an oasis in the desert, a place of light and refreshment, and my heart clicked into place. Then I heard you call my name and I knew I was home at last.

CR

JUNG SAYS OUR SHADOW REFLECTS THE DEEPEST LAYERS OF OUR PERSONALITY: our strengths, weaknesses and unacknowledged gifts, inner forces that shape our behaviour and beliefs. We don't like to peer directly at the darkness and our unexorcised demons, but sometimes they push their way into consciousness and we experience altered states. Your paintings that last year took on a darker tone, an air of foreboding. The nude where you placed the woman upside down on the canvas was particularly sinister, her skin deathly grey, the colour of putrid flesh, and to add to the ghoulishness you put a black swastika in one corner. The painting had a whiff of evil about it, gave the children and me the willies and made us feel you were lost in some dark dungeon of the human psyche.

And then there was the disturbing portrait you did of me on the deck that last summer that made me look so unforgiving and judgmental. Edged with menace, these paintings gave me the same feeling I had as a child, when Mom and Dad would go to the Empress Saturday afternoons and park my sisters and me in the lobby until closing. Just waiting, not knowing who would emerge from the smoky interior of the beverage room filled me with dread, almost as though I sensed something terrible was about to happen but didn't know what. How did I miss the clues?

The Long Wait

Saturday afternoons they'd park me
in the lobby of the hotel

promise to
be back soon, then disappear

into the clouded liquid light
of the beer parlour. Every time

the door opened, releasing a jet
of stale air, I'd look up, hoping

it was them. Sometimes a stranger
would lurch past, pat my head,

tell me I was a "good lad."

When I got bored reading comics
I'd slip outside, down to the river,

listen to the wind whooshing
in the willows, the shadows

creeping behind the tenements on Water
Street. As closing drew near my dread

grew, for I never knew what flicks
would be playing inside their skulls,

what monsters would emerge.

To Cast a Spell over Time

YOUR SUICIDE WAS AN AXE BREAKING THE FROZEN SEAS WITHIN ME. LONG-forgotten memories and trauma surfaced from the depths.

A drowsy summer evening. Earlier it rained and I can feel the moist air on my skin. My sisters are playing hopscotch at the front of the tenement; I can hear the scuff of leather on concrete. In the fire hall lane I'm bouncing an India rubber ball — plock, plock plock — off the brick wall, anxiously waiting for Mom to come home from work. I look up at the trees; the sun has set the tops of the maples at the corner of Simcoe and Aylmer ablaze, the breeze stirs the leaves randomly and gently as it sometimes shirrs a quiet lake. I hear the rustle of leaves, the clang of horseshoes from the fire hall yard. Every so often my sisters peek around the corner to see if she's come yet. Now she's rounding the corner of the fire hall clutching three dripping vanilla cones in her small fist, black leather purse tucked under her arm. She holds the cones away from her black uniform with its white collar and cuffs and big round buttons. A nimbus of gold surrounds her as she strides towards us, her sensible low-heeled shoes clacking on the orange bricks. The firemen who know and like her stop their game momentarily to smile and wave, but she looks straight ahead, chin slightly raised, and pays no attention as though she cleaves to some invisible tightrope of duty from which she never swerves. "She's here," I yell and letting out a big whoop race towards her, my sisters close behind. She stops to steady herself before we wrap our arms round her hard, sinewy thighs. She smiles, gives us each a cone. Our joy is complete.

CR

Pie-faced Mrs. Butcher never knocks, barges through the front door, breathless. "The cocktail hour, Florie!" she cackles. She digs into her big brown purse, pulls out a mickey of rye, pours each of them a shot. I look up anxiously at Mom's face, hear myself pleading, "Please, Mom, don't."
"Just a short one, that's all," she answers, and raises the glass to her lips.

"Please, Mom, please, I beg you."
"Don't worry, Jim, I'm just having one."
That's what she always says: "I'm just having one."

CR

Early Sunday morning; the tenement is quiet as a tomb. I rub my eyes and slip out of bed, tiptoe downstairs and observe empty beer bottles everywhere, cigarette burns on the kitchen oilcloth, a pile of dirty dishes in the sink. The linoleum chills the soles of my feet. I swig some leftover beer from a half-empty bottle; its warm sour taste makes me gag. An unpleasant nicotine tang lingers in the air. From the front parlour the Black Forest clock, Mom's pride and joy, chimes out seven a.m. — the silvery notes sharp as glass in the stillness. When someone stirs in the downstairs bedroom I feel my heart sink. Edging over to the bedroom I ease open the door and peek in. Dad's snoring quietly on his side of the bed, mouth slightly open; Mom's soiled white slip is rumpled above her waist, bare white thighs and dark nest of pubic hair exposed. I feel sick and recoil backwards as though smashed in the teeth by something unnatural, forbidden and obscene. I race upstairs, crawl back into bed; my body begins to tremble all over. As I pull the covers over my face I can feel the hot tears burning my cheeks.

CR

WOKE UP THIS MORNING INSOMNIA-FOGGED, FEELING FLAT, LISTLESS AND uninspired. Is my journalling just an effort to create meaning out of your death, give grief a form I can stand back from and look at, make it observable as the weather, digestible, maybe even comprehensible? Creativity's the thing that's supposed to make us like God, theologians say. Every morning when

I peck away on the keyboard about our life together do I breathe in his/her creative spirit, become a co-creator, trying for a few brief moments to untangle the torment that binds me, unriddle the mystery of death? Antoinette Bosco in her book *The Pummeled Heart* recounts how her son Peter killed himself one morning by putting a bullet into his brain, and how two years later another son and his wife were found slain in their bed at their home in Bigfork, Montana – victims of a senseless murder. Both tragedies caused unbelievable grief, but she made a distinction between them. While suicide leaves survivors with questions of guilt – an unforgiving and remorseless list of "if only"s, yet, there is the reality of choice: someone in desperate straits has decided to end their pain, and therefore it has a kind of built-in closure to it that keeps it a private and personal act. If the survivors can grow to accept that, they can come to peace. But murder is different, she writes:

> Murder shatters the peace of one's life. For murder is
> the entrance of the worst evil imaginable in your home,
> into all the safe places of your life, forever blasting any
> illusions you might have had that good can protect you
> from Evil. Evil is real and never again can I question its
> power.

Will I ever grow to accept your choice to "go home," I wonder? And can there be any true closure until your body is found?

First Snowfall

The morning of the first snowfall, Brendan,
my friend, was not at school. Sister Lucretia

visited our classroom, told us Brendan's mom
had gone home. That night I dreamt

of a long black snake, eyes green & glittery &
woke up coiled in sweat. As we trudged

to the funeral home next day in our highjacks &
galoshes, snow was still falling, huge wet flakes

dropping like lead from the flat grey sky; inside
where it was warm, grownups didn't know

where to put their hands. I was afraid
to look at the shiny box at the end of the

room or at Brendan in his new navy blue
gabardine next to his dad. The sickly smell

of flowers made me want to choke. Why was everyone
so quiet? When it came my turn to kneel

beside the box the Hail Marys stuck in my throat.
I thought everyone could hear the paddling of my heart.

After supper I asked Gaby what it meant to go home;
she told me to go out & play. Later when Mom

got back from work she explained that after
you die your soul flies straight to heaven &

that's where Brendan's mom was now, safe
with Jesus, Mary & Joseph forever. That

night as I lay in bed listening to the snow
gusting on the window,

the soft shirt of whiteness wrapped me
round & warm, a winding sheet.

CR

WHAT WAS OUR MARRIAGE, ANYWAY? A PENNILESS YOUNG MAN FROM THE wrong side of the tracks and a young fashion illustrator, equally penniless, who'd been lucky enough to have been adopted by a good couple looking for a child to fill the void in their lives. Two outsiders joined together by the grace of God. Initially, I'd planned to set up law practice in Peterborough – a hard-enough sell for a person like you who believed that the real world ended at Toronto's city limits, but when I announced a last-minute change of plan, told you we'd be going to Cobourg instead, it was too overwhelming; you let out a deep groan and dissolved in tears. And the day, dark and drizzly, we drove down King Street, its old Victorian facades dripping wet – your first visit to the town – the sobbing broke out again and didn't cease till we got back to Toronto.

No, I wouldn't change my mind, I told you and a few days later you called off the wedding. "I can't live in the sticks," you announced. "I intend to pursue my art career and stay in the city." Your mother set out your options starkly: "You can marry Jim, a good man, and raise a family," she told you, "or you can have a career and be lonely all your life in an expensive apartment in the city."

Thanks to her influence you changed your mind and the marriage went ahead as planned.

During your first pregnancy, when you began to bleed early on (placenta previa, the doctor called it) and were bedridden six months and I was so preoccupied with establishing the practice that I wasn't around as much as I should have been to comfort you, how often must you have asked yourself if you'd made the right decision. The day the funeral director had me sign the burial permit I noted the name he'd given our stillborn child: "Baby Girl" was the terse description, but for you the loss couldn't be shrugged off so easily. In retrospect I often wonder if you ever fully got over the loss of your first baby. And when Adele came along a year later and I did a little jig and skipped up and down the corridors of the hospital in a numinous haze of happiness, so overjoyed at the miracle of her birth I buttonholed everyone I met to proclaim the good news, the nurses smiled, but must have questioned my daft behaviour. But a few months later when Adele fell ill with a strangulation of the bowel that threatened to turn gangrenous (our good friend and family physician Graham Stratford fretted all one night till he came up with the correct diagnosis) it seemed our miracle had turned to ashes. And when the specialist, a solemn sallow-faced fellow, asked for our phone number as Adele was being wheeled into the operating room "in case of bad news," my heart froze and I felt a mountain had just rolled over us. Several hours later, when the call came that Adele had pulled through and was on the road to recovery, it felt like a second miracle; I was moved with joy to the verge of tears and had the doctors been present I would have planted a kiss on all their faces.

℞

WOKE THIS MORNING TO AN UNEXPECTED APRIL SNOWFALL. OUTSIDE THE sunroom the snow drew squiggly chalklines across the silent and still cedars. Whiteness transfigured the dull brownish lawn, braided the branches of the harlequin maple. As the minutes ticked by, the woods echoed with distant crows and the small dry ring of dark earth round the base of the Scotch pine slowly retreated and disappeared. Mornings are prophetic; sunrises promise new beginnings – the gift of light, clean and lucid – calling me to wakefulness and change.

Do you remember those letters we exchanged when we first dated and I was stationed at Camp Borden, completing my Canadian Officer Corps training, and you had a job back in Toronto illustrating Eaton's catalogues, how you emblazoned your bright red lips not only on the letters but on the envelopes, too? Much later, after we'd started a family, I collected the letters (there must have 40 in total) and tucked them in a cardboard box somewhere in the basement, but when I searched for them recently I couldn't find them and I remembered that once you threatened to burn them in the fireplace. "They're too mawkish," you told me. Our love was in its infancy and it's true the letters were full of sappy endearments and dreams.

When I took my new position with Jack German in Cobourg a few months before the wedding, he suggested I stay with Valerie, who operated a boarding house opposite St. Michael's church on Division Street. Short and spry, Val lived alone with her two enormous cats who roamed freely the dusty and untidy rooms. She had stubby fingers and a clear white complexion, and her fluffy thin hair sat on her head like puffs of cotton batten that could blow away any second. She loved to sit in her front room, hands clasped over her ample girth, small feet dangling just above the carpet, and observe the world parading by her window. Val had lived in Cobourg many years, knew everyone, and her alert almond-shaped eyes never missed a lick. She kept a photo of her deceased husband (they'd had no children) in his WWI officer's uniform holding a swagger stick on the side table beside her chair. Val had strong likes and dislikes and freely dispensed her opinion about small-town life. "So-and-so's the only decent men's clothier in town," she'd say in her high-octave, almost squeaky voice. Or "I'd never eat there," if I'd mention a certain restaurant she didn't approve of. But though opinionated, Val never spoke ill of anyone, was fiercely loyal to her friends, and I grew to love her open and kind heart. "I love love" was her favourite expression. Remember how we'd often drop by for a visit after Mass on Sunday for tea and she'd treat the kids to pop and cookies and sometimes she'd plop herself down at the upright piano with the cracked and yellowing keys in the dining room and pound out two or three lively ditties for them? And how when we'd rise to leave she'd invariably insist we stay longer? I sensed she was lonely and hated living alone. Though you loved her dearly I remember how her parochial views on everything under the sun irked you; you thought she was a bit "bossy" and like most young brides and mothers wanted to make up your own mind about things, be your own person and you always were.

Be Quiet Heart

At this equinox
of the year,
sun turns tender,
snowdrops poke their
heads above the earth,
snow, an old nightgown,
lies tattered in the fields.

But early Easter morning,
soft and grey, winter
nudges back, crows
put away their brassy horns,
doves meditate,
snowflakes whisper
above the cedars in the park.
Be quiet heart, the white words say.

◌

FRIDAY, A GREY DRIZZLY DAY; THE PAVEMENTS ARE SLICK WITH WET; TRAFFIC lights trace long red, green and amber lines in the wetness. As I drive to court along the 401, rain crackles on the car roof like static electricity or cedar logs in a fire and I am reminded of other rainy days: Simcoe Street where I grew up, the road in front of the tenement shiny as foil, all dust and grime and horseshit sluiced away and the air washed fresh, invigorating and begemmed with light. Even the battered sheet metal fence of Moldaver's across the street gave off bright red glints. And the rain that swished across Limerick Lake at the outset of a big storm, leaving craters and eddies on the blue-grey water, enamelling the greenery of the forest, drops tinkling on the shiny leaves and needles. And the patter on the cottage roof after we made love, always so peaceful and soothing. Remember our trip up the Saguenay, the time we left Adele with your mom and dad? It rained the whole trip, but we didn't care. We were snug in each other's arms in our tiny cabin, lost in love and counting our dreams, content to watch the shore lights swirl by through the porthole and feel the rumble of the big engines beneath us. We made out on the hard cabin floor (the berths were too short for our long limbs, remember?). As we stood on the deck and the boat glided past the walls of the Saguenay shrouded in fog and wetness, high and forbidding, the wind gusted in our faces and you could almost touch the ancient granite. That night we docked at Chicoutimi, where we danced madly for hours at the shore pavilion – a barn really – and after returned to the ship to continue our lovemaking on the cabin floor. Our second child, Paul, was conceived on that trip – truly a love child, desired and worked for. When we got home we discovered your dad had fallen in love with Adele. Every morning he rose early, your mom said, made coffee and shuffled off to her bedroom in his red bathrobe to baby talk with her for hours. "I'd never seen him so content in years," she said, which made you so happy because that was the last summer of his life.

CR

IN 1968 I TOOK A YEAR'S SABBATICAL FROM THE LAW PRACTICE AND WE decided to go to France to work with Jean Vanier and the mentally and physically disabled at L'Arche – an adventure and challenge, for the world of the disabled was new to us, remember. During our year (abridged to nine months by your unexpected pregnancy with Mira) we lived in the small village of Trosly-Breuil, a cluster of yellow stones perched on the slope of the Compiègne forest about 70 kilometres northeast of Paris. The village boasted a hotel, a butcher shop, a bakery, a tobacco shop, a school and, halfway up the main street, a small grocery store, "Le Comptoir Français," where you could buy anything from Bordeaux wine to Palmolive soap.

The unpainted stone houses had slate roofs and miniature gravelled yards and gardens enclosed by stone walls or wrought-iron fences with signs that warned "Méchant Chien." Pebbled pathways criss-crossed gardens adorned with plaster gnomes and rabbits. Remember how the village used to shut down at night: shutters slammed shut, gates banged close and the watchdogs, those ubiquitous guardians of the French peace, crouched in doorways. The women of the village were always sweeping twigs, leaves and chaff from their thresholds or washing in the public laundry basins on the rue du Lavoir – two rectangular pools, one slightly larger than the other, divided by a low wall, pitched roof on six concrete pillars overhead not far from our dwelling. The village women were polite but distant and you'd often comment that you felt you were being spied on by eyes concealed in the shadow of doorways. Evenings, the men of the village returned, the baskets of their motorbikes laden with bottles of *vin ordinaire*. When the streetlights went out, the village was thrown into almost pitch darkness, and on moonlit nights the old stones of the village shimmered with pale light. The village was an ageless old lady, grey and decrepit, but honourably clean.

Our new home was a cream-stuccoed tenement at the end of a ramshackle terrace hidden behind a 10-foot stone wall opposite the village bistro. Bounded on the north by the Compiègne Forest, it overlooked a clutter of rabbit hutches, chicken coops, tool sheds, outhouses and gardens. From the yard you walked directly into the beamed bedsitting room, which also served as our dining room. A mahogany bed with a lumpy mattress, a dark oak dining table, five chairs, and a scratched and chipped buffet crammed with cracked china comprised our meagre furnishings. In front of the fireplace, a brown box-shaped oil stove with a round glass aperture, on the mantle a silver-plated chime clock. On the left, French doors led into a damp bedroom with a double bed and a cot that the children shared. On the right, two steps descended into the kitchen, a narrow dank space of unpainted plaster ceiling and walls, bamboo wainscotting and dull red-tiled floor, a sink, gas stove, floor cupboards, and at the far end a bamboo curtain that concealed a portable chemical toilet. Remember how the toilet stank up the house and we had to pinch our noses as we lugged the slop pail through the brambles and stinging nettles in the garden to the pit I'd dug in the back? There were few diversions or even comforts: no TV, no doorbells, no telephone, no hot water, no fridge, no plumbing, nothing to distract us from our selves and in the fall and winter the cold was so penetrating that we had to don sweaters indoors and dive under the covers at night in our wool pyjamas to ward off the bone-chilling cold. Winter mornings our breath appeared in white flags. This, then, was our inconvenient, humid, but cozy home in France.

That year I worked in the workshops for $1.00 a month (your standing joke was that I was vastly overpaid). After breakfast of French bread, jam and coffee, I'd escort Adele to the École Maternelle (kindergarten) and then head to the workshops while you stayed at home with the pre-schoolers, Paul and Marilyn. At noon I'd toddle up the road balancing our pre-cooked dinner on a two-tiered portable aluminium tray (all our meals were prepared in the L'Arche kitchen and had to be reheated on our gas stove). Sometimes I'd spot you on the road in front of the courtyard chasing the honking milk truck for our daily litre of unpasteurized milk. We got used to the taste of yellow-skinned warm milk but never to the smell of the scalded milk when the milk pot boiled over. In the afternoon, with Paul and Marilyn bundled into bed for their nap, you'd be free to read, rest, design mosaics for the mosaic atelier or host visitors. Our home became a popular drop-in spot for both the disabled and the assistants. With its few diversions you always claimed that our life at Trosly-Breuil was unjustifiably idyllic.

During the sabbatical we bought a 1963 Anglia (that never started without a push, remember) but despite its capricious disposition we did a lot of sightseeing on weekends and holidays. Though neither of us had had any previous experience with the mentally and physically disabled, by the end of our sojourn our eyes were opened and we'd grown to appreciate not only the depth of their sufferings but also their gifts of the heart: openness, sensitivity and capacity for moral and religious insight. I'll never forget your comment after we viewed the great rose windows at Beauvais Cathedral on one of our jaunts. "How forbidding and uncomely on the outside," you said, "but how beautiful and colourful on the inside." Then you paused and added, "Just like the disabled." According to Vanier, we shun the physically and mentally disabled because their condition reminds us of our radical weaknesses and mortality. They wear their shadow on the outside and we instinctively recoil from those disfigured parts within us that we think mark us as unlovable or unbearable to others. You always found life in Canada running a large household hectic and enervating; the simplicity of L'Arche, with its absence of amenities and its emphasis on one-to-one relationships appealed to you deeply. My grandfather always said that the simplest life was the sweetest, and when we got back to Canada we decided to create our own Shangri-La, see if we could replicate the L'Arche experience, find our own peaceable kingdom, unreachable and safe, and that's how it came about that we bought the cottage and our love affair with Limerick Lake began and we entered the black and boundless world of stars. L'Arche was one of the happiest periods of our life. How often over the years did I not catch you standing at the kitchen window on College Street, a wistful look on your face, remembering. "Maybe someday, when the children are gone," you'd muse, "we'll go back."

ॐ

THAT SPRING MORNING AFTER BENOIT, ONE OF THE YOUNG RESIDENTS AT L'Arche, choked to death in his sleep (he'd had an epileptic seizure) I met Père Thomas, Vanier's spiritual mentor and godfather of L'Arche, swishing to chapel along the rue Principale clad in his long loose Benedictine habit, the pale sun shining on his pate. "Too bad about Benoit," I said. He glanced at me kindly, lifted his pale blue eyes to the sky and said, almost as if I'd missed the point, "Benoit is now with the Father in Heaven." Then he smiled at me and added, "Death's our real birthday."

Benoit was laid out in the administration building beside the workshops, and as the undertaker nailed shut the lid of the plain wood casket, the boom of the hammering bounced off the workshop walls. During the funeral Mass before the whole community, Père Thomas intoned, "Benoit has returned to his Maker, the God of all mercies, mercy within mercy within mercy."

A short time after your death, when I told a visiting priest from Sri Lanka that you'd leapt to your death at Niagara, he said, eyes suddenly aglow, "Wow. Imagine being swept into the arms of Jesus; it takes my breath away." His voice rose as he urged me to make a retreat at the Carmelite monastery there. "Let your prayers mingle with the mighty waters," he said.

Oh, how I sometimes wish I had that depth of faith and instead of the grief and gloom that surrounds me could see your death in that prophetic light — your body stripped clean by the holy currents, your incandescent spirit released like a dove from its cage and winging heavenward straight into the waiting arms of the everlasting Mercy, but the ache in my heart is too strong and that vision eludes me. Some days in the valley of grief it's hard to see the sun. But one day, I promise, I'll make the trek to Niagara, not to forget, but to say goodbye and set us both free.

Compline

Coppery light fluttering

on the cottage wall,

waves lapping

on the shore:

summer and sunset

and the long arms of contemplation

reach out to me

        as I write this poem,

recall your face,

        long to hear you say:

All, all is well,

        the sun – a crimson star

dying in my eyes.

❧

I ALWAYS BOASTED YOU WERE OUR IN-HOUSE PHILOSOPHER, FULL OF OPTIMISM and encouragement, forever dispensing wise counsel to family and friends, never revealing the depth of your own pain. How blind and deaf we were! We dressed up in our Sunday best for your memorial service at the church; Paul rented a tux ("Mom would have liked that," he said), and we put on a brave front as friends hugged us and encouraged us take heart, but what else could they say? Words, even well-meaning words, are such poor comforters! You were not there and death had struck us with the brute force of its mystery, leaving us numb-dead. A blown-up photo of you on the altar, encircled with roses and carnations and smiling, was the only tangible evidence you ever existed – no casket, no body, no mock facsimile of your face, no skin to touch, nothing; it seemed you vaporized at the Falls and slowly floated away, disappeared from the face of the earth as though you'd never been born. How do you grieve a memory? Bring closure to a bad dream? How do I stop you from fading into the sepia-coloured past? The day the police came with the news, Joy screamed, "Why did you do this to me!" stormed upstairs, ripped her beloved Madonna posters from her wall, smashed the bed, swept books, clothes, paper onto the broadloom and, piling up furniture, barricaded herself in her room, sobbing uncontrollably, refusing to speak to anyone; when I tapped on her door she shouted "Fuck off," said I didn't love her and cranked up Madonna full tilt on her stereo till my temples throbbed.

From the beginning, adoption had been your personal project; as an adopted child yourself you felt you owed something to society and I went along. After a thorough vetting by the Children's Aid Society we were finally approved and waited impatiently for Joy's arrival. The Vietnamese airlift was in full swing. In the orphanages of Saigon the organizers found toddlers who spent hours in their cribs, wet and crying, some with permanently sloped heads from months of lying unattended. The wood playpens outdoors had slits on the floor that allowed urine and faeces to drip to the ground. In some institutions, meals meant 20 children lining up to be fed by one nun, often with one bowl and one spoon.

On April 4, 1975, the first authorized Babylift plane crashed 65 miles from Saigon, killing more than half the 300 passengers, mostly children. Canada's only official Babylift plane, a Canadian Forces Hercules aircraft, touched down in Montreal. Fifty-three of the children flew on to Toronto and were bussed downtown to Surrey Place Centre, near Queen's Park. In the space of four days the orphans had flown from East to West with stopovers in Hong Kong and Vancouver. Many were severely undernourished and carried parasites. When we got the call we drove to Toronto, nervous and excited. How disorienting and distressing it was when a black male nurse in the hospital approached us with a brown baby girl in his arms and thrust the infant at me: "Here's your baby, daddy," he declared, grinning. But it turned out he was mistaken, it wasn't Joy but someone else's baby (I confess shamefully I was relieved, for the baby had a badly misshapen head) and we finally found Joy, dragging herself along the floor, quiet and expressionless but beautiful (she had been eighteen months in a crowded Saigon orphanage and the nuns hadn't had time to teach her to walk, the nurse explained). After we got her home she continued to propel herself on her bottom, a dull blank look in her eyes, seemingly oblivious to her surroundings. When loud noises startled her she'd let out a scream and for a while I questioned if she wasn't brain-damaged, would ever walk normally. Using her delicate but dexterous fingers she picked her plate clean to the last grain of rice. For months we took daily stool samples for the lab – she had intestinal problems caused by bacilli – until the doctor gave us the all-clear signal.

After your suicide, thinking that a change would be beneficial, I got her a summer job at the fruit farm of a friend (a former client) near Grafton, but the experiment proved disastrous; Joy resented being told what to do, said she hated picking apples all day in the hot sun; she began to sass my friends and slacked off. It got so bad I finally had to fetch her home. The truth is she wanted someone like you, a new mother, who loved her more than anyone else in the world and no one, no matter how well-intentioned, could ever measure up. She was your special baby and your abandonment of her (and me) hit her especially hard, for she must have felt I couldn't love her the way you did, that her place in the family was no longer secure.

This drizzly Good Friday, one year after your death, my fear that the gas stations would be closed (I was almost out of gas) proved false; this morning's headlines told us in so many words that the world was still screwed up and that as Canadians we should count our blessings, the rosy-cheeked maid in the old-fashioned white bonnet on the big blue-and-orange Schneider neon sign on the 401 seemed to wink at me as I drove past; and outside the sunroom at home three glossy starlings jumped from branch to branch in the harlequin maple, loosening little buttons of rain. Nothing changes. The world carries on as usual.

CR

WHEN I WENT ON THE L'ARCHE EASTER PILGRIMAGE TO TAIZÉ, FRANCE, IN 1973 I accompanied Ralph, a gangly, good-natured disabled man from the L'Arche community Daybreak. On the first leg of the trip, to Canterbury, I met Susan, a L'Arche volunteer from Manitoba. I wore that blue jacket with the red and white stripes – St. Joseph's coat of many colours, you named it – that you'd selected for me at Joe Feller's in Ottawa because you said I looked like a hick and needed a sartorial upgrading. Susan had bleached-blond hair, a friendly face and a bubbly, outgoing personality that reminded me of you. We struck up a conversation and hit it off immediately. On the walk to the Cathedral she smiled at me and locked her arm in mine. After that, we began to look for occasions to meet and talk. Crossing the channel on the ferry we stood together on the deck gazing at the cold green water and the wheeling gulls – I remember how the breeze stirred wisps of her hair and the strong sunlight made her large blue eyes squint. On the bus in France we sat together and talked about our lives. She was married with three children, she said, but confessed the marriage wasn't going well. Her husband, a businessman, was a cold fish and a controller. Her story roused my sympathy and I held her hand. At Taizé I bought her a small silver cross and had all but forgotten about Ralph, who seemed to be getting along fine without me in any event. I felt alive and different. Then one sunny afternoon (all the days of the pilgrimage, I recall, were warm and sunny) while we were out strolling together I asked her – it felt so natural and innocent at the time – if I could give her a friendship kiss; afterward when she told me the kiss had made her feel like a schoolgirl being kissed for the first time my ego skyrocketed. Later we had dinner at a four-star restaurant in the village – an exquisite French meal with wine and candles – and I reached over the table and kissed her again. By this time I was smitten. After, we held hands and meandered through the narrow cobblestoned streets, a starry canopy over our heads, and it was like walking on an airy carpet; every cell in my body tingled with excitement.

The mix of romance and pilgrimage cast a spell over me and I convinced myself that my strange and delicious feelings were the fruit of spiritual kinship. On the plane home we sat together and held hands, promised to write to each other. And write we did (I even phoned Winnipeg once but hung up when a male voice answered). She sent letters to the office – how devious we'd become – and in one revealed she was thinking of moving to Toronto (nothing to do with us, of course) – what did I think? The day you caught me writing her at home – deluded fool that I was, I'd showed you the letter in which I extolled her wonderful mind, the fineness of our friendship, etc. I tried to argue how perfectly legitimate (and enriching) it was for mature couples to have platonic relationships with members of the opposite sex, but you'd have none of it. "You're infatuated with that woman," you stated, tears in your eyes, claimed I was having a midlife crisis and though I denied it vehemently, deep down I knew you were right. My heart had been shipwrecked by another woman. And when you found the cache of her letters in my side cabinet at the office and wrote her that you had a good marriage, that you loved me and demanded that she back off, my brief romantic dalliance burst like a bubble. Remember the long walk to the open field at the cottage when you told me, tears staining your cheeks, how much I'd hurt you and how terrible, terrible I felt, tried to assure you it was only you I loved, and begged forgiveness for my foolishness, the heartbreak I'd caused you. I promised that I would never see or write her again and I never did.

CR

WHEN TEETAW, YOUR MOTHER, BOUGHT US THE YASHICA CAMERA FOR Christmas in 1980, I plunged passionately into photography, shooting everyone and everything that moved (or didn't move), forcing you and the children to pose at the most awkward and inconvenient times and places, all the while ignoring your impatient, surly glances. Yes, I confess I became a nuisance, especially when I turned "artsy" and began to move everyone about like props. Remember how the children would stick out their tongues behind my back (I caught them several times) and you'd scold, "Jim, could you lay off?" but being the obsessive person I was, I was impervious to your protests, took hundreds of pictures, and carefully arranged them in albums (close to 30 at your death). How you hated having your picture taken! You disliked your skin, as though a stranger had foisted a garment on you, a castaway you'd never have chosen yourself, judged your legs unshapely (though you gave your thighs a pass), your hair frowzy and the colour mousy (you tinted your hair red and threatened to let it grow grey, but I liked it the way it was and you never did). Why did you, an attractive woman, shrink from your body? Did being born out of wedlock to a mother who didn't want to hold or even touch you stigmatize you (you were three months in a foster home until Teetaw came along and claimed you), leave you with a feeling that you were unwanted and unworthy? Or was your critical attitude towards having your picture taken linked to how you perceived me: a carefree husband, indulging another of his many hobbies (sketching, tennis, woodcarving, snooker, chess, reading, and now photography) while you were chained to the house – a galling reminder of your satellite existence and your thwarted ambitions as an illustrator? In hindsight it seems so unfair that for most women of our generation marriage was not so much a change, but an earthquake displacing their ambitions and gifts while the goals of men remained largely unaffected. Sometimes I see your suicide as a form of unarticulated anger, a way of evening scores. And was my entering a new relationship so soon after your death my own way of getting back at what appeared like a cruel and heartless abandonment of me and the children?

Monday evening I saw Mira, who was flicking through the albums, begin to tear up (I've observed all the children do the same). The photographs no doubt evoked memories for her of the happy days when you were the heart of the family – those vivid blue, sunlit days at the lake when life stretched to the sky and death was not even a speck on the horizon. How the children cherish these freeze-frames of our life together. My puny effort to cast a spell over time has proven fruitful in a way I could never have imagined nor desired.

CR<

How DIFFICULT TO WRITE UNMASKED FROM OUR DEEPEST SELVES, TO be skinned and nerve exposed. Here I am again at 6 a.m. before the blue confessional trying to slay my dragons, a little intimidated by the extent of my self-disclosure. Natalie Goldberg in her book *Wild Mind* recounts how searing it was for her to reveal she slept with women – her Jewish background was not kind to lesbianism. A writer has to be a samurai, she writes, ruthless in the pursuit of truth. In exposing my grief, fears and desires I realize I am trying to lift my "private patienthood," as Erick Erickson puts it, to a universal level. I believe that my private pain has, if deeply and honestly expressed, a human value beyond the private that can make its way from heart to heart, help bridge the gap between our solitudes.

Lately I've been visited with recurring dreams involving water: images of lakes, streams, rivers, waterfalls and drownings. A few days ago I dreamt I saw your body, no longer solid and fleshy, but some transparent aquatic creature I could see through like a clear plastic sack. In another dream you were at the kitchen sink of our old Cobourg home washing dishes in a daffodil-print blouse and I entered and stood beside you without a stitch, naked as a worm. Instead of reprimanding me you smiled and said in a quiet voice, as though you were talking to a child, "Go upstairs, Jim, and run your bathwater." In still another dream you're standing on the bottom of a lake, your feet firmly planted on a rock, upstretched arms holding up the roof of a watery house (ours? I wondered); somehow I knew that without your support the roof would collapse. Water, the symbol of baptism and rebirth, engulfs my dreams and is now forever associated with you: when I dive into the cool limpid waters of Limerick Lake I think of you; when I gaze on a stream, river or lake or see a flood on TV in some faraway part of the world I think of you and every time I hear the word "Niagara" a small electric jolt travels through my body. Water, water, water, thirst quencher, respite from the burning sun, my joy and pleasure, now and always a reminder of you and your body and

floating red hair washed back to atoms, scrubbed white and clean as a baby's,
O my shining watery angel how I sometimes crave a watery death!

☙

THE HIGHWAY BRISTLES WITH PERILS: ON THE HANLON THIS MORNING A
raccoon freshly killed, the pallbearer crows not yet arrived for the cleanup,
vehicles whizzing past, drivers on their cell phones already plotting the day.
When life was simpler people had more time to pause and ponder their
problems; today they have wheels and are always on the go, but death still
tailgates them with the same tenacity. The highway between Guelph and
Milton is full of risk and beauty. The sky's always changing – today it's
a blanket of grey; sometimes the sun shines, other times the pavement is
shrouded in fog or snow and I wonder if other motorists, who seem half
asleep, staring into space, or chatting on their cell phones are aware, like the
sleepless Schneider Maid, that their lives are being clocked and measured.

Years ago when we were at L'Arche one of the assistants, an idealistic
young man, suddenly turned to me in the atelier and declared: "Now, I
know, you're a goddam pessimist, Clarke." I was taken aback for I'd never
seen myself in that light. Since your suicide I dread answering the phone;
every time it rings I flinch as though in the back of my mind I half-expected
more bad news. Why do I always anticipate the worse? Is this fear rooted in
my lack of trust in God? Or is mistrust just an occupational hazard of being
a lawyer and judge all my life with a front-row seat at the raggedy parade
of humanity? Do you recall the story I once recounted of the middle-aged
woman with honey blond hair and enormous dark brown eyes, bedecked out
in gold – gold bracelets, gold rings on every finger, gold pendants, even a
gold brooch pinned to her white blouse – who'd come to my office with her
husband to make wills? "My husband loves to buy me gold," she explained.
Married for fifteen years, the couple had no children. The husband had been

a cabinetmaker who took great pride in his work but had developed palsy and the trembling had forced him to give up his trade. One sunny morning not long after this visit he shot himself in the head with a .38 in a sugarbush near Hastings. "I don't think I can live without him," the wife told me later. "He was the only person who ever loved me."

She went back to Europe hoping to find a reason to live, but quarrelled with her sister and found she had no more friends. "I want to join my husband," she said after she got back. One week later her nephew contacted me to say she'd shot herself in the heart with her husband's pistol, wanted me to hear her last tape. We listened in silence in my library as the woman explained in a calm, resigned voice that her husband's death had sapped all the meaning from her life, that she desired to be with him in the next world and had confidence God would understand and forgive her. "Poor woman, Jim," you said when I finished the story, "but life is sacred, she had no right to take her own life." How quickly things change. I judge neither you nor the unhappy woman. My task is to salvage meaning out of the wreckage of your suicide, get over my feelings of being ditched by you and God. Sometimes I feel death is just another name for God, a black hole in the sky swallowing our waking and dreaming hours. Prospero said it best: "We are such stuff as dreams are made on and our own little life is rounded with a sleep." Despite the unanswered and unanswerable question "why?" I want to believe God will be there for me (as I believe he/she's there for you); I know that love is the heartbeat of creation and that I must become the maker of my own soul, make friends with my shadow.

Lord, help me to grow, become a better person and love more every day. Amen.

Roadkill

As the sun hooped through
the branches of the trees
on the Hanlon this morning
– the same road you took three years ago –

I saw two blobs of blood and fur
on the pavement – a raccoon
sliced in two by someone's light,
another night victim –
amazed at how the sun
could suddenly grow cold,

like the October afternoon
north of Eldorado
we came upon the smoking wreck
– back wheel spinning still,
dead boy in the ditch
staring at the sky,
eyes full of gold.

Did the light surprise you too
or was Death an old friend
you took along
for the ride?

CR

You dreaded the prospect of getting old, becoming a dependant. "Imagine falling into the hands of one of our children," you'd joke, but I knew you were serious. You watched the slow decline of your mother in a nursing home: the deep bedsores raw from lying in bed too long (the overworked attendants couldn't turn her enough), the deterioration of her mind and speech as Alzheimer's took over her body cell by cell and ravaged her nervous system. You were horrified at the thought of a similar fate, returning to the helplessness of a child, the sunken world of bobbling heads and slurred speech, becoming dependant on family and strangers for your very survival.

Your love of me and the children was all balled up with mothering, and you were only in your element nurturing and giving to others. How many times did I not protest when you'd offer to drive for friends or a social outing? "It's not your turn," I'd say. "You drove last week." But you'd ignore me, insist you didn't mind, that the others couldn't afford gas, etc. You had a tremendous need to pay your way, earn the love of others; it seemed just being yourself wasn't good enough, that your passport into life required that you make no demands. Whenever you were sick and laid up you felt useless and chafed to get back into harness. You bridled at the tyranny of the body, regarded your proneness to boils almost like leprosy and at one time even contemplated cosmetic surgery. The prospect of becoming a paraplegic like my mom, turned your blood cold and when she caught pneumonia during her last stay in hospital and they pulled out all the stops, put her on life support to save her (which to my regret I approved) you were aghast.

"Promise you'll never put me through that torture," you said, and I saw from the look of horror on your face that you meant it. Was it that last week in hospital when the agony you were going through was etched on your face that you made the decision to end it all? It was not a question of cowardice — by nature you were stalwart and brave, even stoical, but pain had a way of undermining your personhood, your sense of entitlement to life. "If this back doesn't get better," you said, "I don't want to live," but your portentous words didn't penetrate my thick skull and again I missed the signals that might have saved you.

CR

THAT AFTERNOON IN BARBADOS TWO YEARS BEFORE YOU DIED WE SAUNTERED hand in hand on the beach, the blue-green flash of ocean all around us, felt the sand being sucked from under our bare feet by the retreating surf, the hot sun and balmy breeze on our skin, little suspecting our paradise was about to change. After the hurly-burly of life in Canada we were beginning to relax and feel restored in this turquoise water world, or at least so I thought. Back in our room you peered out the window. "Come here quick," you said, pointing at a group of men and women gathered under a palm near the kitchen.

"They're government spies," you said. At first I thought you were joking but when I saw the deadpan look on your pale face I knew you were serious. The "spies," all attired in white jackets, were standing around smoking and bantering; every now and then a burst of laughter would erupt.

"They're employees of the resort," I said. "See their uniforms." But you ignored my words (or maybe you weren't listening.) Nothing I could say could change your mind. Later you asked if I would lie down beside you on the bed and hold you. I felt your pounding heart, heard your faint gasps of breath. Through the parted curtains I glimpsed palm trees awash in sunlight, listened to the papery rattle of fronds, the muffled thunder and hiss of the surf. Inside me a deep hollow was widening. Afterwards you rarely left the bedroom except to eat and your face took on a fixed glazed expression. The burly Ulsterman with rosy-veined cheekbones and his broad-shouldered wife who was always rattling on about her horses back home in county Antrim must have suspected something was amiss, for every time we ran into them their concerned glances conveyed the message "poor woman." I persuaded you to take a tour of the island (I thought the change of scene would do you good) and hired a taxi, but you sat slumped in the back seat, a blank faraway look on your face, almost totally oblivious to the passing cane fields, the yellow, pink and blue chattel houses, the brilliant displays of bougainvillea on nearly every wall. In the rock garden we visited you scarcely noticed the frangipani and orchids (you who adored flowers of every variety). Your mind was in some other world, scary and unreachable, and I felt a growing alarm. Even our driver grew worried. "Your wife needs help, man," he whispered to me. I didn't realize the depth of your paranoia until the end of the holiday at the airport, when we were queuing up to board and you turned to me and said: "The passengers are secret agents." Lowering your voice, you added, "And they intend to arrest you and put you in a concentration camp." As our jet stormed down the runway, tilted and lifted, I tried to assure you we wouldn't be arrested, that there was no conspiracy, and once we were airborne and on our way home I said, "See, darling, we weren't arrested and the passengers are not spies," but from the brief sphinx of a smile you gave me and the way you sheltered your head against my shoulder I knew you were unconvinced. It was then I noticed for the first time you weren't wearing your grandmother's yellow canary diamond that you treasured so much, the amethyst I bought you at the Talisman for your 40th birthday and your wedding ring (which you'd combined with your mom's in a common setting), and when I asked why (for you rarely took them off) you informed me matter-of-factly that you'd had to get rid of them because the police intended to use them as instruments to torture me and you'd tossed them out the taxi window on the way to the airport while I was in the front seat chatting up the driver. How often I've regretted I didn't sit with you! In shock and half-disbelief I groaned, "Oh, Mary, please tell me it isn't true," and when you made no reply I knew it was and my anger flared but not for long, for the full gravity of your sickness had finally sunk in and I realized I was in the presence of a new, strange and frightening reality, one for which I was totally unprepared, and a great wave of love and pity engulfed me and I gripped your hands in mine, kissed you on the cheek and told you the rings didn't matter. "Rings can be replaced," I said and you smiled wanly, oblivious to what you'd done (for those rings were more precious to you than life itself and I knew you'd never forgive yourself) and we rode through the heavens hands clasped, on our longest trip ever, towards an unknown and fearsome future.

CR

WE TOOK THE RED CAR HOME FROM PEARSON. WHEN THE WOMAN IN the seat ahead sporting a wide-brimmed straw hat with bright blue ribbon (another island holidayer like us) turned to ask about our trip and noticed your graveyard expression she immediately stopped the small talk and turned her head back. At home the children met us at the door with hoots and hugs but they too soon noticed your lifeless eyes and mechanical responses to their eager questions and grew subdued. "What's wrong with Mom?" Joy whispered to me on the side. "Didn't she have a good time?" I said you were a little tired, that's all, not to worry. Once I'd gotten you into bed I phoned our friend Dr. Robbie Fishburn, who immediately rushed over. From the moment he observed you in your pink satin nightgown, propped against the pillows, lips white and complexion pasty, he knew something was seriously wrong. After talking to you alone for a few minutes while I paced back and forth in the hall downstairs, trying to fend off the children's anxious questions, he descended to tell me you were terribly sick. "This is serious, Jim," he said quietly, and added he would make arrangements to get you into Homewood psychiatric centre the next day. Before he left he uttered something that really chilled me: "She could be suicidal." I thought he'd pushed the panic button and exclaimed, "You gotta be kidding, Robbie," but he assured me he wasn't, that you needed professional help. "Watch her carefully" were his parting words. That night thinking you needed quiet and rest, I slept in another room. In the morning when I entered our bedroom and observed an exacto knife on the nightstand beside the bed and the cut marks (they looked like scratches) on both your wrists I was furious with myself for having left you alone, but at the same time greatly relieved the wounds were only superficial and you were still alive. That morning we signed you into Homewood. During your stay there I visited you twice a day and the children and I showered you with hugs, kisses and bouquets of yellow roses (your favourites), told you how loved you were, believing that love alone was enough to bring you back to life. Gradually love and drugs did their work and you began to improve, but as your illusions dropped away another reality set in: the loss of the rings. "How could I have done that?" you kept berating yourself, tears in your eyes. "You were sick, darling," I tried to assure you, but you kept repeating over and over, "I can't believe it," and wept as though you'd just amputated your right arm or betrayed the persons you loved most in the world. I tried to console you by promising to buy another wedding ring but you were inconsolable. In retrospect, I'm grateful that the children and I were able to pour out our feelings, tell you how much we loved you, how much you meant to each of us. Slowly you regained your sense of humour and your room floated with so much laughter the staff must have wondered what was going on. Two months later when the hospital said you were ready to go home my joy was boundless, for I failed to see the profound and lasting change in our lives the loss of the rings signified and believed naively you'd return to your "old self" and with a little tender loving care our life would be back to normal; and all this happened just two years before you took your own life.

Relic

The last I saw of her alive
she was in bed; she blew
a kiss, waved farewell, she'd
see me when I got back, she said.

Almost ten years to the day as I
rummaged in our dresser drawers
preparing for a holiday, a perfume
bottle — amber, the colour

of her hair — poked up from under
a mound of socks and underwear,
fluted, hard, like an ancestral bone
breaking through the sod, or

a dark shell you'd find upon
a beach, ground round and smooth and
bare by the scraping of the sea, a relic
from another world, empty of all

being, the long ocean in between.

CR

SCIENCE AND PSYCHOLOGY HAVE MADE GIANT STRIDES IN UNDERSTANDING
mental illness, and recognize how circumstances, even genetics, can prevent
the mind from thinking clearly and drive people to commit acts, often with
the best intentions, they wouldn't normally even dream of. That's why the
law exempts persons from criminal liability where mental illness is of such a
magnitude that it stops them from appreciating the nature and consequences
of their actions and knowing they are wrong. In court today I presided over
the trial of a woman accused of attempted murder who had plunged a butcher
knife into the chest of her six-year-old son while he slept. The woman was
obsessed by spillage in her home of a plastic liquid from one of her children's
toys; she was convinced the substance was poisonous and had contaminated
not only the house but also the children's bodies, destining them to a slow,
painful death. Interpreting normal childhood aches and pains as evidence
that the deadly toxin was doing its work, she couldn't bear the thought of
their impending suffering and doom. Fixated on her delusion, she came to
believe she had no alternative but to put an end to the family's ordeal and
afterwards take her own life. Like you, delusion pushed her over the brink and
I found she was exempt from criminal liability.

Suicide's a cancer of the mind. Although the suicide appears to be in
control and the author of their death, twisted logic impels them to act. I will
never fully understand the "why" of your death – whether circumstantial,
psychological or chemical – I only know you had little or no freedom of
choice. I'm scandalized (and saddened) that in the past the Church would
have denied you the right to burial in consecrated ground as though you
were a pariah, someone beyond the reach of God's mercy, a scandal to the
community. In Dante's *Inferno* the souls of suicides are trapped in the bodies
of trees so that they can do no more mischief to themselves, but that is not
the end of their punishment. Harpies (birds with the breasts and heads of
women) tear off twigs and branches, which bleed, and with the blood comes

the moans of the suicides, the only way they can express themselves. If such a netherworld were part of God's plan I would no longer be Christian. I refuse to believe in a devouring God.

Too Soon, in Retrospect

❧

SOON AFTER YOUR SUICIDE – TOO SOON, IN RETROSPECT – I FORMED A NEW relationship with Nicole. Your suicide left me emotionally shipwrecked; yes, I could make everyday conversation and was rational enough to perform my work, but inside I was riven with grief. Within two months friends had introduced me to her; she was dark, French and elegant, as well as kind, intelligent and empathetic (she'd lost her husband a year or so earlier). She loaned me a sympathetic ear whenever I rambled on about you, never betraying resentment or embarrassment even when I'd suddenly break into tears dining with her in some fancy restaurant (as I often did). Unlike you, her paradigms were fluid; she was open-minded on most subjects, especially religion, which at times made me feel uncomfortable and put me on the defensive. "I'm cosmic," was her favourite description of herself. Once I remember becoming so unstrung by her liberal ideas I got up and huffed out of a restaurant in Ottawa in the middle of dinner. "There are no dangerous ideas," she told me after we'd reconciled. My headlong rush into a new relationship hit the children hard – how could they not view it but as a cold betrayal of your memory or a sign I didn't love you (which of course wasn't true) and in the ensuing weeks, months, even years their hurt and resentment would rear up again and again to confound me. In spite of my vehement denials you always predicted that if you died first I'd soon find another woman; it became a running joke in our marriage – me protesting that you were wrong, that one good woman in a lifetime was enough for any man, that I would devote the rest of my life to study and contemplation; you rejoining that I was deluding myself, that you knew better, that I needed someone pliant and maternal to dote on me. Occasionally, when you'd add that in marrying you I'd picked the wrong partner, I'd become greatly agitated, for despite our differences of upbringing and your mercurial tongue I loved you deeply and faithfully.

Writing this journal is my way of diminishing loneliness and helping me to relive and understand our journey together. The story is an imperative, not a choice, and I mustn't flinch from sharing the fears and flaws that link me to the wound stripes of others. Rising most mornings at 6 a.m. to troll the waters of our past together at the word processor is tricky navigation, for

I'm often distracted and the waters are often murky and unpassable, but I persist for I'm writing to save my life and keep your memory green. The first Christmas after you left I gave each of the children a reproduction of your painting *The Family*, a hymn to the sacredness of family life. Every eye was wet. Last year I gave them your painting *The Birthday Party* of the family dining together, as well as a composite reproduction of pencil sketches you did of the children when they were young. The table is the place of intimacy for a family. On Simcoe Street Dad never ate at the table with the rest of us. In contrast to Van Gogh's *The Potato Eaters*, where the peasant family sits around eating potatoes and drinking coffee, no one making eye contact, each member isolated and mirthless, your painting exudes warmth and joy with you, the server, adorned in the bright laurel leaves of hope, the focus. Adele and I also put together a booklet of 40 or so letters you wrote to her when she was away in Mexico and gave a copy to everyone. I asked Marilyn, who has matured into a beautiful, caring person, if she wanted to share some of your letters to her but she decided she wanted to keep them for herself. "They are the only things of Mom I have for myself," she said, and I respect her decision.

Sharing the intimate details of our life in this journal will help others, I hope, slay their own dragons, open up new possibilities for tenderness on their journeys. Your death can lead to either growth or bitterness. I chose growth.

CR

I SIT BEFORE THE BLUE CONFESSIONAL TRYING TO TAP INTO SWIRLING FIRST thoughts, keep the pettifogging internal censor at bay, never knowing exactly where my thoughts and feelings will lead. I want to be borne along with the flow like the red-suited jogger I saw this morning swinging arms and legs in perfect harmony: a kind of automatic pilot. Today in court I listened to the testimony of an expert, an accident reconstructionist. Relying on skid marks, measurements, impact, testimony, and other arcane scientific data he described with impeccable logic how the accident occurred – a bravura performance, but in the end just a hypothesis only as valid as its supporting facts, a bit like me looking at you and our life together through the selective lens of memory. In quantum physics scientists have concluded that an observer alters the nature of what is observed, that at its core nature is essentially random and fluid which explains by analogy why I feel equivocal about putting our life under the microscope. Doubtless everyone who knew you would have a different story to tell. It's as though I see you in the rearview mirror standing at the side of the road, waving goodbye, but as I gather speed and distance you begin to diminish and after a while I can no longer see your face. And then the long last curve and you're no longer there. Am I, like the reconstructionist, trying to recreate your reality from the scrapings and scraps of memory?

Last night two vivid dreams: in the first, a powerful flood swept through our town and I was carried far out to sea on the roof of our house and when the storm abated found myself staring into a vast emptiness, you and the children gone.

In the second dream Nicole and I are sitting on your mom's sofa in the old house on College Street when you suddenly walk in, a knowing smile on your face, wearing a blue skirt and scarlet brocaded blouse. Acting very much like your "old self" you appear undisturbed by Nicole's presence, as though you half expected her to be there. Nor is Nicole embarrassed by your arrival. The children and I are jubilant over the miracle of your return to the land of the living, but at the same time I am burdened with mixed feelings, saddened by the knowledge that Nicole, who has been a good friend and mentor, will no longer be in my life. If dreams are God's forgotten language, the God-given unconscious part of us speaking, what are my dreams telling me? That we cannot live intimately and closely with another person, love them deeply, without at times inflicting pain, that the very act of loving runs the risk of hurt and failure? Maybe it's time I stopped punishing myself with guilt and self-recrimination.

Conscience

After she left that Palm Sunday
the police searched the house,
powdered for fingerprints.
They took out their notebooks.
"Tell us everything," the sergeant
said.
And so he told them everything,
which wasn't much, but they kept
returning to the question:
"When was the last time you visited
the Falls?"
Finally they said they had to go,
but promised to be back.
The next time they took
furniture, books,
letters, old postcards,
even clothes,
left me rattling around the big,
empty house, naked and alone,
with the thought:
"Maybe I did kill her."

☙

YOU OFTEN TOOK ME TO TASK FOR BEING THE ABSENT-MINDED PROFESSOR, complained that often when the kids spoke to me my vague responses showed that my mind was a million miles away. Some of my teachers used another term: woolgatherer. Even my wise mentor Graham Barnett with his elaborate tea ceremony couldn't still the tree full of monkeys inside me. It didn't take the perceptive Nicole long to notice my restlessness. "You're a spiritual glutton," she said. "Try to swallow all experience in one gulp." Like St. Thérèse of Lisieux I want it all. Is this the "spark of the divine" in us, as some mystics say, or an aching hunger for a self-expression and completeness that life cannot yield? Or perhaps both? When life got intolerable on Simcoe Street I'd pack a brown paper bag with peanut butter sandwiches, an apple and a mason jar of milk and strike out down the gleaming rails for Jackson's Park where all day I'd laze around and read under the pines, the fragrance of resin in the air, the sound of the wind sifting through the boughs above my head, and I'd come home late but spiritually renewed. Trudging home Friday nights after a movie or the "Y" was always a scary experience; as I approached the front door I'd work up a cold sweat just thinking of the possibilities, alert for the telltale clues that would signal my fate. The acid test came when I'd poke open the brass mail plate: if the hall linoleum was freshly waxed and polished, it would be covered with newspapers and I'd know order reigned and I'd be safe, but if it was messy and cluttered with beer bottles and I could hear loud voices from the kitchen I'd know the drinking had started and there'd be scrabbling chaos all weekend. Is this why I still hate conflict, a samurai in law but a wimp in private? Remember the time Ruth broke her arm horsing around in the backyard with Paul and you called me, how I hesitated to come at first, fearful I'd find the worst. Maybe speak no evil, hear no evil, see no evil should be chiselled on my tombstone. Though I'm improving, I still have a tendency to shrink from the hard edges of life. To this day I'll wince and shut my eyes when a figure skater on TV tumbles. All those dreams and hours of practice crashing to the ice because of one momentary slip – it seems so unfair. I guess that's it: life's unfair and I don't want my dreams to come crashing down.

Death Row

I lived on death row
when I was small,
never knew if
I would live or die.

I shuddered
when I heard their boots
pounding down the hall
the same hour Friday nights.

I never knew my fate
until the peephole clanged,
and I
smelled the beery stench,
saw the glassy eye.

The black current
twisted through my mind
but they always brought me back to life,
told me I would never get reprieved,
that Friday nights go on forever.

ဆ

GOT UP THIS MORNING TO THE DRUMMING OF RAIN ON THE SKYLIGHT IN
the bathroom. The sky was mostly overcast with a few chips of blue peeping
through and I could hear the swish of tires on the wet street. When I left for
work the orange street lights were still on and a young man in white shirt and
light blue jeans was ambling along Woodland Glen carrying a clear plastic

umbrella. A red banner over Kentucky Fried Chicken announced in big white letters "NEW CARIBBEAN CHICKEN" and promised everyone, "You can't get enough of it." On the 401 the horizon began to take on a rosy hue; dark tracks in the grass led from the westbound lane to a beige car stuck in the median, where a woman nonchalantly leaned an elbow against the hood of her car, hand on cheek, resigned look on face, no doubt wondering why she was in the ditch when everyone else was hell-bent for their jobs and worries; maybe she was meditating, who knows? At the Mac's store in Milton, a tabloid showed a man with hairy wolf face and headline: "HALF-MAN, HALF-DOG" – what a wacko world! Last evening, Nicole told me she planned to see a psychic about her ailing mother, the state of our relationship and God knows what else. Shortly after your death, Gay and Graham went to Niagara, prayed the rosary for you at the parapet where you stood up and leapt. Will I ever be able to visit the Falls again? The thought curdles my blood. But I still have more faith in the rosary than the horoscope.

I worry about the children. Ruth's in a bad relationship and finds it hard to bail out; the other day she told me how you used to anticipate spring and without being asked knew what clothing, shoes and spending money she and the others would need, an area where I'm still so clueless. Adele also concerns me: she'd love to find the right partner and have a child and is always using me as a sounding board for her disappointments and frustrations. Though I admire her honesty there are times I wish she'd lay off. Today I told her to lighten up. But I was consoled the other evening when she related the story of your four days with her in New York City – your last trip, shopping, visiting galleries and generally having a wonderful time and lots of belly laughs. "It was one of the best times I ever had with Mom," she said. You wanted me to come along and how I regret now that I didn't make the time.

Oh, there are days when I need a female shoulder to cry on (Nicole, God bless her, does her best) to quell the anger I sometimes feel towards you for throwing us all into this bottomless quagmire. Gloomy days like today draw out the melancholy in me and I have to remind myself that you couldn't be blamed, that you were plunged in a private darkness and didn't know what you were doing.

CR

NICOLE SAYS I'VE IDEALIZED YOU, FASHIONED YOU INTO AN EFFIGY OF perfect womanhood, wonders if she could ever hope to compete with the icon I've created. Trawling through the waters of grief is like trying to spear sunfish: the sunlight and water distort your vision and the sunfish dart away. In court today the crown alleged a young man stabbed another youth on the wrist with a steak knife. At first blush, the case seemed open and shut: a stabbing in broad daylight in a public park with plenty of eye witnesses, but as the evidence unfolded it soon became obvious that everyone had a different, often contradictory, version of what took place.

The flash and heat of a crime make it difficult to be objective, which is why judges are often skeptical of eyewitness testimony. Is it any surprise, then, that these memories of you and the past should not be distorted by human frailty, especially when I look back on our life together through grieving eyes?

Nicole is astute and I do not take her observations lightly. Yes, I admire you for your courage, your honesty, your devotion as well as your many other sterling qualities, but I don't want to sugarcoat your memory, create a false image. You were very human but for me you were also a rock of moral and domestic stability in swirling waters – a rock on which I leaned for the support I didn't get as a boy.

Minnows

All the eyewitnesses agreed
that the day of the accident
was warm and sunny.

The victim testified that
she entered the intersection
on a green light and the accused
struck the front of her car.

The accused testified that
he entered the intersection
on a green light and the victim
struck the front of his car.

The old lady rocking
on the verandah testified
that the accused definitely
ran the red light.

The young man on the Suzuki motorcycle
testified that the accused
definitely stopped
at the red light.

The pensioner strolling on the sidewalk
testified that everything happened so fast
he couldn't say what colour the light was.

The judge remembered another sunny day
at Jackson's Creek and minnows
shimmering past

his small, awkward hands.

ಌ

THE CARNIVAL MIRROR OF MEMORY STRETCHES US IN ALL DIRECTIONS. HERE are some of the images I retain of you, darling: your eyes open and dreamy as we made love, your monkish concentration at the easel in the screened porch at the cottage, your frantic eyes at suppertime as you rushed around the kitchen to make supper, your body still as stone as you lay in a lounge chair on the deck deep in a novel, your floppy leather sunhat (that made you look like a flower child) as you stooped to pick daisies in a sunlit field, your eyes blazing at me in anger, your single-minded attentiveness as you sewed, the pale blank mask you wore in Barbados after you fell sick, your face, streaky and swollen, at your mom's funeral, your desperate look when we talked in the open field at the cottage and you told me you didn't want to lose me. Yes, images and feelings break the surface like sunfish only to swiftly dive away, and a nimble eye is needed to catch their glistening scales, their cold slippery shapes. I try not to sentimentalize you but often find myself coming to your defense when one of the children (or anyone) criticizes you, suggests you were too moralistic or religious or unstable. A few weeks ago I saw red when Adele, furious at me for what she perceives as my Pollyannaish attitude towards our marriage, blurted out she was glad you had died. Of course she didn't mean it but it hurt just the same. Is it parental pride? Am I defensive because I view any criticism of you as a negative reflection on our marriage and parenthood? Or is it because I don't want you to be judged by others (even children and friends) who didn't love and know you the way I did? When we truly love, we understand and forgive, and when we daydream a grab bag of images and feelings and thoughts tumble out. Though seemingly disconnected, they have their own inherent coherence; the subconscious reveals us to ourselves and it is from these secret places of the soul that we find our compass.

CR

AFTER MASS ON SUNDAY, NICOLE AND I VISITED ANDY'S STUDIO AT Rockwood. His new stainless steel sculptures impressed me, especially one he calls *Banner of the Wind* – two 15-foot pipes with a banner fluttering in between that he's installed in the main courtyard – a tribute to his late mother. The 2000-pound structure exudes a remarkable spiritual lightness. She'd led a heroic life, Andy told us, starting with the Nazi occupation of their native Holland and outlived her husband and two of their eight children. Her secret: an iron will and the ability to shape herself to the winds of disappointments and sorrows without breaking, always accepting and loving.

On the way to court yesterday, fog shrouded the landscape, but this didn't stop Monday's jittery and irritable drivers passing me at breakneck speeds; near the entrance to the 401 I observed a tan and white fawn on the shoulder, mangled and bloody, another night victim. The fog was so thick it was like plowing through a high snowbank, past and future blocked off, with only the flashing red-and-white lights of the vehicles to tell me I was still on earth, relying on blind faith that the highway with its abandoned mufflers, shards of burst tires and grisly roadkill would somehow lead me to my destination. The fog squeezed the green out of the escarpment and at the entrance to Milton triangular phosphorescent orange markers signalled a silver tractor trailer stranded on the shoulder, God knows why. Lately I've become more centred and instead of playing the radio during my shuttles between Guelph and Milton use the time to reflect on our moments of undivided tenderness together in silence, how much I miss you, that if you were suddenly to return I'd collapse with happiness.

In court this morning a young man pleaded guilty to arson. He had torched the matrimonial home in a fit of anger and depression. The relationship had been stormy from the start and the evening before the wife had announced she was leaving, that the marriage was over, and immediately packed her suitcases and left for her mother's with the three children. That's when the young man snapped, decided he had nothing left to live for and set the house ablaze. Sheldon Kopp, in his book *All God's Children Are Lost but Only a Few Can Play the Piano*, describes a joyful person as someone whose house has burned down and begins to build anew from the deep needs of his soul. In a metaphoric sense you burned down our house but I still have a choice: I can lie down and whimper because my dreams have been senselessly reduced to ashes or I can transform my seemingly impersonal fate into my personal destiny. Like Andy's steel sculpture and mother I don't want to crack. How I wish you'd had his mother's resilience; though you were steadfast and brave in many ways the wind finally broke you. Or did it? I like to think you were not broken, that you simply could no longer tolerate the wanton and gratuitous cruelties of life – the culture of death in the world around us – and that your suicide was an inverted affirmation of life and that you've now at last found that place of perpetual light where kindness always blooms.

ೠ

After the barbecue in Thailand, Nicole, Mira and I sat under a cone-shaped gazebo of buffalo grass on the shores of the river Kwai. As this wasn't tourist season the place was peaceful and quiet; we had the river and the starry night to ourselves and I fancied Alec Guinness would emerge at any second from the darkness as Colonel Nicholson to point his swagger stick in our direction and order us to shape up. Disco music, faint and intermittent, wafted across the river from a floating restaurant; yellow and white lights winked on the dark river. The subtle sweet perfume of frangipani blossoms filled my nostrils. I asked Mira about the music: "Rag music," she said, "and the song's called 'Ice, Ice Baby'." Then her face darkened and she said something that disheartened me: "Mom's like music I no longer hear that still rings faintly in my mind." She went on to mention that during the last few days of your life she'd noticed changes in you; casually, almost clinically, you'd warned her that if she intended to have sex with anyone to protect herself, an odd remark given she'd never used artificial birth control and believed fervently in virginity before marriage. And then you added, Mira said, almost as an afterthought:

"I think I've hurt everyone." But it wasn't so much the words that struck her
– after all, you'd discussed birth control with all the girls – but the tone of
resignation and remorse as though you regretted having been so rigid and
doctrinaire in matters of sexuality and were somehow trying to make amends.
"I think she was having a crisis of faith," Mira said. Mira is very sensitive and
astute and I give her observations a lot of credence. The childhood faith that
formed you was a world of few shadows, containing straight lines and a clear
precise horizon. When the tiny truths of that landscape crumbled you must
have felt like a householder whose house is suddenly thrown into darkness.
The American Episcopal Bishop Spong, in his book *The Hebrew God*, describes
the collapse of duality – the wedge between the world and spirituality – in
Christianity as having left believers without a comfortable ghettoized system
to believe in, and how that change has driven many to the edge of despair.
Did you judge your life a mockery? While many chose the slow death of
drugs to escape pain, did you choose the quicker and more honest way? In
recurring dreams you often appear in the guise of a ghost or phantom: grey
eyes, grey skin, grey hair, grey robes, grey everything, as if you belonged to
some Lethean underworld. Or you're a water lady sitting lotus style on a
rocky ledge day and night at the Falls, unperturbed by the mighty plainchant
of the water, blessing star-crossed lovers who stare at your awesome white
curtain. Some dreams are hard to decipher: last night I dreamt Nicole walked
through a field, came upon a clothesline loaded with shirts, underwear, pants,
and decided as a kindness to the owner, an elderly widower living alone, to
take them down. Suddenly a pack of dogs lunged towards her across the field,
snarling and panting, and Nicole took refuge in a shed, but the dogs kept
coming, ran all the way to the highway, where they sat down in an orderly row
along the shoulder to watch the traffic. "People are always taking down my
clothes," the old man complained. "It's a big problem and I wish they'd stop."
What does the dream mean, I wonder?

FOG BLANKETED THE 401 THIS MORNING; BUILDINGS AND TREES SLID BY LIKE shadows and though I was dimly aware of lights and a green aura around me, I felt I was tunnelling through a grey blankness, invisible and unobserved, lost in inner space. Jack Kerouac is called the "Great Rememberer." In trying to snag thoughts, feelings and vignettes of our life together sometimes I feel like a clumsy lepidopterist with a net full of holes trying to catch butterflies in a windy field. Every time I get close, the butterflies flit away and vanish. My net is the blue screen of the computer where I sit most mornings – a sacred circle or tenemous, as Jung calls it – where I let myself go in a kind of psychological freefall and remember. Nicole says that if she ever moved she'd want to turn the page, replace most of her furniture and start anew. I can understand why. There are billions of monarch butterflies and to my undiscriminating eyes they appear the same, but you were unique and unrepeatable and the big house is full of hints and reminders of you: the green floral wallpaper you chose for our bedroom; the Victorian bed where I sleep every night that belonged to your grandmother and where your beloved Teetaw came into the world; the modest paintings and engravings we bought over the years (some from your old professors); the stained glass you designed for the dining room window and front-door sidelights; the plaster walls and extra-high ceilings you insisted on when we built this house; the wood umbrella stand you picked up at an auction for next to nothing and painted sky blue; and the rose Victorian lady's chair we bought at another auction before we were married (I'm sad to report that Kody, that ungovernable cur, has chewed off the ends of the arms); yesterday, I looked again at the portrait you did of me sitting on the deck of the cottage the summer before you died. I look so severe and censorious – is that the way you perceived me? And the sepia self-portrait you dashed off one afternoon that made you look like a slightly demented stranger: the house is a museum of artefacts, an inventory of our 28-year marriage.

But memory is a leaky container and without the impress of flesh – an indentation of fingers on an arm – you've become a blurred figure in a mist. Annie Dillard says that loss is the extortionate rent we pay for staying. One of my few epiphanies since you left was the birth of your eldest granddaughter, little Mira. I was at Bourke's chalet in the Laurentians cross-country skiing when Marilyn rang to give us the news, and I recall the inexpressible joy I felt; it was as though you'd been brought back to life. Later, when I saw her and noticed her remarkable resemblance to your baby pictures, this feeling was magnified. Recently I read about a man who couldn't accept his wife's death – they'd been married 30 years – until he placed a tombstone on her grave; the stone became a symbol of acceptance and only then did he find closure. Your cousin Betty told me about the death of her brother-in-law; he'd been suffering from cancer a long time and when the end finally arrived his wife and five children gathered around his bed, a circle of love and prayer, and before he died he said his goodbyes and blessed them – the classic Christian deathbed scene. You had no such edifying end and I cannot give you a tombstone, but I console myself with the thought that you died in water, the matrix of life and the sign of new birth, that you are alive and well today in the vast river of love where no one is lost forever.

Silver Mercies

"It takes seven years for a suicide,"
the priest said, but I was too numb

to hear his words; that was the black
spring tongues of tulips pierced my

heart and the thought of never seeing
her again was more than I could bear.

Last night when her long beautiful
arms reached across the bed, huge with

desire, and I could not even remember her
voice, that rich resonance that once filled

our home with warmth and joy, I grieved for
all our faithless flesh too small for

even strongest love; but snow,
our comforter, knows us better than

ourselves and covers us whitely, seven
times seven, with soft forgetfulness, and

just as the hibiscus never completely fades
but rises red and radiant always

in our mind, so too the snowy voices
of those we loved live on in our reborning

selves, silver mercies of the dead.

CR

THESE KADDISHES ARE LOOKING FOR A PAST TO BLESS, FOR LIKE A
drowning man my father keeps breaking the surface to gasp for air. Does he
want to tell me something? Nicole's right: I've got unfinished business between
us that begs for a hearing. Or maybe "absence/transience" is my real subject.
Dad left Belfast at thirteen, sent by a widowed mother with five young mouths
to feed who believed there was no future for him on the sectarian streets of
Belfast. For four years he worked as the hired man on a mixed farm near
Bobcaygeon owned by the Thompsons, a hardworking churchgoing couple
who shunned both alcohol and tobacco. Dad grew fond of the couple, who
treated him like one of their own, and in later life always referred to them as
"Mom" and "Pop." He was overseas for four years and when he got back it

was like meeting a stranger. I remember the day he disembarked at the local train station, a stocky man with a grey duffel bag slung over his shoulder and a wide grin on his ruddy face and Mom shouting, "It's him, it's him, it's your father!" and next I recall he'd hoisted me up in his powerful arms and was kissing me on both cheeks, his whiskers like sandpaper on my skin.

Who is the soldier in the house
laughing and drinking and shouting,

who sings out of tune, bangs his fist
on the kitchen table?

Who is the soldier who finds my
hiding place, shoves his whiskers

in my face? Who is the soldier
who tells me what to do, says

he loves me, wants me
to love him too,

the stranger with hairy hands,
the dry kiss?

Over the years his excessive drinking drove a wedge between us, and my only glimpses of the inner man came through the eyes of others. Many years ago I ran into Mr. Thompson, now an aged widower, who reminisced about the night of Dad's arrival. "We went to the station to fetch him," he said, "but he wasn't there. The conductor and me searched up and down the platform and I was beginning to think he was lost when we decided to go through the coaches and that's where we found him, curled up on a seat in the last coach, head leaning on his brown suitcase, face streaming with tears. Sammy was homesick, that's all."

Other memories crowd the surface: St. Patrick's Day parties at the house on Simcoe Street, when he'd invite over all his cronies, north and south, to celebrate, and the beer and rye would flow freely. Dad would dragoon my sister Shirl to play the piano, and the festivities would quickly sink in a bog of sentimental Irish ballads — I recall "Mother McCree" and "I'll Take You Home Again, Kathleen" as two that kept cropping up. Then at some mysterious but definable moment Dad would grab the spotlight and the room would hush. Clasping a beer bottle in his big fist he'd sing — shout would be more accurate — in his big, tuneless bass voice everyone's perennial favourite, "Danny Boy," accompanied by many dramatic gestures, crocodile tears and climaxing with the dramatic flourish of him plucking his mom's portrait from the wall over the piano and pressing it close to his heart. By this time everyone would be misty-eyed with memories of their own mothers. The party seemed to go on forever and next morning the floors would be littered with empty bottles and cigarette ashes, the air rank with the vestiges of stale beer and second-hand smoke.

Once he dragged me across the street to pray in Latin for ailing Mrs. O'Sullivan. Stretched out on a filthy bed in a kind of unnatural repose, partially naked, complexion chalky, eyes half-shut, she looked as though she didn't have long for this world. A black crucifix hung on the wall above the bed and there was a half-empty bottle of Bushmill's Irish whiskey on the floor. My nostrils burned with the reek of urine and vomit. I dutifully recited the Confiteor as commanded (I was an altar boy at the time and knew all the Latin prayers by rote) while her husband, old Irish, unkempt, grey-stubbled and hairy-chested stood by and let the tears roll. When I heard Dad exclaim after I'd finished, "I told you, Irish, he can pray in Latin," I realized he'd dragged me there not for the powerful magic of prayers, but to show off my skills as a linguist. The old lady survived another five years until one Sunday morning, blue and bright like the day you went to Niagara, Mom found her in bed, cold as a block of ice, a mickey of Johnny Walker's grasped in her white fist and old Irish beside the bed, mumbling, "I think poor Kathleen's gone."

Last weekend, I visited my sister Marilyn to pore over old photos and reminisce about our childhood. As you know she's a big-boned woman, the image of Dad with his round jovial face and strong Northern Irish facial bones except for the eyes, which are big, blue and soft like Mom's. As I gazed at her huge glass cabinet crammed with expensive collectors' dolls she must have noticed my look of puzzlement for she said, almost apologetically, "As a child growing up on Simcoe I always dreamt of owning a china doll but Mom could never afford it." And then she went on, "You know, I don't remember much of my childhood. I hardly remember Dad at all." Flipping through the family albums that evening there was one picture we couldn't find – a family portrait of Mom, Dad, Shirley, Marilyn and me all together. It doesn't exist. "It was like he was never part of the family," she said. "A ghost." I picked up a faded Polaroid of him standing in a ditch on Aylmer Street, big hands folded over the handle of a spade, a pile of earth in the background, and he appears like a stump rooted in the ground. But the strongest impression is dust: dust covers his yellow hardhat, checkered flannel shirt, green pants, and skin, erasing all the features of his face and melding him with the street. Even to this day I have trouble seeing him clearly; it's as though the alcohol contained some secret potion that rendered him invisible. Marilyn is right: he is a ghost.

Dying Alive

When he finished the box
he stuffed himself inside,
closed the lid.
But not before he threw away
the key. Early on
he must have decided
(don't ask me when or why)
that this was the safest way.
How could it be otherwise?

All our lives we stood
outside the box and
peered into the breathing dark,
hoping to glimpse his face
in cracks of light,
begged him to come home,
listened to the unravelling
of his heart,
his slow surrender to advancing night.

&

A BUSY DAY AHEAD; ONE OF THE CONSTANTS OF MY LIFE THESE DAYS ARE these bleeding dialogues before the computer. I try to brush everything aside, keep the monkey mind in check, pluck first thoughts and images from the swift current of the subconscious. Talked to Nicole on the phone last night: she's worried about her eldest son, a gifted young man who's having domestic problems. "Maybe all the emphasis on giftedness was wrong," she mused in a wobbly voice. Nicole's a good person, a supermom like you, and I felt sorry for her. Morning light careens across the Hanlon, setting the grassy banks and crowns of pines and maples aflame; the blond light on the 401 makes you feel you're entering the brilliant white tunnel described in near-death experiences, so strong it strikes stars off my eyeballs and the chrome of the big tractor-trailers. At times I think I must have a pagan soul. Like Horace the ancient poet on his farm in the Sabine hills, I'm always extolling the beauty of nature and its ability to comfort and heal. Odd, too, how we come to depend on particular roads, signs and landmarks like the escarpment to keep our bearings, but nothing stays the same for long; something is always cropping up to turn our lives topsy-turvy. Sometimes I'll be sitting in court listening to the drone of lawyers when, despite the blunting of time, out of nowhere the stark finality of your suicide washes over me like a rogue wave and I'll have to call a recess to regain my balance. At such times I ask myself: How could you have done it? Did the collapse of your childhood faith demoralize you, throw you into despair? You were the last person in the world anyone would expect to join the band of Canadians — estimated at 1200 per year — who decide to take their own lives. How can I make the shock I felt plain? It is as though a veil was torn away, exposing me for the first time to the cruel face of reality. And when this happens I'm never far from tears and begin to wonder if the world isn't just a gruesome nightmare. And of course the ubiquitous attack dog of guilt is never far away, always ready to pounce. Nicole sometimes gets my ire up when she reminds me I must take ownership for my part in your suicide. Her words make me feel complicit with the icy waters that drowned you.

As I peck out these words, sunlight dances on the row of maples beside the courthouse, a white transport rolls into a parking lot and in the distance against the backdrop of a seamless cobalt sky a grey concrete factory belches puffs of dark smoke into the air, the scene solid, permanent and familiar. If suddenly one bright spring day all these sights we take for granted should vanish, the pavement of the 401 disintegrate and shoot skyward or the light of consciousness wink out, or if they discovered all members of Parliament are pedophiles or that McDonald's is serving human flesh in its hamburgers or that Jesus Christ was only a medieval concoction like, some claim, the Shroud of Turin, this would convey some inkling of the impact your suicide had on me. But now I yearn for shocks of a different order: that someday we will discover that everyone has a secret angel or that you and all departed loved ones will descend to earth one starry night to tell us you are happy, that all, all is light. Oh, if only I could find the mountain of Zion, the key to the hidden garden where death hunts us in vain and all summer long roses sing to the heart and joy knows no season.

Oh How I Wish It So

morning tips
                the dish of night
spills her beads
                of blue and rose and white
last night
                I rode the dragon of sleep
across the long ocean
                deep into
your watery cave
                watched you rise
unfold your glassy wings
                and say
all all is light

Oh how I wish it so.

☙

MY MORNING RENDEZVOUS AT THE COMPUTER HAS BECOME A KIND OF
meditation. I try to write with clarity and depth from my deepest centre,
hoping to find my voice and trust it, which means trusting myself. How hard
to tap into the original stream of the subconscious where we all swim naked!
I seek to embrace life holistically, don't want to shirk unpleasant memories,
ideas or feelings, accept my shadow without fear or censure, but my left brain,
the censor, keeps trying to take back control, staunch the flow.

These kaddishes help me trust the process. Daylight always brings a
sense of renewal, the mind freshly skinned and alert; despite Joy's irritating
behaviour last evening (more on this later) and the prospect of a complicated

medical malpractice suit with two hotshot Toronto counsel this morning I felt my mood lighten. The beautiful filigree of sunlight cast on the garage doors by my neighbour's ornamental locust helped: the thin long leaves, clearly etched against the brightening sky, fluttered in the breeze; the scene reminded me of a delicate silkscreen I'd seen somewhere and brought back all the enchanted interplays of sun and shadow of my life. On the way to the Hasty Market to get my coffee and *Globe* I spotted a happy-go-lucky youth with freckled cheeks riding a bike with no hands, arms folded across his chest (something I loved to do as a boy). He was wearing a white T-shirt and black shorts and looked as if he'd just woken up to a wonderful new day and wanted to celebrate. Last evening I treated Joy to dinner at East Side Mario's – it was the end of her exams – and afterwards we went window shopping at the Stone Road Mall, where we separated: I was looking for new sandals and Joy wanted to check out the video store, but when I returned at the appointed time to the agreed meeting place, Joy was nowhere to be found. I spent the next three quarters of an hour trudging up and down the long central concourse peering into stores, wondering what had happened to her (my overheated imagination even toyed with the idea she might have been kidnapped). I was tempted to have her paged but closing time arrived and I drove home to find her instead in bed. "God, Joy, you could have at least told me you were going to walk home," I said, trying to conceal my annoyance. "I thought you might have been in trouble of some sort."

"Don't get mad. You know I hate malls," she responded in a petulant, put-upon manner, and I dropped the subject. Joy has a sweet nature and I love her deeply, but at times she can be very irritating. You always claimed I didn't love Joy like the others (which was untrue), but I'll admit I find some of her ways vexing and inscrutable. And Joy is more adept than the others at finding the chinks in my armour, twisting the knife. When she pulls off a caper like last evening I have to remind myself she's still a teenager who's just lost her mother, the person she loved most in the world, not to mention peer pressure, the rivalry of siblings and being coloured in a still-racist society. Next year Joy goes off to university in Montreal and a new start. Oh, how I miss you sometimes; the children loved you dearly and you had a way with them I can never match. But I won't give up.

C℞

In a disturbing nightmare last night, Paul took the law into his own hands, shot a vicious child predator and buried the body in a secret place and now the predator's father, seeking revenge, persuades Paul to board a boat and enter a lock that turns out to be a deep elevator shaft. Suddenly water gushes in and it appears Paul will drown, but at the last moment two strangers in the control room with the father overpower him and drain the water just in time. The dream had a sequel, which I don't remember.

I told Nicole about my plans to go to Niagara someday to make peace with your death and she concurs, thinks it's the best thing I could do provided I was ready. D.H. Lawrence says that creativity requires a vicious streak. I want to describe my bereavement journey as honestly as I can, but sometimes I worry about hurting feelings. Nicole agrees with Lawrence, says that unless I'm ruthlessly honest I won't touch human hearts. If this journal were ever to be published (I have no plans) I am not blind to the reality of human nature: no matter what I say, some are sure to find offence. She's also read stories of the dead returning in dreams and visions to plead with survivors to release them, let go of their obsessive mourning. How curious that water rises so frequently in these kaddishes! Perhaps there's a nexus: like your presence-absence, water's sheer liquidity appears tactile and solid, but the instant you step into it it gives way underfoot, try to grasp it and it trickles away into nothingness and if it floods, beware, you can founder and drown. You and I were on the baptismal team at St. Joseph's for many years; your role was to explain the symbolism of water as a drowning to the old Adam and a rebirth in Christ. Remember the primary school teacher you loved years ago, a gentle woman, sensitive and kind, who one bleak November evening decided

155

to take her own life and waded into the icy waters of Lake Ontario, never to be seen again, and how devastated you were? "What a dignified way to leave the world," you commented. I've told Nicole, whom I've been careful never to compare with you, about this journal (it's hard enough for her to live in your shadow and I've never let her read it) and how important it was for my healing – and she didn't appear perturbed. I also told her that the river of love is wide enough to carry many loves. Is it the love of the Trinity – complete, undivided, holistic – I crave? A seed planted by God himself/ herself and a plenitude which you are now enjoying? Maybe I should accept the limitations of my creatureliness, recognize that all our symphonies in this life are incomplete.

☙

YOURS WAS NOT A FAIRYTALE ENDING. YOUR PRECIPITOUS EXIT ALLOWED NO time for farewells, not even a hasty note. We were cut off in mid-flight, like a novel whose last chapters have been expunged, or a family album with half the pictures ripped out. I felt cheated, hung out to dry, suddenly plunged into the vortex of the absurd where nothing made sense: no plot, no meaning, no catharsis. And worse of all no chance to say "I love you." Two items caught my eye in the evening paper: a photo of a 58-year-old man who'd just made his third jump over the Canadian Horseshoe Falls in a black steel barrel inscribed CHALLENGING NIAGARA FALLS ONE LAST TIME and the story of a 24-year-old veterinarian student reported missing whose car was found abandoned in a Niagara park. Two days ago a tourist spotted his body near the Steamship Company Dock, the same place where the smiling photo of the 58-year-old survivor was taken. Your suicide, though a mystery, is at least partially explicable, but what would compel a young man with a promising future to kill himself, I asked myself. Nicole wonders if my grieving will go on forever, if I'll ever find closure. This morning in the sunroom I gazed at the azure spring sky and the grass bejewelled with dew and spied what seemed like a brown bag or clump of brush in the middle of the lawn. Closer observation revealed it was a tawny cottontail rabbit sitting very still, basking in the sun and flicking his long butterfly ears. Occasionally he'd twitch his nose, lick his breast, nibble a blade of grass. His dark beady eyes were half shut and I could tell he was totally immersed in the moment, relishing his patch of sunlight, the cool breeze, the thick carpet of green. I watched for a long time and felt a burgeoning sense of peace until he shook his long ears one last time and skipped away. I think I'll mimic the rabbit: soak up the sun and enjoy the fleeting minutes, let life wash over me like a fresh clear stream. One reason for writing these kaddishes is to emerge from your shadow into the sunlight, to find the dawn.

CR

How difficult to let go, capture first thoughts and feelings before the internal censor gets out his eraser. The right side of my brain is starved. Friday morning: the end of the week and everyone is looking forward to their barbecues and gardens. The sky is milky blue, the sun a pearly smudge on the horizon that is gradually turning into a shining disc as I get closer to Milton. On my right the GO Train traced a chalk line through the burnt umber of the escarpment. I was hesitant to show these kaddishes to Nicole, fearing she might be jealous at all the references to you. She's a kind, super-sensitive person and I don't want to hurt her feelings. But when I gathered enough courage to show her a few the other evening I was pleasantly surprised by her reaction: instead of taking umbrage she was supportive, said I was writing from the heart. I have to learn to trust people. Why am I always fearful people can't take the unvarnished truth? I went to bed early.

Dream

I write Nicole two long love letters, but then Mary, who has been in a coma, wakes up and begins to get better. At her bedside I tell her about the letters to Nicole, but she already knows about the relationship and isn't upset. We both realize, though, that it will have to end. One time Nicole expressed her fear that Mary might not be really dead and would come back into my life; now that fear has come true. I know I will have to visit Nicole and break the news. I feel deeply sorry for her and wonder where I'll find the courage to tell her. I'm torn between two loves.

℞

WEIRD WORLD. EVERY DAY THE MEDIA REPORTS OUTLANDISH STORIES: yesterday I saw a two-headed boy in the *Sun*: two sets of lungs, two spinal cords, two pairs of shut eyes and two faces, serene, even cherubic. One face was olive-skinned and had a shock of shiny black hair; the other, fairer skin and blond hair – a legacy of Chernobyl. When Nicole and I visited Mira in Thailand the Thais were preparing for the imminent arrival of Michael Jackson and his entourage, and you'd have thought from the hoopla that it was the second coming of the Buddha. At this moment while he's still on tour in Thailand doing his moon walk I read an item in the paper that he's been accused somewhere in the states of child molestation. The *Globe* tells me this morning that there's a cult in California that worships the atomic bomb and that 48 civil wars are currently raging around the globe. Sometimes I think you were wise to bail out when you did. But when I see the brief, brilliant fire of autumn, hold little Mira in my arms, walk through a field of goldenrod or see an old mare switching her tail in a sunny pasture or a crescent moon pinned above the blue streets of Guelph, I'm awed by the luminous beauty of creation and glad to be alive. Paul's wedding is still a ways off, but already we're beginning to feel the adrenaline rush that comes from fresh beginnings. All our daughters are planning new outfits. Gabriella's your type of woman, traditional, intelligent, talented – she speaks Italian, knows art and has a great zest for living – and she and Paul will make a great couple. Your daughter Adele is still on the *Beauty Myth* kick; today when I showed her photos I took of Nicole in Thailand – the Thais were smitten by Nicole, thought she resembled their Queen – something tripped a fuse. "I've seen enough of this beauty pageant," she sniffed, and walked away. When I went to our daughter Marilyn's for dinner the other evening and saw how much her happiness revolved around her little Mira it made me realize how quickly we find substitutes for our deepest losses and how soon the dead are nudged to the wings of life. You would have understood this, as you were always a bit cynical about human vanity, the craving to be remembered. Graveyard visiting was never your style. But I'm still sad that you'll never have the opportunity to hold little Mira in your arms, cuddle and play with her. You will be the unacknowledged guest at Paul and Gabe's wedding and the children and I will feel your presence-absence deeply, for the wedding has become a defining moment in the family; the old order is passing away and a new one beginning. Oh how the beautiful moments slide by our hearts like water. Soon I'll be rattling around the big house alone with my memories and someday no doubt I'll sell and move into smaller accommodations and even bring these kaddishes to a close. We ignore the flow of life at our peril.

CR

NICOLE AND I SQUABBLED TODAY. EVERY TIME SHE SUGGESTS I'M PARTLY responsible for your death she tweaks a nerve and I react badly. Of course I know she doesn't mean I pushed you over the Falls, but only that all of us – spouses perhaps more than others – are complicit in each other's lives and that by our insensitivities and emotional absences wound each other. Having read Alice Miller's *The Drama of the Gifted Child* I have no problem accepting her point, yet her reminders of my fallibility are like slow drops of pain, unseating my heart.

"Quit pushing my buttons," I tell her. "I've got enough neurotic Catholic guilt to last a lifetime."

In an article entitled "Advice to the Next Generation," Frederick Buechner related how after his father's suicide he swallowed hook, line and sinker the belief — a belief never explicitly articulated but woven into his relationship with his mother — that he had no right to be happy as long as she was unhappy. Consequently he grew up believing that there was something shameful in being happy not only when his mother, but anyone else he felt responsible for, was miserable. After many years of self-torment he concluded that this attitude was dead wrong and that everyone has the right to be happy, no matter what, and because happiness is infectious, the happier you are inside your own skin the better your chances of spreading it to others. It is why at creation itself, according to Job, the morning stars sang together and all the sons and daughters of humankind shouted for joy.

Lord, help me to be stronger and happier so that I can be available to others.

CR

ANTHONY DE MELLO BELIEVES MOST PEOPLE ARE SPIRITUALLY CATATONIC. Since your death, thanks in large part to Nicole, I've opened myself to new ideas, become less dogmatic and legalistic in matters of faith, but at the same time, I hope, more compassionate and caring as a human being. I've tried to learn from the truths of others, move from the known to the unknown without feeling threatened or insecure. Jesus said the truth will make us free, and it's the freedom that wakefulness brings, no matter the cost, that I seek.

I know I haven't been my old self since your death. As Ron Mitchell, a kind, practical friend, put it, the bloom's off the rose.

All my life I dreaded the display of raw emotion, especially anger and its twin, violence. Maybe I've always harboured anger and your suicide brought it into the open. The anger I feel is mostly diffused. I'm angry at everyone: my family, my friends, God, you, and not least myself. I feel as though I've been violated and robbed of the gold wedding ring that gave special meaning to my life. Oh, how it stings sometimes to hear friends talk fondly of their grandchildren, knowing you've cheated yourself of that rich experience. And how hard to get beyond our own pain to rejoice in the blessings of others. Sometimes, though, the anger is focused on things and people you'd least expect. The anonymous phone call from a male neighbour last evening, threatening to poison Kody because of her barking, got my hackles up. I seethed at the caller (he refused to give his name) and was also pissed off with Paul who took the call and who, instead of rebuking the caller for being the cowardly cretin he is, sounded mild and apologetic. After we talked Paul felt bad about his milquetoast reaction and realized he should have taken a harder line, released some of his own dammed-up anger. That the dog has become an unholy nuisance – yesterday she got loose again and only with luck and persistence was Adele able to catch her, has cost me $300 in fines to date, and chewed the knobs off the arms of our Victorian lady's chair – only exacerbates my feelings. And it doesn't help that Ruth's wrath hangs over our collective heads like the sword of Damocles ready to descend should any harm befall her pet. Ruth's an admirable, intelligent person with a hilarious sense of humour, but when it comes to her beloved Kody she's hypersensitive and protective. When I awoke the morning after the call I was still bristling inside; the sun, a fiery ball above the Hanlon, changed to a white glow on the 401. The light was so strong I had to lower the visor, the Schneider sign said 6.44 AM and just before Milton I drew up behind a beige Dodge pickup with a license plate that said "CHEEKIE" and a woman in a tan check work shirt and pink plastic loop earrings at the wheel and a small brown teddy bear spread-eagled across the inside of the rear window, glaring mockingly at me. The woman glanced into the side-view mirror and shot me a bold, sour stare and I don't know why but some of the rancour I felt towards the caller, Paul, Ruth and Kody got deflected to her. No, I didn't feel very civil and by the time I got to my chambers I was beginning to feel culpable about my unchristian attitude, so much so I made a conscious effort to summon the better angels of my nature and rein in my feelings. Trudeau's motto "Reason above all" never struck me as very realistic.

Adele, Ruth and, to a lesser degree, Joy have been loud in their grieving; the others – Paul, Mira and Marilyn – more muted. All have been deeply wounded. Nicole suggested that there could be a genetic explanation for your suicide, a frightening possibility since it is known that those closely related to a suicide have seven to eight times greater chance of taking their own lives. I'm sure the children have pondered this possibility, for one day Adele let it out of the bag during one of our conversations: "And don't think I don't worry about having a baby," she said. Leaving us the way you did robbed the children of their birthright; they will never have your companionship, wisdom or encouragement as they grow into mature adulthood and start families of their own; their children will never know your nurturing presence and you will never be part of the baptisms, birthdays, graduations, weddings and other defining moments of their lives. Marilyn told me the other day that one of her abiding sorrows was your absence during the birthing of little Mira. You bequeathed us a dark legacy and like a tree that grows around a lightning hole in its trunk we will have to grow around your absence. I hope that writing these kaddishes as honestly as I can will force some of our unexorcised beasts into the open and be a catharsis for us all.

I'm attending a judges' conference in a skyscraper in downtown Toronto. I meet another judge, a keen self-important type who has a collection of stallions that he has just led into the elevator. The animals will be riding with us to the conference on the top floor. I'm hesitant to enter the elevator, the horses frighten me. I dread their flashing hooves and big teeth. If they should start to rear and kick in the confined space of the elevator I know

we'll all be killed. Although I'm anxious and scared the other judge
finally convinces me to enter the elevator, assures me I'll be safe.

Elephants on the Loose

Yesterday at the barbecue hour
my elephant got loose in suburbia,
slipped through the gate unseen
while I lay dreaming on the deck.

"Be a good elephant," I said,
trying to coax him back,
but he was like a kid just out
of school,
crashing through hedges and gardens,
toppling flowerpots and sundials,
while neighbours watched, aghast,
steaks and hamburgers going up
in smoke.

And when he bellowed like ten thousand
foghorns in the night,
all the doors of all the cages
sprang their locks
and hippos and hamsters,
giraffes, goats,
lions and lambs,
monkeys and bears,
every species, great and small,
trooped out to join the fun.

And when my neighbours saw
that all their animals were free
wives screamed,
husbands accused me of breaking all the rules,
pointed bloody spatulas
at my heart.

❧

OUR ELDEST DAUGHTER POUNDS HER FISTS AGAINST MY HEART, BEGS ME TO
open up; she hates my willful blindness, my chauvinistic tics, wants me to fess
up to my role in your suicide. On Simcoe Street I'd escape chronic angers of
the house by hiding upstairs in the bedroom closet, my only refuge. All the
significant others in my life were women. Sometimes I wonder if I've always
had a secret fear of emasculation. Why am I still hiding, Nicole wants to
know. "You've outgrown the need for hiding places," she says. And how long
can I take the lashings of guilt's long whip? Oh, if only I could untangle it
all! Has the time now come? Maybe I should confess my part in your death,
say my mea culpas and get it over with. I always believed you were good (and
still do), even noble, in giving up your dream of an artistic career to raise our
family. Only now do I know the price you paid. One of my most poignant
recollections was the time we both entered works in the Northumberland
Open Juried Exhibition. You submitted two exquisite period costume sketches
and I, a couple of watercolour landscapes. When I discovered that both your
drawings had been rejected I felt terrible for I knew how much your art
meant to you (the curator later told me that though brilliantly executed the
jury found them too academic), but I felt even worse when I learned that
both my submissions had been accepted, one a "Unanimous Choice." What
should have been a jubilant moment for me turned out to be one of my most
dolorous, for I would have gladly burned my watercolours if it meant you

would have gotten into the Show. Last night I dreamt of Peggy Atwood: she wore a black yet very sexy beard and was pushing a homely child in a stroller. We met on College Street and she greeted me with a wry smile; we sauntered downtown together, arms linked, talking of life's vicissitudes and the shock waves of failure, but there was no danger of a romance: I was a Jesuit priest.

Kafkaesque Dream

"My guiding principle is this: Guilt
is never to be doubted."
Franz Kafka

Darkness hunches over him
in the alley of the neon city.

He's far from home, without
papers, hemmed in

on all sides, the rigging of
his bones rocked by icy stares,

accused of some ulcerous
crime. His good name

has been lopped off and maimed,
passed roughly round, sprayed

freshly on clay brick walls,
a hate-name, red like blood.

He's innocent but it doesn't
matter. His appearance is

disturbing. No one understands
his strange dialect. Though he

protests loud and long no one
listens to his voice. In this

stone-coloured underworld how
could it be otherwise? No one

can explain the sick green
shawl of shame that wraps him

round, the inner trickster who
makes him yearn to confess,

cry for forgiveness, not
knowing why.

CR

YOU ALWAYS SAID I HAD AN EGO AS BIG AS A BARN; I NEVER REALLY
understood what you meant until I read Spong on the nature of sin as
the Hebrews and Jesus understood it – not so much particular acts or
omissions, but a state of being, into which we're born: creatures capable of
transcendence, observing ourselves from the outside and not liking what we
see. The disjunction between our idealized selves and our performance is too
great and we can't stomach the reality. Hence we cover up in order to feel
acceptable, sink into self-centredness, and the greater the deprivation of love
in childhood the more calcified that self-centredness becomes. Is that why my
ego's sprouted into a giant? Who will kill the giant?

I don't feel like writing kaddishes today. I'm upset because my phone bill is high; the kids have been racking up dozens of long distance calls and I also discovered two gas bills for the van charged to my VISA card when I was away. Why do such trivia irk me? All I know is I'm scared and shouldn't be. Since you left I've found the dual role of mom/dad tough sledding. Unlike Elizabeth Smart, who accepted tribulations and wasn't afraid of tomorrow, I'm fearful. My trust is in tatters, I shun suffering, fret constantly over the children. Read yesterday about an accident on highway 19 just outside St. Jean, Quebec; a truck crossed the median and crashed head-on into a busload of seniors returning from a pilgrimage to a shrine near Lac Burchette. A huge explosion engulfed the bus, and almost all the seniors, many trapped in wheelchairs, burned to death. I think, too, of my own mother, returning from a healing Mass, struck by a drunk driver – a paraplegic the rest of her life. And where was he/she when you fell into the black hole and vanished without a trace? Why does God shit on his loved ones? What's all this rhetoric in scripture about God knowing us before we were born, counting hairs on our heads, reading the palm of our hands? Pious claptrap? It seems God gives all his/her creation a drubbing, good and bad, faithful and scoffers alike. As a judge even I try to be just, protect the innocent, punish the guilty. Maybe that's why I'm so angry; I want things to be different. The giftedness of being human is a double-edged sword: just as we despise impotence and weakness in ourselves so we despise impotence and weakness in God. We can't accept that God can't make us happy, save us from harm, protect us from death or even deliver us from our imperial self-centredness. Is there any hope for anyone?

Silver Mercies

I'VE BEEN FEELING DISMAL LATELY. A FEW DAYS AFTER YOUR DEATH I WAS walking in the conservation area behind the house with Bourke Smith when the aftershock of your suicide walloped me again, a psychic force so powerful it buckled my knees and sank me to the ground, breathless, unable to get up. Today it's not the dramatic manner of your leave-taking but your absence I feel most acutely. Being a "dad-mom," as Ruth now calls me, hasn't been easy; how many times when a crisis erupted I wished you were here to give me the benefit of your wisdom. Like a week or so ago when Ruth phoned, sobbing and distraught; she'd had another spat with her boyfriend who's always niggling at her about her weight, her driving, the way she dresses. As if Ruth needed negative nitpicking at this time in her life. Or Joy last evening who phoned me at Marilyn's, panic-stricken and frightened because a "big black bird" was loose inside the house. "Come right away," she pleaded. "I'm scared." When I got home I found her cringing in the kitchen, afraid to go upstairs to her room. "It's in Mira's room," she told me, but I searched everywhere and no big black bird. "You've been studying too hard, Joy," I said, half-jokingly, pointing out that all the windows had screens and the dampers on the fireplaces were shut. "But I know it's here," she insisted. "Maybe your mom's come back," I jested – in retrospect, given Joy's overwrought imagination, a thoughtless remark – at which she threw up her hands and groaned, "Oh, no!" Even I was beginning to feel edgy until I discovered the bird in the closet of Joy's room, as skittish as any of us, and let it out the window. "It was only a starling," I told her, but the incredulous look in her eyes told me she didn't believe me. Later when I showed her a photo of Mira in Thailand, a boa constrictor round her neck, she shrieked and bolted out of the kitchen. The idea of you returning morphed into a big black bird is irrational, but your presence continues to haunt the house. How you died isn't important, it's the yawning hole you left behind. Whether suicide, cancer, heart attack, accident, etc., there's no hierarchy in the republic of death – in the end it isn't important; you were swallowed by the emptiness of a vast snow field, all differences erased, and that's how I, dumbstruck by the fate that befell us, have come to view your suicide. No one dies better than another.

ℭℜ

ONE YEAR AFTER YOUR DEATH, ANOTHER HOLY WEEK ARRIVES AND WE'RE still searching for the sweet comfort of hope; emotions run high for it's a touchy season laden with memories, sorrow and guilt. Last evening Paul exploded at Joy because she wouldn't help search for Kody, Ruth's Jack Russell terrier who'd gotten loose again. "You're too damn lazy!" he shouted, all his pent-up fury pouring out; I hadn't seen him so upset in a long time. Joy stormed off to her room and cranked up her stereo to top volume and blasted us with rock and roll, her trademark tactic these days. I felt guilty, too, for not helping (I told Paul I'd had a hard day in court, was too exhausted) but it ended up with me going to the dog shelter again and forking out another $30 – the third fine this year – for our canine delinquent.

When I was appointed a judge you rejoiced with me (you always said I'd make a good judge), but at the same time you were sad to leave our old home in Cobourg and the many close friends we'd made over 23 years. Many happy memories were graven on the walls of the big house on College Street: Paul and Stephen and their friends playing floor hockey in the basement, a frenzy of pucks thunk-thunking off the walls, the din so loud we could hardly hear ourselves talking in the kitchen (oh, how we cherished those intimate moments of undivided tenderness at the end of the day); hot summer afternoons on the cool side verandah, the breeze riffling the Dutchman's Pipe and fanning our faces; ushering in the New Year with our friends Chris and Dave Stewart, Peter and Ann Kolisnyk, and Gay and Graham Stratford when we'd gather in the attic, uncork a bottle of Champagne, clink glasses and toast the changing year, then fling open the dormer window and Dave would blast his dad's First World War brass bugle into the frosty midnight air. Oh, for the elixir of those youthful days when skies were full of endless blue possibilities and we believed we could control our lives like a beautiful kite at the end of a string. Remember the time we paraded around the house, me holding aloft a lighted candelabra and all of us belting out "Auld Lang Syne" at the tops of our voices, not caring a fig what the staid neighbours might think; and our heated arguments on the lawn – the time you threw an aluminum pot at me as I came up the walkway and called me a momma's boy (you and I had a penchant for conducting our fights in public). Many of our quarrels related to gardening, for I hated the grunt work of digging in the earth, caring for shrubs and flowers and yard duties generally and you always felt (rightly) that I never pulled my weight in that department. No, it wasn't easy raising seven kids in a big house, with shopping, meals, chauffeuring, piano, ballet, hockey, mending and sewing, birthday cakes (children's birthday parties were your specialty) and the million other loving details that had to be tended to make a house a home. It's small wonder you found the task debilitating. Time was your *bête noire* and there was never enough of it to accomplish all the things you planned. By evening, your physical and emotional resources drained, I'd often catch you nodding on the den sofa or in bed, a book in your lap.

That last day after we'd packed and were ready to leave forever the place we'd called our home for 23 years, I felt empty. Without furnishings and the other bric-a-brac of living that tie a home together, the house had a cold and derelict look, seemed stripped of meaning. I went down to the basement to carry out one final rite of passage; using a black marker pen I scrawled in large letters on the whitewashed wall of the root cellar: JIM, MARY, ADELE, PAUL, MARILYN, RUTH, JOY AND STEPHEN SPENT MANY HAPPY YEARS IN THIS HOUSE for this is how I felt, a parting testament before we drove away into the unguessable future. If we'd never moved, I sometimes ask myself, would you still be alive?

ॐ

ON THE STONE ROAD THIS MORNING A HUGE WHITE GLOW EMERGED FROM the misty sky, the sun a glittering nickel inside – a light so unalloyed it looked as though it'd been newly minted, was the first light created ever; along the

Hanlon, long thin shadows from passing vehicles striped the pavement and pebbly shoulders all the way up the green embankments into adjoining fields where russet-coloured cattle adrift in patches of blue mist were munching grass. More and more I find it difficult to shoulder the problems of the children; you carried the brunt of them for years and remember how I'd catch you in bed late at night still wide awake fretting because one of them had dumped their heartaches on you. "The worry won't seem so big in the morning," I'd always say, urging you to get some sleep. You were too sensitive (or was it caring?) to shrug off their concerns and you left yourself vulnerable. Recently Joy informed me that Adele was so upset over a quarrel she'd had with her current boyfriend that Paul had to drive to Toronto to settle her down. Call it survival instinct, but I'm glad Adele hadn't told me about it. One of the tender mercies of aging is the diminished capacity to absorb the pain of others, especially loved ones. Or is it weakness? Stephen Levine says, "The distance from our pain is our distance from God" and growth means walking into our pain and embracing it. All I know is I don't want to vibrate any longer to the daily woes of the children, that a certain detachment is necessary for my peace of mind. Oh, the high cost of parenting!

I'm still feeling uneasy about my relationship with Nicole. All our married lives you and I (especially you) cleaved to the teachings of Mother Church, especially in matters of sexuality, and tried to raise the children with similar beliefs. All the answers to life were filed away in that repository of unfaltering authority, the big white box of religion; we were married to the ideals it contained (virginity before marriage, motherhood, etc.) and never knew when we'd be ambushed by Catholic scruples. We were probably typical of parents of the pre–Vatican II generation. Sometimes now I feel spiritually disoriented, as though I've wandered out of a safe place into alien and dangerous territory, at a loss for what to say or do. When I told my good friend Gord about my pangs of conscience he scoffed, asked when was I going to grow up, said God wasn't a prurient bookkeeper and had better things to do than track my sexual peccadilloes. Nicole has no problem; for her, love is the path to God and personal fulfillment and it's hard to disagree.

In hindsight I realize that you and I leaned too heavily on the institutional Church and perhaps not enough on God. After Ruth's birth – an unplanned pregnancy, for we were still playing Vatican roulette and hadn't yet discovered the Billings method of natural family planning – you got so depressed you raged against the patriarchal Church, remember, and when Father John, a pious traditional priest visited you in the hospital to cheer you up you gave him both barrels, unloaded the full charge of your accumulated fury: "How dare you celibates dictate my sexual life?" you roared and poor Father, taken aback by your passionate outburst, turned pale and retreated as diplomatically as he could; later you sent him an apology but your rage continued to burn like a red-hot coal for a long time. Not only the children but I, too, with my restive spirit must have been a burden for someone like you, overtaxed and exhausted; my brain was a whirligig of new ideas and projects: yearly improvements to the cottage (bunkie, screen porch, extension, new deck, installation of electricity, skylights, etc., etc.) and the hassle of planning and preparing for holidays each year and worrying about the children. Thank God for Nanny, who was always there to pitch in; sometimes you'd sigh, "Do we really have to go?" All this must have been at times too much for you. You would have preferred we channel our surplus funds into Horizons of Friendship or some other third-world development agency where it could do some lasting good. At your urging we set aside 10 per cent of my annual net income for worthy causes (you always said there was more at stake in the world than our own small happiness) and it seemed as the years rolled by that every charitable organization in Canada must have got wind of our project for we were swamped with importuning letters that we found hard to refuse. Yes, I was a restless dreamer and you tried to keep up and I regret now that my restlessness got you so frayed and sometimes made you unhappy.

Inquisition

Sister Victorine made us learn Butler's Catechism
by heart, all the big riddles of life – Who made you?

Why did God make you? Why were you put on
earth? What happens after you die? etc. etc.

decoded & packaged into handy, seamless boxes,
pressing down on our puny noggins week after

week like huge stone tablets. Every Friday morning
Sister would summon us to the front of the class

where, donning the holy breastplate of Grand
Inquisitor, she'd grill us on our spiritual progress.

Our rote had to be letter-perfect. No paraphrases.
No excuses. Sometimes she'd banish us to the cloak

room one benighted heretic after another,
take the black leather strap from her desk &

lash away in the dungeon dark till small hands
burned like the back of Christ.

CR

A DARK DRIZZLY DAY. IT POURED ALL NIGHT. I COULD HEAR THE TATTOOING
on the bathroom skylight. I had a series of dreams that I kept breaking off
to go to the bathroom. The details elude me but in the morning I felt I had

been put through the wringer. The 401 mirrored a shinier version of the dull sky, except for the dark smudges of tire tracks, and the Schneider sign said 6.50 AM 6 degrees Celsius. Last evening Adele, John, Marilyn, Bruce, Mira, Gabe and Paul came over for a steak barbecue. All your children have guilt-tripped themselves over your suicide, some more than others, but last evening the atmosphere was cordial and relaxed, no rancour, no finger pointing, no arguments, a welcome moratorium on intensity. Paul mentioned he'd always tried to please us. "Didn't you know that, Dad?" he asked incredulously when I expressed surprise. Lately he's been able to show his feelings more, let off a little steam, and feels good about it. "The world doesn't fall apart when you get angry, does it?" I joked. Why don't we ever measure up to each other's expectations? Adele related a couple of spooky and bizarre incidents connected to you: how one night not long after your death, a force, like powerful hands, grabbed Ruth and pinned her to the bed, and another that my sister Marilyn told her: how the pastel portrait you sketched of me before our marriage (which we'd given her as a Christmas gift) fell off her bedroom wall the same day you took your life and when she picked it up she found that the hooks and picture wire, including the wall attachment, were still intact. Adele, who believes in the paranormal, found the incidents disturbing. Only poets and the wise find angels under rocks – the rest of us are blind. Is that the purpose of religion, to tame the terror of life and death, make it bearable? If we were truly conscious of the transience of life, how it sometimes hangs on a thread – a weak vessel, a rogue cell, or a stranger's carelessness – would we have the courage to go on living? I come back to my question: Why do we never fully measure up to each other's expectations?

Remember that stormy night in December after our *Who's Afraid of Virginia Woolf?* session at the Mitchell's (they were new to Cobourg and must have been scandalized by our bellicose behaviour) when you got so incensed at something I said – to this day I don't know what the row was about – that on the drive home you demanded I stop and let you out of the car, and after you'd gotten out and were standing by the side of the road, I accelerated quickly and unintentionally splattered your coat and beautiful white dress with slush and when you got home you were so furious you threw a pie tin at me? My father had an explosive temper just like yours, especially when he was drinking. When I was about sixteen, having defied his wishes to quit school and get a "real man's job," he challenged me to a fight. When I refused he slammed his stone fist into my sternum and sent me flying over the sofa. "Get up, you Fenian!" he shouted, clenched fists upraised, but when I tried to get up he slugged me again, this time harder on the shoulder, and I knew I was trapped, that he wanted to duke it out and would never relent until I fought him. It was as though he needed to put me through some archaic rite of passage, so when he pulled his fist back to strike again I beat him to the punch, my right fist landing squarely on his belly, but it might have been a leather punching bag for all the effect it had and only succeeded in inflaming him further. We grappled and thrashed our way along the hallway like two clumsy bears until we came to the open bedroom door and fell onto the bed, panting and speechless, and for a brief, still moment we lay face to face, hearts beating in unison, locked in our savage embrace, eyes meeting, as close as we'd ever get. I could smell his beery breath on my face as he tried to squirm free and hit me again, but finally out of sheer exhaustion we both gave up, and though neither of us ever mentioned the incident again, I remember it with shame. A son should never strike his father.

Wartime Daddy

I dreamt I opened an attic trunk
and found the oddest odds-and-ends:

an album with the pictures torn out
save one of me, perched on a wire fence,

saluting him across the sea;
a batch of pale blue

promises, never kept, bound in package
string; a row of tarnished

medals — "Give me a thousand Irishmen and
I'll lick the world" — souvenirs of glory days;

an envelope full of praise I never got;
an empty rye bottle, Seagram's circa 1945.

Then to my surprise and shock his dimple,
— "Dimple in chin many women to win" —

beautifully carved, wrapped in cellophane;
a mason jar with blarney smile

gleaming through two large front teeth;
and at the bottom of the heap, proof that he

was still alive and well, his wild red fists.
At night I still shiver when I hear

those wild red fists pounding to break out.

CR

THIS MORNING THE SKY WAS A SPOTLESS BLUE BOWL. ON THE 401 A BUMPER
sticker on the Ford ahead of me invited me to take Jesus into my life and the
sun, show-off acrobat that he is, tiptoed between two black poles spanning
the side of the highway, a halo of silver daggers round his head. On the
horizon a duck chased a sparrow and two faint braided vapour trails began
and ended nowhere. If you glanced at the sun you could see inside its eye, a

bright nickel, playing peek-a-boo in the shimmering folds of light. The circle is the symbol of wholeness, a mandala, a rose window of dreams, ringing together the joys and sorrows of our fragmented lives. After I proposed you contacted a friend of a friend who peddled rings on the side and we met downtown near City Hall on a windy autumn evening; you selected a plain white-gold ring with a solitary diamond, and years later I gave you a large pale amethyst in an ornate gold setting for your 40th birthday. In court yesterday I noticed the identical ring on the finger of a magisterial woman with a large sharp face; she had dark upswept hair (your style for a long time), wore a red linen jacket with a pleated black blouse underneath and I wondered what sad tale hid behind that cold face. I never had a wedding ring until the day you gave me an antique gold band incised with turtle doves that once belonged to a beloved uncle, and when I lost it one evening shovelling snow at Teetaw's during a heavy storm you were livid. Another example of my carelessness, you charged (the ring was too loose and I'd ignored your requests to get it sized). Next day we searched the snowdrifts for hours and again in the spring after the melt but we never found it. It was almost as though I was never meant to wear it. But I still have the 14-carat gold band you chose with Ruth's help for our 25th anniversary; we renewed our vows at St. John's church and our kids invited a few Guelph friends back to the house afterwards for a celebration, remember? Our marriage meant a lot to you and it saddens me to think of the enormity of pain that made you sunder the bond. Nicole is less sentimental than me; after her husband's death she removed her wedding ring and suggested the other day that I put yours on my right hand to show I'm no longer married, but I don't intend to take it off for it is the ring you gave me, a sign of our covenant.

℃

ALFRED ALVAREZ, IN HIS BOOK *The Savage God*, DESCRIBES DEPRESSION AS a kind of spiritual winter, frozen, sterile, unmoving. Lately I've been thinking about your leave-taking and your failure to leave a note. Would it have made any difference? I've since read that you belong to the majority: only one in five suicides leaves a note. I've also learned that suicide notes, as communication, are dismal failures and rarely meaningful. A person contemplating suicide is not thinking clearly, for if they were they would recognize immediately that suicide was a bad idea and no solution for their pain. While the note can be rife with meaning, it is the product of a disturbed mind and not the meaning intended by the deceased. So in a way I'm glad you chose not to leave a note.

I've also learned that the suicidal state can be Janus-faced, that suicides are often ambivalent about taking their life. In one recorded instance, a man who survived a jump from the Golden Gate Bridge explained how from the moment he leapt off and was airborne he understood with horror that he'd made a terrible mistake and felt a strong frantic desire to live. Sometimes I lie awake at night in a cold sweat wondering if you too had second thoughts as the powerful current swept you along on your back towards the rim of the Falls.

The mere thought that you might have changed your mind in those last few seconds chills me to the bone.

CR

YOU'LL BE HAPPY TO KNOW MY RELATIONS WITH JOY ARE IMPROVING. Yesterday we shopped amicably together for groceries at the mall, sharing the job. After, I bought two sugar cones at Baskin Robbins — she had chocolate mousse royale, I raspberry cheesecake — and we listened to the Suzuki String School of Guelph play Bach and other classics in the rotunda. All the musicians were young, wore jeans, cords or slacks, and casual shirts and pullovers; the bass player sported a red baseball cap backwards, just like Joy. At first I thought the heavenly music was out of place in the mall, but the rapt faces of the shoppers and their applause made me change my mind; the music gave dignity to the mundane and relentless business of "getting and spending." If Bach, whose music speaks to the spiritual in us, can be appreciated in the marketplace, I reckoned, there's hope for us all. You hated the mall and only went out of dire necessity. In one of your last paintings you depicted it as a vast modern cathedral with orange blobs – phantom people, emerging from a vast sea of cars to pay homage to the god of consumerism.

Yesterday I heard the case of a young Bible student who pleaded guilty to dangerous driving causing bodily harm. Late for a prayer meeting, he'd run a red light and collided with another car in an intersection, severely injuring the passenger, a young boy, and was racked with remorse. Law punishes the crime, not the consequences, and I knew that no penalty I could impose could restore a brain-damaged child or heal a guilt-ridden heart. Guilt punishes more brutally than any car or whip or legal sanction. When I woke this morning, rain beaded the windows and it was dark; I could feel the nip of approaching fall. After getting my usual coffee and newspaper at the Hasty Market I was driving south on Scottsdale when a small group of children unexpectedly stepped into the crosswalk and I had to jam on the brakes, tipping my Styrofoam cup of coffee and causing the van to yaw sideways on the wet pavement. Though I was able to stop well before the crosswalk, the incident shook me. After, I berated myself for not having detected the children sooner, and the possibility of injuring a child set my imagination whirling. I imagined an officer showing up at the courthouse, black notebook and pen poised, and hearing her crafty question: "Now, Justice Clarke, what happened?" What would I have said? What could I have said? I thought of the Bible student and it struck me forcibly that there but for the grace of God go I.

Verdict

As he left the housewarming he made
a quick calculation; three, maybe

four beers, two toasts of champagne,
the "one for the road" – a scotch

on the rocks. Too close for comfort,
he thought, remembering the legion

of hapless drivers he's sentenced for
crossing the line. But he decided

to take a chance. Halfway down
Waterloo Ave. he realized too late that

the commotion on the road was not
an accident, but the RIDE Program and

the police were out in force, dome lights
whirling, stopping everyone. His stomach

clenched, hands trembled. An officer
waved a red flashlight, he pulled to

the side of the road. "Just a couple"
he heard himself saying, scarcely believing

he'd just uttered the courtroom cliché
he'd heard a thousand times

– a sure indicia of guilt.
For a second he thought of saying he was

a judge but immediately rejected the
idea. Some officers, he knew, would

have no mercy on a judge who broke the
law and besides he'd always believed

in equality. The officer produced
the Roadside Screening Device

inserted a fresh plastic mouthpiece:
he knew he had no choice.

Heart pounding, he took a deep
breath and blew, then closed his eyes

waited for the verdict.

CR

LAST NIGHT I DREAMT I STOOD IN A SHALLOW RIVER WITH A WOMAN ABOUT
to give birth; a typhoon tore through the landscape sweeping leaves, branches,
bits and pieces of housing before it. When the woman gave birth on the shore
to a beautiful long-legged baby boy who smiled and spoke to me I knew
immediately that the boy was the long-awaited Messiah and my heart leapt
within me. The dream left me with a feeling of hope in the morning.

Do you remember how worried we became when Paul came back from
Cursillo and floated around the house in a blissed-out state hugging and
kissing everyone, telling them how precious they were in the eyes of God?
Mental illness is insidious and some become God crazy. Like the man in
court, beatific look on his face, charged with robbery – he claimed he'd only
taken the money to distribute to the poor – who said the court had no

jurisdiction to hear his case. "You have no power over me," he said. When the judge inquired why, he looked at him at though he were a child. "Don't you know who I am?" he said. "I'm Jesus Christ, come back to judge the world." Every day in court I'm exposed to the chicanery, greed and capacity for self-deception of humans and have to guard not only against their machinations but also against becoming jaded and cynical. Most judges I know are full of decency and earnest good intentions, but a few become too preoccupied with their performing selves, adopt a cool, clinical attitude more concerned with legal niceties than matters of the heart. The true test of a judge (or doctor, or lawyer) has as much to do with the humanity he or she brings to the work – Martin Buber's sense of I-Thou – as judicial expertise and this test necessarily implies a healthy dose of self-knowledge and humility. Without the touchstone of humanity our spirits wither and die. Nicole says that growing up in a dysfunctional home where drinking made life unpredictable and chaotic, even dangerous, taught me early on that I couldn't rely on adults and made me skeptical of them. "You learned the art of ostrichism," she says.

For a long while after your suicide I felt like a blind man bumping and fumbling in a strange house and it's only lately that I've begun to dig myself out, open my eyes and see the world. Last weekend I helped Ruth move in Ottawa and as I stood outside of the Donair restaurant below her apartment, staring at the rhododendron in the window, I noticed a strip of fresh torn wood on the door jamb of the entrance. Thieves had tried to break in last night – the third time this month – Ruth explained, to steal the new TV the owner installed for his customers. While Ruth was upstairs packing, a thin dark-skinned woman with raven hair parted down the middle and wearing brightly flowered spandex pants approached me. "Do you have any money to spare?" she asked in a quiet, dignified voice. I immediately dug into my pocket and fished out a loonie, for which she thanked me politely. "You're welcome," I replied. The transaction seemed so dignified and natural and right. A little later another woman in blue slacks and jacket, a green beret on her head, came by and began to gather up flyers someone had scattered on the sidewalk. She wore rimless glasses and had a kind, serious face and when she raised her head our eyes met: "People are so mean to do this," she said before walking away with the sheaf of flyers under her arm, looking no doubt for a trash can.

Yes, darling, many kind and beautiful people flow around like a strong warm current if only we were awake enough to see them. On the way to Ottawa the earth seemed dead, the branches of the trees black and lifeless, the fields the colour of straw. The big transports kicked up clouds of spray, which sometimes made it difficult to see. Driving back, rain poured, mist hung over the fields and highway and when I told Ruth, who was driving, to slow down, she got annoyed. "You're a worrier. Relax " she said. "Anyway, I'm a better driver than you." But after the rain abated and we'd travelled a few more kilometres I observed that the landscape was transformed: patches of liquid light glittered through willows and poplars, streams brimmed their banks and pencil lines of blue brightened the brown plowed fields. Buds created a misty green haze in the trees and even the yellow grass was now lime green. A tapestry of green, rust and gold was unfurling across the earth and it was as though we were seeing spring for the first time "Look, Dad," Ruth exclaimed, "the world's turning green even as we drive." I felt uplifted and alive, like Adam must have felt on the first blond day of creation, spinning in newborn light.

First Spring

"Let us sing long live the sun who gives us such beautiful light."

Cézanne

Gasquet reports it was as if he'd erupted into happiness,
the weight of age and suffering fell from him like a train
casting off freight. "He took me to the Jas de Bouffan,

showed me his paintings; every morning he'd call & we'd
set out for the countryside where he'd explain his ideas
of beauty & art, his face transfigured, as though

a bird of paradise had shot through his whole body. It was
spring. The first pale buds touched him deeply. He'd stop
to gaze trance-like at the white road or a dance of clouds,

pick up a fistful of moist earth, squeeze it like he wanted
to bring it closer to him, mix it with his blood. To slake
his thirst he'd lie on the ground, scoop up handfuls of

water from shallow brooks. It was as if he'd been reborn &
the world was blessed & beautiful. 'This is the first time
I've really seen the spring,' he said."

CR

ONE EVENING AS WE WERE LYING IN BED YOU SAID YOUR VISION HAD
suddenly gone black, as if someone had just switched the lights out in a
room, and you rubbed your eyes like you wanted to brush the darkness away.
I suggested you see a doctor but you scoffed at the idea and the subject was
never raised again. Once or twice (or was it more often?) you claimed you'd
be "better off dead," but I attributed it to the pressure of living and running
a busy household. When Pierre, our friend from L'Arche, visited Canada we
took him to see the Falls and I remember gazing at that giant curtain of white
water, marvelling at the sheer animal power of Nature, and thinking how the
spectacle must have appealed to your artistic soul. Many years later you told
me (I thought it was a morbid joke) that drowning was the sweetest death
and that if you ever decided to take your life you'd go to Niagara. "It's cheap
and it isn't messy," you said. In retrospect I realize the idea must have taken
root in some alcove of your brain, just as it's taken root over the years in the
minds of many others who chose the Falls for their final exit. I read that when
the engineers diverted the river in the 1950s – they wanted to remove the

unsightly rubble at the base of the American Falls (which they never did) – they found in a crevice halfway up the massive cliff the remains of an elderly man, and at the base amidst huge boulders the body of a woman in her 20s. You would have preferred a clean watery death, for physical violence of any sort was foreign to your nature and you hated guns and violence and blood with a passion. Once when I brought home some fine replicas of American civil war rifles to hang in our snooker room in the basement you objected vehemently, vowed they'd never hang in your home and made me get rid of them. And when Paul went through the hunting phase with some of his friends – it lasted two years, remember – and bought himself a fancy Italian partridge shotgun (his only bag a hapless inedible Merganser) you made him disarm it and stow it out of sight under his bed. Remember too the time just after my appointment to the bench – these free-association memories stray all over the map – we piled everyone into the station wagon and drove to Milton to reconnoitre the town. After the tour you were not impressed, described the courthouse as a monstrous grey hangar, and I agreed. Before leaving you suggested we drop into the local church for a visit and when you spotted a banner on the church wall – THE GRACE OF GOD WILL NEVER LEAD WHERE THE GRACE OF GOD CANNOT KEEP YOU – in big red letters your considered it serendipitous and your spirits lifted. Later you inscribed these words in perfect roman lettering on a Bristol board and had it framed for my office as a birthday gift, a reminder, you said, that we must always trust God no matter what happens. And the other day when I took it down and read the note you'd written on the back "To my dear Jim on your birthday, December 14th, 1983" my eyes swam with tears.

CR

IN THE VAN LATELY I'VE BEEN PLAYING OVER AND OVER THAT LOVELY BALLAD of the Waterboys "How Much Do I Love You," which incarnates my feelings about you and our loss.

How much will I love you
as long as stars are above you,
and longer if I can…

I remember the autumn afternoon when Marilyn and I drove to St. Jacobs (little Mira was still in the womb) and I heard the song for the first time. As red, orange, and yellow foliage swept by, it touched a tender nerve and both of us lost our composure, melted into tears. Am I becoming morbid in continuing these kaddishes and resurrecting your ghost? Maybe I should heed my friend Ron Mitchell's advice and forget you. "Mary's dead," he reminded me bluntly not too long ago. When he asked if I wanted to read the statements of the witnesses at Niagara who saw you jump, a glacial current ran through my body. "I'm not a glutton for punishment," I said, and told him that maybe someday when I was psychologically and spiritually ready I would, but the time wasn't ripe. The other evening I took down from the shelf in the closet the two cardboard boxes filled with your memorial service memorabilia and as I riffled through the pile of sympathy cards, letters, death notices, Mass cards, tapes of the service, a copy of the eulogy I'd written for Gord Kelly to read, a mauve booklet from the funeral director with inspirational readings from the Bible, I could feel my eyes begin to burn. But it was when I looked at the Bereavement Book and read what someone had written after their name, "Thank you, Mary" that I burst out crying. Perhaps Ron's right; maybe I'm too hooked on your death and should stop this self-lacerating introspection.

Perhaps these kaddishes are nothing but a futile attempt to staunch the flow of forgetfulness, those immense drowning waters that threaten to engulf us all. When I was a boy in Peterborough I evaded the half-blind old caretaker of St. Peter's Cathedral and found the trap door leading to the steeple. As I climbed the ladder past the windy belfry and slowly inched my way up the wooden scaffolding inside the dark interior, splinters nicked my fingers, nails snaggled my T-shirt, dust smarted my eyes till at last I reached the apex, bumped my head on the ball and cross. As wind shrieked through the cracks of the metal sheeting I could survey the entire city, including our shabby tenement on Simcoe, snug and safe, from my aerie in the sky. Change or perish. Now that I've begun my journey through the dark forest the view may not be so sweeping, but I know God dwells not in steeples but in the innermost recess of the common human heart.

Lord, give me an honest mind, a clean heart and the courage to seek you always.

CR

THIS MORNING THE WORLD IS GREY — NOT JUST ORDINARY GREY, BUT GREY, grey, grey — the way I feel inside, with rain-threatening clouds overhead, and the rough breath of winter in the air. Orpheus the Greek god, disconsolate over the death of his wife, Eurydice, descended into the Stygian underworld past Cerberus, the three-headed dog with snaky hair, to find and retrieve her, but when he returned to the upper air broke the one condition of her release: never to look back at her. Is this what I'm doing in these kaddishes, risking my own three-headed demons to bring you back alive, and will I, too, like Orpheus, when I reach out to embrace you find only empty air and forgetfulness?

I've just returned from Montreal with Nicole and Joy, where we got Joy registered at Concordia and found her a large room close to the downtown campus with fridge, hotplate and a grocery store just a short block away. The affable landlord promises to install new carpeting, and best of all Joy is happy. But as usual Joy and I bumped heads when I told her she couldn't install a telephone — I'm still rankled over the huge long-distance bills the children racked up since your death — until she got a part-time job. "You can think what you like, I'll do it my way," she snorted, and our quarrel quickly degenerated into an exchange of insults that only ended when Nicole intervened. After, I felt ashamed that I, a father approaching 60, could still act like a child. Since your suicide I've become the whipping boy for the family and have had to absorb the brunt of their anguish. How I dearly wish sometimes you were here to cushion the blows, you who were always more patient and understanding with the children than I. I've just finished Rosemary Sullivan's brilliant biography *By Heart*, the life of Elizabeth Smart, a passionate woman like you who wasn't afraid to tackle life with flair and two-hearted enthusiasm. Nor was she hesitant to seize the moment. Once, when some English friends brought her a gift of 20 bottles of good French wine, she uncorked them all, to hell with tomorrow. And she didn't shrink from responsibility or suffering, either. She showed great courage in breaking out from the shadow of her domineering mother to fall head over heels in love with the Englishman George Barker, a talented egocentric poet. Like you she sacrificed talents and ambitions on the altar of motherhood, and though she succeeded in clinging to her identity, it was at great personal cost. Surrendering your career as a fashion illustrator must have been traumatic for you. At school, Teetaw told me, you showed scant interest in other subjects and the acceptance of your application for admission to the Ontario College of Art at seventeen was the high point of your young life. After graduation your full-page fashion illustrations appeared in the Toronto newspapers, and for a while after we moved to Cobourg you freelanced, trekking back and forth to Toronto until Adele and the others came along and you had to put your artistic career on permanent hold. Yes, you sewed and made dresses for the children, cards for birthdays and posters for the church and other organizations, even found time to do some sketching at the cottage in the summer, but it wasn't the same. You were a perfectionist married to the idea of the "good" mother and were never able to compartmentalize your life to carve out time for yourself, and if you had you would have reproached yourself mercilessly. You were always playing catch-up and how galling it must have been for you when I managed to squeeze out leisure time to do scores of watercolours (it was you who got me started, remember). Though I tried I regret to this day I wasn't the most helpful mate.

But as an apologia let me state that I

a) always encouraged you to make time to pursue your art,

b) agreed to a weekly cleaning lady to free up your time,

c) set up a studio in the basement of the rented bungalow on Cedarmere and later in our home on College,

d) and after the children were older encouraged you to enroll in the Fine Arts program at Guelph (which you did).

Reading this over, it sounds both like a self-serving lawyer's brief and a plea for clemency. Though I know I wasn't emotionally available to you enough, I also know that I'm not responsible for the happiness of others. Like Elizabeth Smart you tried to find your identity. But when we suppress our gifts they don't die but go underground and bide their time to rise into consciousness when we least expect, confront us face to face. "Why didn't you let us live," they'll say, pointing an accusing finger. In denying our gifts, the authentic in us, we murder our souls.

☙

RUTH PHONED THIS EVENING TO GRUMBLE ABOUT JOY'S ACCOMMODATION IN Montreal. "It's a shit box," she said. As you know, Ruth has for years taken on the role of Joy's guardian angel and protector, but sometimes she goes too far. I told her I hoped she hadn't expressed her opinion to Joy, who likes the room and location. The last thing I need is another malcontent. The children constantly criticize me for being too tight-fisted. Every time there's an argument over money they invoke you and trot out the same old line: "Well, Mom would have spent the money," conveniently forgetting how frugal you were. When I attended McGill in the '50s Mom had to scrimp and scrape to be able to send me a $10 weekly money order that I counted on to cover all my living expenses: meals, transportation, dry cleaning, pocket money, etc. When she fell off the wagon and missed a week I'd have to scrounge till her belated catch-up order (invariably accompanied by a painful apology) arrived. I taught myself to live close to the bone, found a restaurant on St. Catherine Street where for 25 cents I could get breakfast with two eggs, bacon, hash browns, toast, jam and coffee – but when I talk to our kids who were raised in middle-class comfort about my hard times they're not impressed. "We had a privileged upbringing, you didn't," Mira says tersely.

September's here and I'm back in legal harness. As I drove to court this morning, nature's familiar furniture was all there: on my right cirrus clouds sliced the sun into white ribbons and by the time I got to the Schneider sign (40 degrees Celsius, 7.14 AM, HAVE A GOOD DAY) the sun had morphed again and was now a disc, fierce in its brightness, with a small dark-ringed sphere spinning inside. Before leaving the house I glanced at the latest *National Geographic* in the den. On the cover was a Somali woman with a pinched, weathered face and a stick-thin body. She carried a kettle and was dressed in a rose-and-yellow ankle-length sarong blazoned with exotic birds, trees and mountains, and on her wrist wore a silver bracelet. An orange headscarf that ran to her shoulders covered her head. Yet despite her wraith-like appearance her face radiated serenity and detachment. When two obese middle-aged women jogging along the sidewalk, one in green shirt and black shorts, the other in white top and blue shorts, caught my eye this morning, the image on the cover came back to trouble my conscience. After your death I turned inward, sunk in the desert of my own bereavement, lost sight of the larger suffering world. I even toyed with the idea of selling the big house and buying a bungalow or even a small condo, giving my excess money to the poor and devoting myself exclusively to physical, intellectual and spiritual goals – simplify, simplify, simplify, as Thoreau wrote. But alas, my idealistic intentions came to nought and I fell back into my psychological sinkhole. Now I wonder sometimes if I've become desensitized to poverty and hardship. Maybe our children are trying to tell me something, that my financial worries are a thing of the past, that I'm living in a time warp, need to loosen up, toss away the security blanket. Yes, dear, I need a metanoia, a change of heart.

CR

AFTER COURT TODAY I DROVE INTO AN AFTERNOON SUN SHOWER. LIGHT gilded the tops of fluffy clouds and the sun burst out as rain splattered my windshield and the pavement turned into a light blue ribbon. Rooster tails of spray from passing cars sparkled in the sun. Sun showers symbolize my life; my natural disposition leans towards happiness, but then out of nowhere I feel the cold cheek of death and the numbing nullity of the first few months after your suicide, when knowing you were gone forever was like shutting the lid on my life, surging back. Even nature seems washed out in the late afternoons; the vivid greens of the morning fade and a haze, like an airy forgetfulness, envelops the farmhouses, fields and trees, with only the tops of clouds sending glyphs of light earthward. Like an old man with rheumy eyes, nature becomes dim and forgetful. To escape the bedlam of an alcoholic home I sought solace in nature with the companionship of a book at Jackson's Park, strategies that served me well at the time, but in the end I always knew there was no escape, that I had nowhere to flee and had to return. Once or twice during our marriage you expressed the desire to leave, said you couldn't take it any longer, a sentiment myriad spouses must have uttered in moments of discouragement and frustration. Once you even disappeared for a day (or was it overnight? I don't remember) but came back and carried on as though nothing out of the ordinary had happened. But your leap into Niagara was a final and irrevocable step and left a wide track of grief, guilt and anger in its wake. Since your death I've often played with the fantasy of escape, entering a monastery (if they'd accept me) where I could pursue the life of the mind in the spirit in tranquillity free from the grit and grind of everyday living. I'd spent weekend retreats at the Cistercian monastery at Orangeville and revelled in the orderly life and the beauty of the Gregorian chant. When I mentioned my fantasy to Nicole she wondered if I was gay or simply looking for an easy way out, a flight from responsibility.

As Thomas Merton and St. Thérèse, the Little Flower, discovered there is no unspotted haven in this life; we take our problems with us and even in a monastery trials await. Not only does the perfect comfort zone not exist, but even if it did it would probably be a trap. As I enter the narrowing tunnel of time, the last phase of my life – the period of synthesis and mellowing and the most enriching and profound in many ways, according to Jung, I must prepare for death, but I know it can't be done by distancing myself from loved ones and others in the here and now. As John Shea says, the only way to prepare for death is to live less narrowly, stretch your arms wider and wider in love and be more fully alive each day. Readying ourselves for death means an ever-widening entry into life.

CR

YOUR GREATEST QUALITY, ACCORDING TO RUTH, WAS YOUR ABILITY TO SEE good in others. That's why, despite strong differences on religion and morality, including such issues as abortion, you kept all your friends. With Patrick, my alcoholic boyhood friend and nemesis, your were particularly gentle and understanding, until that Monday morning he rang us at 3 a.m. (he'd long been in the habit of phoning at any hour day or night) and embarked on one of his self-pitying harangues about how broke he was, how unfairly life had treated him, etc., and you finally exploded, scolded him for his lack of consideration, told him you were weary to death of his sodden rants and that he was never to phone us again unless he was sober. Your outburst had a salutary effect: he stopped phoning and we never heard from him until the day almost a year later – it was your birthday, remember – a dozen long-stemmed red roses materialized at the door. That was the trouble with Patrick: when sober he was a perfect gentleman, had so much wit and charm and could be so disarming you couldn't stay mad at him for long. A few days after your death he phoned; I could tell from his slurry voice he was sloshed again. "I went over the Falls with Mary," he whined and broke into deep sobs. A few weeks later he rang again, complained he had no money for rent or food (I'd already bailed him out numerous times, to the tune of several thousand dollars) and in a weak moment I suggested he come live with me in Guelph (an egregious mistake I immediately regretted, for I knew I could never tolerate him rattling around the house at all hours in a stuporous state and that eventually I'd have to call on the police — I knew he'd never leave voluntarily — to get him evicted). But fortunately he politely declined my invitation and I was off the hook. A few months later when he phoned again to say he'd reconsidered my kind offer, my reply was swift and unambiguous: "Impossible, Patrick!" "I guess no one wants old Patrick anymore," he lamented in a lugubrious voice. "Goodbye, Jim, it's the end for me." Though I've learned never to take any hints of suicide lightly I didn't believe his veiled threat, thought it was just another one of his conneries, and though I told him only cowards committed suicide and that I still loved him, I went to bed that evening twinged with guilt and slept fitfully.

CR

LAST NIGHT I DREAMT I ATTENDED A FORMAL BALL, BUT THE INSIDE POCKETS of my tux were so bulky with wallet, papers and other paraphernalia I couldn't dance properly. I left the dance floor to find a locker where I could store my belongings, but was unsuccessful. Then the scene changed abruptly and I was outside in the cold, the winter sky the cold clean colour of ice, wrapped in a blue blanket, shivering. Two snarky police officers came along and confiscated the blanket: "We'll have to test it before we give it back," one of them said, and when he mentioned the cost I yelled, "Exorbitant!" When I told them

I was naked and asked how I was to get home, one of the officers replied, "That's your problem." I felt vulnerable and panicked, but mercifully the dream ended.

In bed at the cottage after I'd returned from Ottawa, where I'd helped Ruth move into her new digs (the big panic's over, she's got a good apartment on Laurier Avenue, swimming pool, washer and dryer, sauna, whirlpool, and she's happy), I listened to the rain lashing the metal roof in gusty waves, sometimes loud and drumming, sometimes so scattered and scratchy it sounded like chipmunks scurrying on the deck. Wind sifted through the cedars, thunder rumbled across the lake and occasionally light blue flashes lit up the bedroom window where raindrops skated down the glass. Snug and warm under the thick comforter Adele bought me, I remembered Ruth's words when we went out for dinner in Ottawa and talked about you. She was glad you did it the way you did, she said. "At least I didn't have to see her get sick and suffer for years." Then she added, "But I'm still mad at her. What she did was selfish." "Your mother wasn't selfish, darling, " I said, "just sick, that's all." Why am I always defending you? Defending you seems to be an automatic reflex; Adele claims I'm in a state of denial, refuse to face up to the truth. "I get nightmares all the time," Ruth went on, "that you or Paul or Adele have died and I wake up sweaty and crying. Sometimes I dream I meet Mom in downtown Toronto disguised as another woman and she doesn't recognize me, it's awful." When Ruth talks like that her eyes get teary and she tenses up. She's also furious at the doctors. "They did nothing for her," she said, "except push those goddam pills." As I listened to the rain my concern gravitated to Adele. Worry must be stamped on my genetic code. Did she get her old job back? I wondered. And the next day when I found out she didn't I felt bad. One teacher on the interviewing committee told her she was too passionate. Too passionate! Who do they want as teachers — a clique of bloodless mediocrities? I tried to comfort her. "It'll all turn out for the best," I said. "They've just lost a terrific teacher, that's all." "That's bullshit, Dad, and you know it," replied Adele. Sometimes I feel like a hypocrite. How much do I pray and how much do I trust, like St. Paul, that all turns out for the best for those who love and serve the Lord? Why do my children's problems, real or imagined, get to me? Someone wrote that there are only two lasting bequests we can hope to give our children: one is roots; the other, wings. Why don't I give my children wings? And why don't they grow them? As a self-conscious pimply-faced teenager growing up on Simcoe Street I felt like a pariah, an outsider, too poor and too ashamed of my parents to have a social life. On weekends when my friends were out on dates I'd be stuck in my room, my nose in a book bitterly aware that life was passing me by, that I was missing out on what it had to offer. Is that why Nicole says I'm always trying to squeeze every drop out of life, live every moment to the full? Is it my fear of rejection that gets resurrected through my children, causing me to feel the sting of their every setback and humiliation, a case of déjà vu? Your suicide has caused the children and me enough suffering and sometimes I want to curse God, but don't. Though reason keeps telling me chance rules our lives, my heart rejects this verdict. In the deep wakefulness of faith there are no accidents. I want to believe that love determines our fate and gives meaning, and that if we follow where it leads, all will be well, all will be well.

A Clean Death

She had wild-grown hair that
                cascaded down her back in rivulets,
the sheen of sun-dipped oranges,
                looping in curious folds, waist-long.
"I've never seen such beautiful hair," my daughter said.

That afternoon she went
                to her father's new house,
climbed the narrow stairs to the dark attic and
                taking her mauve Gucci belt, the one
he gave her that year for Christmas,
                hanged herself, but

not before she'd gone home one last time,
　　　grabbed the butcher knife
from her mother's kitchen drawer,
　　　slashed off all her locks and made
a bonfire on the floor,
　　　stayed till amber turned to ash.

"We were lucky in a way," my daughter said,
"no fanfare, not even a strand of hair."

CR

YOU WERE A RESCUER, SOMEONE WHO FEELS RESPONSIBLE FOR OTHERS, often puts others' needs first. Every rescuer needs a victim, and in Stephen, my sister's 11-year-old boy, you found a perfect candidate. Stephen's father had died of cancer, an aggressive variety that shrunk his 200-pound-plus frame to under 120 in the space of a few months, and afterward my sister found she was unable to control their son. Not only was he playing truant and failing at school, but he'd begun to pilfer – he once pinched $120 from his grandmother – and to hang around with a gang of older toughs who were experimenting with drugs. When the cancer of the cervix that would ultimately kill her flared, Shirl, my sister, grew desperate and that's when we (at your initiative) decided he should come live with us. Although reluctant at the beginning, my sister finally agreed that it was best. With Joy and now Stephen our family had expanded to seven children (plus the dog and cat). At first Stephen balked at having a part-time job – an unwritten code in the family; naturally, after his mother had forked out $40 or more weekly to pacify him and get him off her back, $5 or $6 dollars weekly for delivering papers on the streets of Cobourg every evening, rain or shine, must have seemed spartan, even mingy. He sniffed, too, at the modest weekly allowance we allotted to all the kids, called it "chicken feed." How difficult for him it must have been to be thrown in with a bunch of over-achievers! And to make matters worse he was two or three years behind in school and had a propensity for getting into mischief. Remember the call we got one blustery September evening that the Eaton's catalogues he was supposed to deliver had been found in a ditch, and how he'd insisted that he delivered them all and that the discards were only "extras" and stuck to his alibi until I took him out into the rainy evening and made the rounds of his customers who one by one denied ever having received their catalogue; I think we'd reached the tenth customer before he, standing there sopping, in his squishy running shoes and clinging wet jeans, finally caved in and admitted that he was lying through his teeth.

You always said in those years that he got half our attention and the other children had to divide up the other half between them. For a long time after his mom's death Stephen was sad; the photos I shot of him at the time show a glum-faced adolescent with rumpled forehead and a blank look in his eyes. But we persisted, taxied him to track and field, hockey, volleyball (sports were his sole passion), and Paul and he grew close as brothers. But when after five years we'd reached the end of our tether and decided we could offer him nothing further we lit upon the solution (on the recommendation of the bishop) of sending him to Assumption College at Windsor, a school run by the Basilians, with a good reputation for dealing with troubled youth. But that initiative didn't work out either and after two years Stephen quit and struck out on his own. Last Christmas, when he visited us for a few days, Stephen told me that coming to live with us was the best thing that ever happened to him, that it probably saved his life and that he was especially grateful to you. You often told me that you'd grown to love him like one of your own and he knew it.

☙

LAST EVENING I MADE THE FOOLISH ERROR OF PHONING RUTH IN OTTAWA to tell her Kody had escaped again and had been found by the animal control officer in someone's yard near the intersection of the Hanlon and Stone Road, yapping at 3 a.m., and according to the officer might have been run over. I could almost feel her wince on the phone. "Please, I don't want to hear this," she said and immediately launched an anguished attack on Paul and Joy, labelling them "dipsticks" for having neglected her dog. While I wasn't specifically singled out I sensed from her tone that I was included in the indictment. When we adopted Joy, Ruth's world fell apart. Until then she'd been the baby, the fair-haired child in the family, and suddenly she was shunted aside to make room for a brown-skinned Vietnamese infant over whom everyone made a big fuss. You and I believed at the time that the reason many of our friends and acquaintances, even strangers on the street, made such a commotion was because deep inside they disapproved or were ill at ease with the idea of adopting a foreign child and were only covering up their uneasiness. In those years, adoption of foreign children was uncommon. Remember how we'd drop heavy-footed hints to them to pay attention to Ruth, standing on the fringe, overlooked and forgotten. Eventually Ruth would become Joy's chief critic and staunchest defender. Teetaw, God bless her, saw the problem. While remaining even-handed and never neglecting Joy or the others, she tried to redress the balance by shifting some of the spotlight to Ruth, bestowing little gifts and attentions on her, and over time a special relationship developed between them. When your mom was in the nursing home Ruth visited her daily after school, smoothing her blankets, brushing her hair and later, as the Parkinson's advanced and she began to dribble her food, helping to feed her. Near the end Teetaw's body became transparent, almost skeletal. Her death was a crushing blow and night after night for many weeks Ruth cried herself to sleep. And when you took your life it was the final straw; her universe collapsed (she loved you dearly) and since then the spectre of death has haunted her dreams. That's why I regretted I hadn't kept my mouth zippered about Kody; she'll be upset all day.

You know how I hated hunting and cruelty to animals, but there was a brief period in my youth – I'm ashamed to admit – when I indulged cruel fantasies. After I purchased my first BB gun I shot birds, chipmunks, frogs, squirrels wantonly and indiscriminately for no other reason but to sate the bloodlust to kill. At Jackson's Park I recall shooting bullfrogs as they sunned themselves on the smooth wet rocks (their flesh exploded like punctured tires on the impact of the pellets), thrilled to watch them hurtle high in the air and flip-flop on their backs, goggled-eyed and still, the pellet bulging like a piece of shiny shrapnel from the creamy chests. I recall one bright summer afternoon hiding in some bushes with a friend to pick off grackles as they alighted in the branches of a nearby maple – ping, ping ping – and hearing the rustle of the leaves as one by one stricken birds tumbled through the foliage to the ground, black feathers splayed and scarlet. My hunting came to an abrupt and shameful end after I had bought my first .22 and shot a rabbit point blank as it munched grass in a field and buried it on the spot. When I related my exploit to Hubert, Dad's chum who also was an avid hunter, he grew livid. "You don't shoot and bury animals like that," he growled, eyes blazing. "You eat what you shoot or you don't kill." His words humiliated me so much I stored away the .22 and never hunted again. Where did this savagery come from? Does cruelty beget cruelty? Was I, at that stage in my life, anaesthetized to pain and finer feelings, immersed in a world where violence was taken for granted? Or did my cruelty emanate from some shadow side of the human psyche? Despite millions of years of evolution, the human heart is still in its infancy.

Grackles

The boys crouch near the shed,
BB guns in sweaty hands,

ammunition stockpiled, adrenalin
rising, waiting.

Suddenly the dogwood darkens,
iridescent wings glisten through

the foliage, and the sport begins,
grackles falling like tipsy

acrobats from their perches –
such a humorous dance – staining

the ravine below, into the night
and next day, volley after volley

and still they come, bloodlust
stronger every year,

guns bigger and deadlier, corpses
spreading like an oil slick to every

continent, all the white blossoms
turned to blood.

CR

GORGEOUS DAYS AT THE COTTAGE; SUN SHINING AND AT NIGHT LOONS singing their lonely operettas. I rose at 6:00 every morning, breakfasted on cereal, toast and coffee and then struggled with reserve judgments upstairs. The breeze stirred the cedars and shirred the surface of the lake; red-winged blackbirds chittered in the big poplar by the shore and occasionally a gull arced across the blue. One morning a great blue heron perched on my dock on one leg, stone still, a model of mindfulness. The greenwood scent of the forest filled the cottage with a delicious aroma; every afternoon I sawed and hammered on the deck and front porch, replacing rotten planks; the rest of the day I put in napping, reading and swimming in the cool satiny water. Most evenings I went to bed early under the silent white stream of the Milky Way.

Since your suicide I'll admit that I've become a nervous Nellie when it comes to the children, lapsed into spells of low-grade depression. Paul has had a rough time. On Sunday after Mass he drove off to get a fishing license, or so I believed. When 5 p.m. came around and he still hadn't returned I grew concerned. Since he arrived with Gabe he'd been unnaturally subdued: no smiles, no laughter, no exuberance, not the old Paul at all, responding in monosyllables and looking downhearted. I thought of you and became restless, poured myself a rye and water, wandered around the cottage outside, cursorily inspecting my rough carpentry and gazing at the whitecaps on the lake. After, I retreated to my room, tried to read some Raymond Carver, but found I couldn't concentrate. Wild thoughts stampeded through my mind: what if he's done something drastic, I asked myself. I got up, made myself another drink and sat on the porch staring down the driveway; every time I heard the crunch of tires on the main road my hopes rose, only to fall again when the sound faded. It was now close to 6 p.m. and I was growing alarmed. Sweat beaded on my brow, my stomach clenched. Your last words to Joy when you dropped her off at St. Joseph's: "I'm just going for a little drive," returned to keep me on edge. I mentioned my worry to Adele and her face clouded. She began to trim her toenails and said: "After what happened to Mom anything can happen." After a while she added: "He shouldn't be doing this to us. If he's not back in a half hour I'm phoning the police." Finally, at 6:30 p.m. Paul's blue Tercel barrelled up the driveway and I let out a sigh of relief. I climbed into the passenger seat and told him how worried we'd been; there were tears in my eyes and he could see I was shaken. "Dad, I get upset when you talk like that," he said. "I just needed a bit of time to myself. Don't you trust me?" "It's not that I don't trust you, Paul," I replied. "I just don't trust depression." I promised I wouldn't worry so much about him in the future.

When I got back to Guelph and noticed that Joy hadn't mowed the lawn as she'd promised I gave her an accusatory look and asked why. "Too busy," she said petulantly. "Besides, I had an essay." When I countered that the essay was no excuse, that the grass would have taken less than a half hour, she ignited, called me an asshole. "No wonder Mom killed herself," she snapped and rushed upstairs, fingers jammed in her ears, revved up the stereo to top volume, her classic defense, so predictable these days it's almost laughable. Adele shoots with a blunderbuss, Joy aims her darts straight for the heart. One of the first rules of judging is never to descend into the arena with counsel, to always stay above the fray. Sometimes, as you know, children can suck the adult out of you and your child pops out in the white heat of the moment to utter the meanest and most unforgivable sarcasms – words you can't always take back. When we quarrelled you sometimes fired off the most hurtful remarks – your rages were blazing hot conflagrations that consumed everything before them. That day you would have been proud of me. Despite black thoughts I held my ego in check and didn't replicate in kind. After our dust-up Joy phoned me from Nicole's (Nicole has the knack of smoothing ruffled feathers) and asked if I'd correct her essay. I accepted her olive branch and spent last evening poring over it as though nothing unpleasant had ever passed between us.

CR

ADELE PLAYS THE GADFLY IN THE FAMILY, GOADS ALL OF US HER WITH HER critiques, wants us to question ourselves and look deeper into your tragedy. She's a ballsy person, intelligent, direct and amazingly well-read with a keen eye for spotting humbug. Though her criticisms often rankle, I admire her passion for authenticity and love her dearly. Before bed last night she phoned in a testy mood. She wanted to know why I'd cancelled the traditional cottage Thanksgiving dinner with the neighbours.

"I think we should have it," she said. "Mom would have wanted it."

"But there are practical reasons...," I started to explain, but she cut me off.

"What did you mean? You never did any of the work."

Then out of the blue she changed the subject.

"When are you and Nicole getting married?"

"Why do you ask?" I replied. "There are no plans."

"Well, I was just wondering. You spend all your time with her."

That's when I saw red and hung up, another instance of the child in me getting the upper hand. Maybe I shouldn't be so disappointed with myself, and instead of disowning my inner child, embrace him. After all, we're all radically weak and I know with God's help we can always pick ourselves up again. Despite the Black Dog who regularly nips at my heels, my journalling goes on. Bringing pain out into the open somehow loosens its hold over me. Recently I read in the weekend paper about the Ganzfeld experiment, which claims that humans can transmit images to each other. I'm not sure I believe in ESP, but the day of your death when Gord told me Joy was on the line, I had a premonition that something terrible had happened and before I ever spoke to her felt a trap door open beneath me, pictured myself plunging headlong into darkness. And I keep coming back to the same question: What does God mean when good people commit suicide? On Simcoe when I was a boy, the sight of the scrawny and cruel bread man mercilessly lashing his equally scrawny mare because it wouldn't move fast enough to suit him appalled me (Mom phoned the police but they did nothing). Is God like the bread man, a sadist who enjoys inflicting suffering on the innocent? Or maybe the policeman who elects to stand by and do nothing?

Cosmic Silence

After the ten o'clock news
(another chronicle of doom)
my ulcer flares, I go outside:

stars are peeking from the roof
of night, moon is full,
Hale-Bopp shoots across

my sight, a heart of ice, its
radiance, like ours, borrowed
from the sun. Leaning on

a pillow in a corner of the sky
I spy the Great Huntress;
"Who'll chase away the gloom?"

I say, but she won't reply,
refuses to look me in the eye,
shuts her eyelids tight,

chews her pearly fingernails and
prays.

CR

ONE OF THE THINGS WE GOT RIGHT AS PARENTS WAS TO TEACH THE CHILDREN
a sense of responsibility. Each of them was allotted duties around the house
such as cutting grass, helping with dishes, making beds, vacuuming, and so
on, and when they were old enough we insisted they get part-time jobs. I'm
proud of the spunky, autonomous persons they've become. Recently, when I
offered Mira financial help to buy a second-hand laptop, she politely declined.
"I prefer to pay for it myself," she told me.

For four years as a boy I delivered the *Peterborough Examiner* door to
door, good weather, foul weather; my territory (65 subscribers) covered
the downtown and to this day I can still hear the crackle of car chains on

snowy streets, the soggy hum of tires on wet asphalt. I loved the job and my customers (at least most of them), even Mr. Bogue, our curmudgeonly circulation manager (we nicknamed him Bogie), who wore a beige hearing aid and always looked worried and harried as though the fortunes of the paper rested solely on his shoulders. Complaints were posted every day on a small bulletin board in the circulation room and if you were unlucky enough to be the recipient of one, Bogie would cock one eye and in his booming voice give you a dressing-down in front of the other carriers, make you feel you'd just committed the crime of the century. "*The Examiner* relies on you, young man," he'd always state before stalking away and leaving you with the dishonourable feeling of having let down the side. An old couple who lived in the upper apartment of a red brick tenement on George Street near the CPR station, my farthest delivery point before I doubled back, would always invite me in for a glass of milk and homemade cookies, an invitation I rarely refused, especially during inclement or wintry weather. I recall the steep dark stairs and the musty smell of the small apartment, but mostly the snug feeling of security, sitting in their tiny parlour and hearing the sound of their soft solicitous voices: "Did you get enough to eat, Jim?" "Make sure you button up your coat, Jim, it's cold outside." The paper held regular circulation contests and one year shortly after the war ended I was lucky enough to be among those who'd won a weekend trip to Rochester, New York. We embarked on the big white ferry, the SS Ontario #1 at Cobourg, and in my young imagination, never having travelled far from Simcoe Street, the trip was as exhilarating as crossing the ocean. After the drab war years (electricity was rationed and signs were blacked out) the neon splendour of downtown Rochester dazzled me, made me feel I'd entered a new exotic world, but most thrilling of all were the Dick Tracy cap guns, silver .45s with spools of caps, narrow red strips with powder bumps that fitted into the handle and went bang, bang, bang when you squeezed the trigger, just like in the gangster movies. On the way back we chased each other all over the boat, playing cops and robbers, sniping at each other, dropping to the deck mortally wounded when someone scored a hit. But the trip was memorable for another reason: in Rochester my roommate

George reported $15 missing from his wallet. The revelation that there was a thief among us landed like a grenade; instantly we all became suspects. I've never forgotten the trapped feeling of being suspected of a wrong you didn't commit, how one act of dishonesty can sow the seed of distrust and destroy community. To everyone's relief the thief was soon discovered, a morose, lanky loner, and for the rest of the trip we ostracized him, treated him with contempt, as though he'd committed the one unpardonable sin.

The one thing that riled you more than anything was being lied to. If the children fibbed you'd threaten (but never did) to rinse their mouths with soap and water and insist they own up. You inherited your abhorrence of mendacity from your parents, particularly your dad, a straight-from-the-shoulder scrupulous salesman. I remember accompanying him once on his rounds, observing how he'd enter a store and with a nod and "Hi, Bill" or "Joe," then march directly into the storeroom only to emerge a few minutes later with a gruff "You need three" or "You don't need any" (he sold brake linings) and how the managers accepted his word as gospel, no questions asked, for he had a reputation of never overstocking his product. Teetaw always claimed he was the only salesman in the company who never padded his expense account. While you and Teetaw harped about his frugality and jumped on him for his drinking, you always knew he was a man of probity. And when he suffered a fatal heart seizure at the wheel, veered off the roadway and careened into a verandah (mercifully, no one else was injured), you sobbed for days for you knew you'd lost not only a good father, but a good friend, and your world would never be the same.

The other morning in court, during an attempted-murder trial, there was an unusual occurrence; a sparrow flitted around the courtroom and alighted for a few seconds on my bench as though he was trying to tell me something. At the recess my constable brought me a single feather the bird had left behind as a memento of its visit, informed me it had vanished as mysteriously as it came. Sometimes truth is as elusive as a sparrow, and one of my greatest fears is that I will convict an innocent person. Being condemned for a crime you didn't commit has to be the ultimate darkness: like Jesus on Good Friday you must feel betrayed, abandoned, helpless to explain yourself, stripped naked and mocked. Distinguishing between the truth sayers and the accomplished liars can be daunting.

Falsely Accused

When the judge was a schoolboy a classmate
falsely accused him of stealing seventy-
five cents. The more
he protested his innocence the more
he was disbelieved,
caged in guilt, a victim
of unfairness.

Now when an accused took the stand
he looked for clues: inflexion,
tone of voice, a particular expression,
any reminder of what it was like
to be charged with something
you didn't do.

CR

SATURDAY EVENING I TOOK NICOLE, MIRA AND ADELE TO DINNER AT A THAI restaurant in Toronto. We had a splendid evening, lots of good conversation and laughs but as happens so often lately when Adele is present you become the flashpoint of conversation and Adele chewed away at her favourite subject – gender inequality: how hurried, harried women like you who were locked into traditional roles ended up getting the short end of the stick, while white males (like me) reaped all the rewards. When she gets on her hobby horse like this it brings to mind Jung's comment that what usually has the strongest and most lasting impact on children is the life the parents have not lived. While I admire the courageous and intelligent way she speaks her mind and admit more than a mite of truth in her words, sometimes I wish she'd find other avenues to deflect her pain. Mira said something that saddened me: you were ceasing to be a living presence for her, fading into a memory. "I feel bad about it," she said. I tried to assure her that it's only natural with the passage of time that you'd become a memory, that we could never get on with our lives if our beloved dead remained living presences, but my assurances didn't seem to console her. It was as though she believed her feelings were a betrayal of your memory. Nicole said something sage and discerning: that your eclipse into memory was like a second death for her. I understand Mira's disquiet, for in a sense these kaddishes are an attempt to keep you alive, rescue you from the great indifference of things, name your grave. Having a loved one dissolve into memory is like having her recede from you towards a dark wood, watching her pause every few steps to wave goodbye and smile, but continuing on her journey until she's gradually swallowed up by the greenery and nothing is left but the rustle of leaves. Is love worth the pain of parting? Yes, yes, yes, I say. My deepest instincts long for completion and I refuse to believe that this longing, so strong and persistent, is only nature's cruellest trick, an illusion, that the evolution of self-reflecting life and intelligence on this planet is pure randomness. Faith says death is not the end, that our bodies are only husks for love, a love that finds fruition in a greater dimension. We crave wings, an end to death. Perhaps the real purpose of these kaddishes is to set both you and us free, so that we can find rest. Perhaps what I said to Mira I should apply to myself: "Let it go, Jim, entrust your beloved to the hands of the Creator and live fully the here and now."

As I climbed into the van this morning lugging my customary gunnysack of worries, a woman in a red jacket was marching her small brown spaniel along the sidewalk, leash in fist, arms swinging above the shoulders military fashion, and I got so distracted my tires brushed the curb. On the Hanlon the sun, a gold ball, peeked through the skeletal woods, skimmed over the top of the embankment and tinged the smoke from Sleeman's Brewery a pale orange. At the junction with the 401 I handed in the traffic survey the OPP had given me a few days ago (I'd completed it before I left) to an attractive female officer who smiled warmly and said, "Thank you, sir." The sun flicked and winked off the metal and glass of the big rigs and cars; the Schneider sign told me that April was cancer month, that it was 6.58 AM and 9 degrees Celsius. A few shreds of dirty grey snow still blurred the edges of fields. The ice on Kelso Lake had melted, the surface glittered with diamonds. By the time I'd reached the Milton ramp the sun had risen, a radiant white coin now, to the edge of a cloud blanket and was beginning to vanish again. With all this beauty around us why do we allow troubles to weigh us down? Why do we cease to praise?

Benedictions

Sometimes when the world breaks over you
like a dark wave, distills the last small drop
of hope within your veins and baffled, you no
longer know where to turn or how to pray,

a sudden gift: bubbles of light on the ribbed
hull of a gold leaf along the way; a marsh
hawk, poised and imperious, white rump on
pole in the belly of a bush, kee kee keeing into

the cool and colourless air; or on a bare fall night
furred with frost and just beyond our windowsill
a spill of stars, brilliant as the eyes of children,
earth's sweet-tongued orisons that nudge you

out of self, unlatch the chamber of your cold-
dumb heart, utter your own unspoken prayer.

CR

Drove to Milton this morning with a heavy heart, not only because Kody had escaped again last evening (Joy left the front door ajar after the paper boy came to collect) but also because I'd had a vivid dream in which Adele was telling someone on the phone that I'd been on a toot for a week; I got so enraged that I yanked the phone from her hand and yelled, "It's a lie!" Frost silvered the fields and the sun was a scraggly brightness on the eastern horizon fading into stringy pink strips; before the Guelph Line a black Honda sedan swerved in and out of its lane for no apparent reason and as traffic began to bunch up I feared another accident (last week along this stretch two drivers were incinerated in their charred and mangled rigs). A little later another vehicle, a jeep this time, cut into the fast lane and tailgated another car and I began to wonder if everyone was suffering from Monday morning hangover. The highway between Guelph and Milton is like a parable with beginning, end, and much drama in between. Sometimes bathed in sunlight, other times shrouded in fog and snow, it perpetually surprises you. A few constants remain: the Schneider sign is always there to remind us the company is FAMOUS FOR MEAT and that our lives are being clocked and measured, but the motorists stare straight ahead, looking half-asleep or babbling away on their cell phones, and I wonder if they notice. It surprises me how often these kaddishes evoke images of sun, light and blindness. Do you remember my fascination the first time I visited your home, with the still life you did at twelve or thirteen when you were a student of Dorothy Stevens (the one with apples and pears, a green glass jug and brass and silverware), how I marvelled at the way your deftly placed highlights made the objects so tactile and breathed life into the painting? When I started to paint you stressed the importance of tonal values and why it was always crucial to be aware of the source and direction of light. Remember at Limerick watching the sun shadows as they slid down the hills on the far side of the lake and moved across the water, listening to the gathering nightsong of crickets and frogs? Or lying late at night on the dock and gazing skyward at the velvety black heavens, the breath of stars on our faces. You often said that you couldn't imagine life without eyes. "I'd sooner be dead than blind," you told me. How agonizing and unbearable it must have been for you who always loved and sought the light to have fallen into the watery abyss, hemmed in on all sides by darkness. In our bereft state after your suicide the darkness around us was deep and we sought solace in the physical company of each other by huddling together those first few days in our bedroom, as though physical solidarity could immure us from our common enemy, your friend Death. The rituals of that Holy Week held special meaning for me; for the first time I had an inkling of what the evangelists meant when they described Jesus as being "sad unto death," for that is exactly how I felt. After the Memorial service I dreaded the departure of our kind friends but I knew the world only pauses for tragedy and must move on and I also knew that once the children and I were alone in the big house again your absence would only deepen and the pain grow worse. That darkness tracked us for many months and even at Limerick Lake, my haven and place of centring, it often found me.

Night

I lie on the dock and
        shut my eyes
against the rush of sun;
        a wall of fire
burns inside my skull.

I cover lids
        with both palms,
but still the flames
        peep through.

I press the sockets with
      all my might till
sun's devoured and
      nothing's left,
not even a gasp of light.

Was it Night like this, I ask,
that made you climb the parapet
      and leap?

꩜

DREAMT OF KODY AGAIN LAST NIGHT. I WAS TRAVELLING ALONG THE 401 TO work when I glanced out the van window and guess what? There was Kody in the centre boulevard, bounding through the air like a gazelle, trying to keep up with the van. I was furious for I was late for court and knew I'd have to stop, catch the beast and return her home. My eyes flew open with relief when I realized it was only a dream. Kody's become my nemesis. While showering this morning a host of disparate thoughts and images flitted through my mind: my pestiferous dream of Kody; the surly faces of the parties in the case I was continuing – another acrimonious family dispute over money and custody of children; the fleeting image of Joy's happy face at Christmas when I gave her the framed pastel sketch you did of her sitting at the old kitchen table with the Singer sewing machine base; the remembrance of the lift that Ruth's card, three buttercups and a blue butterfly with the scribbled message that I was the best "dad-mom" ever, gave me last Easter; a stab of remorse because of my insensitivity to your feelings of being excluded when the French teacher came to the house to give me lessons. Driving to Court I could see the western flank of the escarpment once I passed the Guelph Line Road; it appeared like a bluish haze on the horizon and I couldn't distinguish the trees from the limestone because of the strong glare. The rays slashed the tall bushes and grasses at the top of the embankment and backlighted the greenery in the maples. In the morning, shadows lie long, dark and sharp and everything appears clearer and more focused (or is it just that the senses are more awake?), but by late afternoon a milkiness skins the earth, and cedars that looked like dark rising empresses in the morning have morphed into sweltering bathers on a sun-bleached beach. Shadows shrink into cramped spaces. The traffic, too, seems more lethargic. Is everyone just tired? The sun banalizes the earth and erases the mystery of the morning – thank God for the night and the stars. One clear cold evening not too long ago I passed the Schneider sign and how different it looked after dark; gone were the ugly struts and scaffolding; only the brilliant letters and face of the blond and toothsome kitchen maid stood out against the murky background, a bright shard of Las Vegas in the black fields of Pushlinck Township.

The French teacher, who was vivacious and intelligent, possessed a lively sense of humour. It was Adele who tipped me off about how threatened you felt by the teacher's presence for two hours every Saturday morning in our home, the teacher and me cooped up in the small library off the kitchen joking and jabbering away in French, a language you didn't know that well. When you began to insist I accompany you shopping to the market every Saturday before the 10 a.m. lesson I still didn't twig that something was amiss. And even at the market as 10 a.m. approached and I'd say something about having to leave soon (time my old bugbear, remember) and you'd snap, eyes blazing, "The lesson can wait," I still didn't get it. If I had known how insecure and threatened you were I'd have dropped the lessons immediately, for you were more important to me than anything or anyone else in the world. Oh, the dullness of men!

Since your suicide my life has been rife with transitions and dislocations, your death the greatest dislocation of all. Unlike animals, who live in the present tense, we humans are caught up in lineal clock time, seek to interpret our lives as a story. And when we can't find the story we feel lost and disoriented. Someone wrote that we should compose our lives like works of art, weave the various parts together with the thread of continuity, but it hasn't worked out like that for me. Just as the brain likes to zigzag in all directions, my life has taken some abrupt turns and twists and I wonder sometimes if I'll ever find my way again. You pulled the ground from under my feet and I'm still reeling, looking for a clear direction, trying to find that unifying principle that would make it all make sense. Is the golden thread a story of survival? Or something more profound? A God who will not let me, the consummate escape artist, out of his grip?

℞

KODY'S BAD HABIT CONTINUES APACE: HE ESCAPED AGAIN THIS MORNING. To date the mutt has cost me a potful in fines. Rose, our cleaning lady, left the sliding door at the back open a crack, all the beast needed to slip out. I glimpsed her white and tan coat jouncing in the tall grass behind the house as she chased the honking geese from the Kortright waterfowl park. Young Jack Russells are supercharged with energy, almost ungovernable; they should stay on the farm where they can indulge their feral ways. When Joy finally caught her I was so relieved I kissed her on both cheeks. The secret is to pretend to walk in the opposite direction and Kody will follow, she says, then when the dog approaches order her sternly to sit and she'll obey; I'm skeptical but next time I'll give it a try. Knowing how much Ruth loves the dog, my greatest fear is that Kody will get hurt or killed during one of her escapades, and the emotional fallout from that could be devastating. Later in the morning, I raked and gathered up last year's leaves around the back link fence and heaved them down the embankment. On the surface the leaves appeared dry and brown, but underneath were wet and blackish, like decayed gunk – such a contrast to the brilliant yellow-and-red carpet of last fall. In the front, the crocuses are already poking their violet heads through the earth, harbingers of spring and new life.

For a long time after your suicide I'd shudder whenever the phone rang, especially at night, fearful of more grisly news. Like Woody Allen, I'd become a little paranoid and anticipated the worst.

"That's the way it is with parents," Rose said.

"Surely not all parents, Rose."

"If the worse can happen, it will," she replied.

Why am I so mistrustful? Has it something to do with my job? Or is it deeper than that? As a child, not knowing sometimes where our next meal would come from, what angers would erupt in the night, taught my sisters and me we couldn't always rely on the adults in our lives and that to survive we had to learn to be our own caretakers, build our own security systems. Mom had a prodigious memory and when she drank would trundle out every act of betrayal or wrong, real or imagined, that Dad ever committed; the list was long and predictable and my sisters and I knew it by heart. Sometimes, instead of stealing off to our bedrooms (our normal evasion) we'd amuse ourselves by anticipating what she was going to say and reciting it before the words even left her tongue and even, on rare occasions when she overlooked one of her grievances, filling in the blanks. We learned early that life was full of dangers and traps. Your suicide shook my confidence in both human nature and God even further. Yet I know it's pointless and stupid to blame others; in the end I'm responsible for my reactions, as Nicole constantly reminds me, and must take charge of my own life. The gospel says that perfect love casts out fear. Some argue that fear and mistrust are endemic to humanity, but I reject that contention as too cynical and negative. Nevertheless, I've concluded that fear and mistrust sap energy, destroy creativity and prevent me from living fully. Call me an idealist or dreamer, but I desire to greet the world with calm and hope.

Lord, help me recover my faith in your providence and the goodness and beauty of life. Strengthen my belief in your grace, that you will be there for me through all the rough tosses of life. Amen.

CR

THE NIGHT BEFORE PAUL AND GABE'S WEDDING I WAS HONOURED WITH THE
sleep of the innocent. Though I woke several times, I felt a peacefulness I
hadn't experienced since your death, as though I'd slipped back into the warm
womb of love. The next morning I took the van to the car wash and as the
cloudy soap slathered the windows and the big rollers with their yellow-
and-white plastic tentacles thrummed and hissed, water shooting at the van
from all sides, the van roof drumming like a herd of running buffalo, I
thought of you and remembered how car washes always made you fearful and
claustrophobic, wondered if that fright was connected with the coldness you
must have felt in your mother's womb, after she'd rejected you and decided
never to see you or hold you in her arms. I thought of you a lot during the
wedding, too; though I rejoiced in Paul and Gabe's good fortune (you would
have loved Gabe) I had moments of sadness because you were not there to
share in our joy. The wedding Mass was dedicated to you and Emilio, Gabe's
father, and all of us felt your presence-absence deeply, especially when Ruth
sang "Ave Maria" and "Lord of the Dance" in her strong, crystal-clear voice,
and I saw your face reflected in Paul's when his eyes welled with tears and
lips began to quiver at the lectern and Gabe had to finish his reading – tears
of joy, he told me after. And what a banquet! Seafood antipasto, fettucine
with meat sauce agnolotti, grilled breast of chicken with herbs and spices,
green beans, baby carrots, sautéed mushrooms, braised shrimp, and calamari,
mixed green salad with oil-and-basil vinaigrette, selva nera, coffee and tea,
not to mention good Italian wine – a Babette's feast. Everything conspired
– the mellow baritones of the Italians singing across the room, our friends,
the children – to set memories flowing through the heart like the strains of
a cello. Slowly, slowly, not without pain and struggle, my heart is widening
and deepening. Mira, who knows about these kaddishes, urges me to reveal
what's in my heart as honestly as I'm capable, but while the journalling helps
to soften your loss, it's still hard. "The artist's struggle to transcend pain can

become a seed for many others' hopes, transforming a personal journey into a vision for us all," writes Susan Shaughnessy in *Walking on Alligators.* There's no way to outrun grief, and in baring my soul I risk ridicule and rejection I know, but trying to meet my pain head-on in these stream-of-consciousness sessions is the only way I have to show my solidarity with others.

Nicole who, unlike you, is at home in her skin, is often very perceptive. I don't appreciate the little licks of pleasure, she says, am not sensual enough and fear the domination of women. Too often I failed you by my lack of tenderness, my ignorance of the small strokes of love, my inability to accept body and soul holistically. Nicole attributes these failings to my childhood, the absenteeism of my father and the conflict I experienced in my home, which made me withdraw and put up defences. "You're always searching for what is normal," she says, "and that's why you're so referential, always seeking the opinion of a jury." How do I learn to trust that I won't be consumed, swallowed up, destroyed by mother-women, stop the lunatic restlessness that has beset me all my life, slide under the skin of life and make friends with my flesh, and live in the moment, the everlasting all-we-have? I never felt safe in my body. I remember when I was three or four sitting on the cool yellow linoleum in the kitchen of Simcoe Street; Mom was ironing her white uniform for work and late afternoon sunlight angled through the window, spangling the kitchen floor with bright shapes. I felt a wet substance, warm and sticky in my shorts and slid my hand under my bottom to explore, then slowly, ever so slowly pulled my hand back to bring my fingers to my lips to taste. "Dirty, dirty, dirty!" Mom screamed as she ran over and scooped me off the floor over to the sink where she washed my mouth with soap and water, repeating like a mantra "dirty, dirty, dirty!" me sobbing, thinking I'd done something unspeakable and disgusting by trying to taste my own stink. I think I picked up the message that there were parts of my body that were evil and untouchable. Now I want to accept my nakedness, embrace body and soul holistically, thinning hair, small puffy eyes, all my ageing and sin marks, touch the dark ridges of my soul, the gritty stuff of reality. I want to be a Hebrew, bring my body home to God and put an end to the duality of spirit and body, no higher or lower, both good, level, equally loved, be fearless and trusting that I will emerge refreshed and blessed by the God who fashioned us all out of dust and pronounced it good.

Naked

"Life is so short, we must move slowly."
                              Old Thai saying

It took courage
                    to dive naked into
Palma's mountain lake.

Afterwards you told me
                    what I already knew,
that I never let the water
                    touch me,
must learn
                    to ride my breath,
float freely;

learn too
                    the lake is sovereign,
nourished by springs,
                    that there is no water
beyond this.

A Sign of Renewal

CR

AFTER YOU TOOK YOUR LIFE I WAS SO DISPIRITED AND DISTRACTED I TOOK A month off work to gather my wits and strength. At the end of the month I felt strong enough to return to the bench (everyone had urged me to keep busy) and for the next two or three months functioned well enough, but gradually the inner turmoil got too much and I realized I needed more time. I phoned the regional senior judge, a kind, conscientious man, arranged for a meeting. "I can't concentrate on my work," I told him, wiping my eyes with Kleenex. "The pain is too sharp." As I spoke he fiddled nervously with his pipe and stared at the wall. The last words had barely escaped my mouth when he stammered: "Of course, of course, Jim, you take as much time as you need." People have been kind, but I sense the idea of suicide disconcerts them and they're at wit's end for what to say. For many, suicide's an embarrassment and enigma they're emotionally unprepared for.

Yesterday I received a letter from the wife of an armed robber whom I'll be sentencing to the Penitentiary this Friday. The man has a string of convictions for similar offences and the Crown describes him as a hardened criminal. Though his chances of rehabilitation are slim, the wife's letter describes him glowingly as a good husband and loving father. "He wants to make a good life," she wrote. She enclosed a photo of the family: the accused, herself and their three small children in front of their blue-grey aluminum-clad bungalow with lacy white curtains, all smiling, and in the background a tall juniper and old-fashioned lamppost and life-sized cutouts of a Victorian lady in red skirt, jacket and bonnet trimmed in white fur. One of the daughters, a blond toddler in a blue winter coat, was clutching a white-bearded Santa, a Hallmark Christmas scene. To understand all is to forgive all, the French say. In the Buddhist tradition the ultimate stage of love is Upekkha, a detached love that no longer makes or even recognizes distinctions, but loves everyone the same, whether a serial killer or great humanitarians like Mother Teresa. Clearly society hasn't reached that stage in its evolution, and probably never will. A minister friend of mine who worked for many years as chaplain in a major American prison once told me he found deeper spirituality among murderers and thieves than many so-called law-abiding citizens. "They've lost their masks, been reduced to the essentials of life, stripped of supports and illusions," he explained, "are better able to look themselves squarely in the mirror, recognize their need for God."

As judge I sit in God-like judgment of my brothers and sisters, an uncomfortable role at best, and I don't have a crystal ball. Very often I feel I'm only skimming the surface of their lives, a voyeur looking in, unable to plumb the deeper recesses of their hearts. The law is a broadsword, not a scalpel, and I have to constantly remind myself that my job primarily is to protect the peace and good order of society, retain a "lucid indifference," as one judge put it, not engage in some micro-dissection of the soul. While I strive to act compassionately, some things are best left to God, who alone can track the swervings of the human heart.

Last night as I lay in bed in our big empty home, I recalled the time we drove from Cobourg to inspect our new dream house in progress. As we climbed the rickety ladder the workman had erected to the second floor, I remember how scared we were. The framing was complete but the roof was still open to the elements and we meandered through the wall-less, roofless rooms – a jumble of wooden bones, laughing and waving to each other across the empty spaces under a flawless blue sky, giddy with the prospect of a new future in the making. Little did I envisage then that I'd be in this house today alone, you gone, the children scattered – the house once again a skeleton.

෫

AFTER YOUR DEATH I WENT INTO A KIND OF COGNITIVE PARALYSIS. SORROW annexed my sleeping and waking hours and I couldn't concentrate. My sleep was riddled with spooky dreams and three or four times a night I'd get up, wander around the house or turn on the TV. I can't remember the last time I had the charmed sleep of a child, the sort that scrubs clean the psychic grime in one unbroken sweep of oblivion. I joined the "Y" and went to three or four sessions a week: swimming, jogging, workouts on the rowing machines, whirlpool and shower, the same routine each time. At first I sleepwalked through the motions, my soul packed in ice, my mind in limbo. Sometimes the interior pain was so searing I'd stop in the middle of an exercise and turn misty-eyed. For a brief period I even considered resigning from the bench, taking up some other line of work to try to sort out my life, but I'm glad I didn't act on that impulse. Work, in a sense, has been my salvation, permitting me to get my thoughts off you and my grief. I marvel at the ability of the brain to function in the teeth of unspeakable pain and inner turbulence as though it operated on two distinct and separate tracks at the same time. And gradually my time at the "Y" bore fruit: I lost weight, grew fit, and discovered that the exercises had an unanticipated therapeutic effect. You would have approved, for obesity was always your bugbear and offended your aesthetic sense; you liked men with small tight bums, you told me, and for most of our marriage I didn't measure up to your standards. After a while I also found I welcomed the special invitations of dreams, looked forward to my nocturnal movie house with its bizarre clues to what was happening in the rich underworld of the mind. I came to believe with Jung that dreams are pure gold and give access to that shadow side of our personalities where our deepest secrets and wildest energies are stored. When I asked Ron, my old partner, if he was prepared to accompany me to Niagara should I decide someday to go he immediately said yes, but then told me in his matter-of-fact level voice that he'd talked to the Niagara police and it's highly unlikely your body will ever be recovered, the strong currents and whirlpools would see to that, which surprised and dismayed me as I'd nurtured the fantasy that you'd float downstream and one day be snagged by some hapless fisherman. How typical of you, who never wanted to create a fuss, I reflected later, to take leave of the earth in this fashion, you who would have been surprised and horrified at the great crowd at your memorial service. One neighbour described your death the other day as a blow. A blow? A blow strikes in one spot whereas your suicide was more like a seismic upheaval shaking all our foundations, even my trust in a providential God, and I'm still teetering in the aftershock. Will I ever find the courage to go to Niagara and face down my demons? Will standing on the spot where you stood before you plunged into the mesmerizing waters lure me to join you? And if perchance they should ever find your remains and ask me to come down to identify you, will I have the guts? I don't know; all I know is that I must someday grab the demon of your suicide by the scaly reptilian neck, confront his fiery breath and cold sharp claws and wrestle him to the ground; otherwise he'll disappear into the subconscious with all my other demons and snipe at me for the rest of my days.

O God, give me the courage to be!

No Place of Rest

As the identification officer
showed photos of the fatality scene
in court this morning,
the remains of a headlight
where the impact occurred,
a trail of blood to the ditch
where the body came to rest,

I thought of you,
your unclaimed body picked
smooth
by the hungry river,
ribs of cold light,
no place of rest.

CR

ANOTHER DISPIRITING CASE OF "POCKETBOOK" JUSTICE TODAY IN COURT.
After a lengthy trial, a judge awarded the Children's Aid Society permanent
wardship of three young children and the mother appealed; it's a Catch-22,
however; the appeal can't proceed without the transcripts, and the mother,
who lives below the poverty line, can't afford to order them. Legal Aid has
denied her assistance (they claim the appeal lacks merit) and the CAS has
immediate plans to put the children out for adoption (they've already selected
the adoptive parents). The stricken look on the mother's pale face tells me
she's devastated, but without personal funds and without aid from the public
purse her right to appeal is meaningless. Over the strong objections of counsel
for the CAS, who asked me to dismiss the appeal, I gave her an additional 45
days to come up with the money – in the circumstances, a forlorn hope.

This six-bedroom house, which we built in the name of happiness, which
was once a cocoon of love, is now an echoing shell. Often, lying in bed alone
at night unable to sleep I hear strange noises and imagine that there's a burglar
in the house or, more plausibly, a disgruntled litigant out for revenge. In the
morning my fantasy looks silly and I berate myself for being so lily-livered.
The fallout from your suicide continues; I spoke to Adele, who's out of sorts
lately (she misses you greatly), and assured her things were sure to get better,
that time would heal. Sometimes I see my role as a coach trying to buck up
the spirit of a crestfallen team. As I approach my 60th year I'm more and
more conscious of Time's winged chariot – the last gallop before death that
Jung calls the age of meaning. Like those jerky frames in the early silent
films, the days flip speedily past, and as my future contracts every moment
becomes more precious. Or to employ a different metaphor (perhaps more
apt in your case) I feel I'm being swept along on a frothing river knowing
the Falls is not too distant. In his memoir of childhood, *The Sacred Journey*,
Frederick Buechner, whose father shot himself when Buechner was ten, poses
the question that has obsessed these kaddishes: What is God saying when
a good person takes their life? A moment comes into being and it goes on
forever, he writes, not just in memory but as though it had a life of its own
in a new kind of time, what Dylan Thomas described as "below a time" – a

"having-beenness" beyond any power in heaven or on earth, in life or death, to touch – and the people we knew and loved continue to grow and change along with us. What a beautiful thought! – that you will continue to grow and change with us till we finish our days, that you will continue to touch my life and the lives of our children with power and richness.

☙

WHEN I ENTERED THE OFFICE MONDAY MORNING I FOUND THE shrivelled remnants of a hibiscus bloom on the carpet. The previous Friday afternoon, the bud was on the verge of opening and I'd nurtured the hope that I'd be greeted by a beautiful red bloom to chase away the Monday morning blues when I came back. Alas, it was not to be; the flower had blossomed during the weekend, unseen and unappreciated. The plant, which Adele gave me for my birthday a few months ago, follows its own laws and blooms randomly. For me, each bloom is a sign of renewal, a resurrection. Abundance we take for granted, but when beauty is delicate and timebound it's doubly precious. I love the plant's hardiness, too, the way it continues to thrive month after month in this sterile environment. Like Thoreau's crickets, newly risen from their ice-bound beds, nature startles our ignorance, astounds us with her hidden music. Yesterday Nicole and I discovered a moth on the interlocking brick of her driveway near the front of my van; it looked disoriented in the blazing midday sun, but what took our breath away was its unusual colouring; to the naked eye its wings were dun-coloured, until you looked closer and realized they were reddish brown. We marvelled even more at the electric, almost psychedelic blue of its long abdomen, its bright orange head and orange-tipped antennae, a small yet dazzling specimen of God's inexhaustible creation. Last evening I dreamt of you again: you were clinging to the rim of a steep cliff and I tried to save you by grabbing your hand, but my fingers were greasy and you slipped out of my grip. The image of your body plunging straight for the rocks below was the last I saw of you before I broke through the dream, and for a long time afterwards I felt terrible, couldn't get back to sleep.

You always claimed I had an ego problem. Nicole puts it another way, says I'm always seeking to maximize my time, squeeze every ounce of juice out of life, and that I should learn to let go and relax. Yesterday I got miffed at her. I'd loaned her a book by Anthony de Mello titled *Awareness*, which she'd casually flipped through, and when I asked her about it she said, "See, he's only saying what I've been saying for years. I could have written that book myself." Was it the perception of intellectual arrogance that bothered me? Or am I simply jealous of her brilliant intellect? De Mello says we only become aware when we drop our opinionated ways, learn to dance with life. We don't find truth so much as truth finds us; the idea is not to control but to breathe deeply and let life flow through us, become witnesses instead of uptight agents. Yes, Nicole's probably right, I should become more detached, shed my agenda for self-actualization and like the train sign tells us, stop, look and listen. How do you let life sieve through the senses, acquire the quiet lucid eye, the ear that listens, the skin that feels the heartbeat of others, the sensitive nose for the perfumes of nature, the eloquently silent tongue? And, of course, the sixth sense, already there but not yet awakened, to find the better angels of our nature who people the air and enfold us with soft wings? Yes, though I've made progress I've still a long way to go.

Lord, help me to wake up.

The Way Everyone Is Inside

What are you doing with your life?
This is a good Buddhist question.
You didn't buy it.
It's quite sobering, but the way
the world is being organized, bigger parts
of it are sliding inexorably into

smaller, where we live,
we don't even know we're being bruised.

When the raging elephant (or angry
boss, it makes no difference) comes charging
it's already too late.

The old millennium is darkening like a window,
the bus is breaking down:
ball bearings have sprung loose, we're desperately
in need of a cosmic catching mitt – a fresh way
of seeing;
a new sun's begging to be born.

ॐ

FOR A LONG TIME AFTER THE MEMORIAL SERVICE I FELT YOUR ABSENCE LIKE
a dagger. Deprived of your love and companionship, isolated and vulnerable
as an animal licking its wounds at the edge of a field, I distanced myself
from everyday living. The smallest reminder of you – one of your summer
dresses still hanging in the closet that the girls had overlooked, finding the
amber brooch I gave you for your 35th birthday that you loved so much in
one of the compartments of the jewellery box, or one of your long-forgotten
charcoal sketches of the children – burned like drops of acid, evoked tears.
I even began to begrudge the good fortune of others whose marriages were
still intact. In my inward turning I felt one remove from others; it was as if a
bell jar had descended over me, glassing me off from normal life. But while it
may be true that some find relief in the misery of others – the vicarious re-
enactment in movies and novels of the shadow side simultaneously stimulates
and relieves our anti-social impulses – nonetheless, it is also true that a tragedy

(such as your suicide) can create a sense of kinship with others who suffer and eventually lead to greater compassion. Your suicide (I like to believe) has slowly made me more sensitive to the pain of those around me. Even our children claim I've become mellower and more empathetic. Too often we hide our pain and fears, seek to impress others into loving us with our strengths. But I'm convinced that compassion, which catches our hearts in nets as soft as flowers, is the fruit of shared vulnerability, the only escape from our private exiles. Now when people talk to me about their losses and problems, instead of turning a deaf ear I listen not only with my head but also with the ears of the heart. For a time after your death I got into the habit of leaving the house early Saturday morning and driving to Burger King on the Stone Road for an egg croissant and coffee. Observing other Saturday morning stragglers around the room, usually sitting alone like me, nursing a coffee and staring blankly into space set me to wonder about their stories, imagine myself in their shoes. I thought I could glimpse the invisible ball and chain they were dragging just like me. And isn't this the beginning of compassionate wisdom, the realization that in this life we are all works-in-progress and that everyone has his own custom-made ball and chain?

Saturday's Children

Why don't you join me at Burger King
early Saturday morning for breakfast?

The décor's cheery: a white fluorescent
heaven overhead, the air awash with

no-name music designed to keep
the soul from sinking

and room dividers of plastic fronds
to conjure up the illusion of

sunnier climes. See, Santa's still
in the window – though Christmas is

now three weeks old – wearing a black
top hat as he leads a line of merry

youngsters up a hill and if you look
carefully you'll see scattered

around the tables some of your
neighbours, regular customers, like me,

who come for the atmosphere and always
eat alone... the haggard woman

across the aisle, stubbing her
fifth cigarette this morning, squinting

at the snow as
though she half expected someone from

her past to emerge from that
swirling silver and, of course, you

mustn't miss the Burger King basement
playground – if you're taller than the

Burger Chipmunk you can't go down –
and Saturday's children, jostling

each other in the plastic ball pit,
frantic, upturned eyes yearning

for attention from weekend fathers,
awkward, behind glass walls.

CR

TALKED TO PAT LESAGE ABOUT THE AFTERLIFE THIS LOVELY SPRING MORNING in my office over a cup of tea. We agree that it goes against nature to accept that our three score and ten ends in a void, that something visceral inside us rebels at the thought of pure extinction. Once we've tasted love, we want it all – infinite love, another name for God, mercy within mercy within mercy. I glanced out my chambers at the greenish haze atop the birches in the distance and the pale green shoots in the maples close by. Memories of you surged back, overwhelmed me. Tears formed in my eyes and I wiped them with Kleenex, which I now always keep handy just in case. I told Pat I looked forward to the heavenly banquet where I would see you and all my lost loved ones again. St. John says God is love and that he who loves is begotten of God and knows God. Jack Kerouac, a God-seeker all his life, put it even more poetically: we wander through flesh till the dove calls us back to the Dove of heaven. The world floats on springs of grace, I said; God is inside us and death's a doorway, and I expressed my belief that your watery grave would turn into a garden and your eyes would break forth like lilies. Was I whistling in the dark, trying to bolster my sagging confidence? Sometimes I wonder if I'm trying to decorate the horror of your death with heaven, make it more palatable, absolve myself in the holy water of God-talk. After Pat left I realized I'd gotten carried away and wondered whether my lofty and flowery language had embarrassed him. In the strident and divisive arena of the law, poetry gets short shrift, and who can deny that it is a bit incongruous for two veteran judges immersed in the rough-and-tumble of unpoetic human conflict to be talking like this, but Pat being the gentleman he is didn't flinch or betray annoyance; he listened patiently to my tortured ramblings.

Lord, give me the courage to trust you and face my fear of the void. Mary, pray for me that someday like you I'll fall into the loving arms of the everlasting other, mercy within mercy within mercy.

CR

SIMONE WEIL SAID, "ABSOLUTE ATTENTION IS PRAYER." ONE OF THE BENEFITS of my travels between courts is the necessity of paying close attention to what's happening around me on the highway; my brain cells are being constantly engaged by events, a kind of enforced meditation that takes me out of myself and keeps the Black Dog at bay. Leaving court in Brampton today I got wedged in a traffic jam on the 401; two cars, one green, the other maroon, were in the eastbound ditch, badly damaged. Why is it every time there's a highway accident the traffic accordions and drivers crane their necks to gawk? Is it because our neighbour's disasters make us feel lucky, invulnerable, immortal? Clarence Darrow, the trial lawyer and atheist, considered immortality a pipe dream, a refuge for the fearful and cowardly, yet the yearning for immortality is anchored in human history. Stone Age people ate each other's hearts in cannibalistic rituals to confer immortality, buried tools alongside the dead for the next life. The ancient Egyptians turned such practices into an art form, anointing their dead with special oils, wrapping them in cloths in the hope that if they could preserve the flesh from rotting they could bestow everlasting life. Plato believed the soul was distinct from the body, a divine element and immortal. Today, artists seek immortality through their art, parents through their children, and the wealthy through giving large donations to museums and art galleries that will bear their names. Some who take cryogenics seriously even have their corpses frozen for the day a cure is found for death and they can be defrosted and live forever. And the secular immortalists who believe the soul is simply the product of organized atoms like music to a CD are looking to artificial intelligence and other technologies to unload the mind and preserve identity. For Christians, immortality is granted through the death of Christ to those who live the Christ life. Faith is a revolt, a bold refusal to resign before the tombstone facts of life, to be reconciled to the death of those we love. Faith flies in the face of the inevitable and doomsday laws of the universe, proclaims with

Christ that death is not forever, that love is not meaningless and that our instinctive yearning for permanence is not folly. I recall your words when we were on the baptism team at St. Joseph's and you spoke about baptism, the symbol of eternal life. Baptism is the Easter sacrament, you said, the sign of both death and resurrection. When we are baptized we drown to the world without Christ and rise out of the water to the reality of the spiritual. We light the Paschal candle at baptisms and funerals as a sign that the life of Christ is born in us, that in death the life of Christ remains in us. How fitting in a way, then, that when you decided to go home, you chose drowning as your gateway into immortality.

Permanence

After the funeral my granddaughter whispered in her
mother's ear: "I want to be alone with papa," &
so I took her by the hand, led
her into the living room, thinking
we could have a quiet time together.
She leaned the slight weight
of her four-year-old head against my chest, nestled
in my arms, mute & still & safe &

for the longest while we held each other – our
hearts, two shells resonating in the dark –
the wet, white seconds like lanterns soaking up
the night, her life-breath – a small urgent bell
making me promise over & over I would never leave.

☙

DROVE TO A JUDGES' MEETING THIS BRILLIANT MAY MORNING. ON Edinburgh the sun lit up the east wall of the white-stoned Sears building and the windows mirrored a flawless pale blue sky. A middle-aged man in bright red gym pants jogged along the sidewalk, head bent as if weighed down by the worries of the world. How admirable, I thought, despite burdens he's pushing gamely ahead. In the countryside I catch the sweet fragrance of lilacs along the roadsides, pass corn stalks, broken yellow toothpicks strewn in the fields, sun-splashed ponds, stone farmhouses, barns, and small clumps of grass that stand out darkly in the greening pastures. It was only 8:30 a.m., but I spotted a young woman in yellow shirt and jeans stooped over, planting geraniums on her lawn. Combing through the rubble of bereavement, many thoughts percolated through my mind. Though Nicole's fluid beliefs sometimes vex me, I envy the way she floats through life, human and caring, content to be guided by the light of her heart, but attached to no fixed credo except love. The absence of fixed beliefs threatens me; it's as if I've been abandoned in some dark alien field without boundaries. I realize now how much I leaned on you for my religious and moral fences. Nicole likes to say, if you see the Buddha on the road kill him, and encourages me to find my own path to God. The other evening my sister Marilyn visited a psychic, who fingered my gold wedding ring which I gave her to take along and said it belonged to a kind and caring man who'd once been a priest. Curious; I've felt like a priest in my life and have often said how we're all called to be healers. When Adele mentions you she frequently falls silent and her eyes cloud. Paul told me he's grown up a lot in the past year: "It's been hard," he said, "but I'm no longer so afraid." Then he added, "Your dawn hasn't come yet, Dad, but it will." I'm still struggling and my bereavement journey is far from finished; sometimes I wonder if it will ever end. How sad to outlive loved ones. God traps us, it seems, in a no-win situation: the longer we live – normally a wished-for boon – the more we suffer. For some there's no escape except to build ramparts, adopt the fortress mentality, but the price is high: emotional and spiritual impoverishment. I look forward to my dawn; perhaps it will be similar to the other morning, when Paul nudged my shoulder and woke me from a deep troubled dream. Or maybe the new dawn will be like this early May morning, a green world renewed with the windows of the Sears building reflecting a flawless blue sky.

Dream

I'm in one of the great Gothic cathedrals of Europe. I recognize the strong Polish face of Pope John Paul II in the pew beside me. A new pope is speaking in the sanctuary and John Paul looks peeved, even angry, because the new pope has softened the old absolute moral teachings. What strikes me is not so much the look of betrayal on John Paul's face but the flicker of disapproval I see there, so unbecoming and unworthy of someone I admire. Does John Paul lack confidence in the truth of his beliefs? Then I thought, if the old pope is like that maybe the institutional Church is also fearful and I'll have to find my own way through the dark thicket. Do I have two popes inside me?

CR

TODAY IN COURT A WOMAN BROUGHT A MOTION TO DENY HER HUSBAND ACCESS to their son's medical information. The son, age eleven, who was suffering from an aggressive form of leukemia, was in hospital and not expected to live. The parties couldn't even agree on visiting hours, and when they were in the son's room together, sat on opposite sides of the bed glowering at each other in cold silence. Once when the husband picked up the son's bed chart the wife tried to snatch it from him; the appalling spectacle of a tug-of-war over the dying boy was too much and I left the courtroom feeling dejected. That evening Ruth phoned from Dublin in a panic; someone had filched her wallet in a pub. Her big concern was the loss of her class F license, which she needs for bussing junior rangers in the summer. "Please, Dad, please," she sobbed, "you must help me." How inadequate I sometimes feel trying to fill the shoes of the "greatest dad-mom" as she described me in her Easter card. I don't handle confrontations well and the fear of someone else in the family having a breakdown like yours is never far from my mind. Last winter when Paul sat cross-legged on his futon, a gloomy expression on his face, and told me the world appeared increasingly black and hopeless to him, that he could hardly rouse himself in the mornings to go to work, I was alarmed. Why do I persist in making myself sick, lose sleep over the children? Sometimes I think all my fretting and chafing is pure folly. All fathers (and mothers) sooner or later must surrender their children to the wilderness of the world, learn to stand aside, take a deep breath and watch helplessly from the sidelines, for there is nothing in our power to assure their ultimate safety. This is the father/child narrative of the generations and I must learn to bow to its wisdom and entrust them to God, the Father/Mother of us all. Oh, how easily said! But you would have been proud of the way I conducted myself: I remembered that she was only 20 and that this was her first trip abroad, assured her calmly that I would write the ministry that day (which I did) and also get her a new social insurance card and she seemed mollified and relieved.

Growing up, all the significant adults in my life were women: Gaby, Mom, my sisters, the nuns. Dad was overseas for most of the war and when he got back remained emotionally absent from my life. As a result, Nicole says, my adulthood has been a quest for male models and normalcy, with an underlying terror of female domination thrown in. Nicole is always putting me under the psychological microscope. She means well, I know, but sometimes her scrutiny nettles me, makes me uncomfortable. Do I secretly fear emasculation? And do I put you on a pedestal, as Adele claims, airbrush your memory, refuse to see your humanity, acknowledge the narrow paradigms that killed your spirit and hope? Oh, if only I could comb the tangles from my life! Sometimes I ask myself if these kaddishes are simply repeating an archetype of female sacrifice and male redemption: the woman (you) redeems the man (me) through her death. In his grieving, old wounds are reopened and ultimately healed and he is restored back to wholeness and health – a narrative deeply embedded in our culture? But our story has no such facile and artistic denouement. Your suicide conjured up a host of ghosts, especially from my childhood, but I don't feel especially whole or healed. If any good has come of it, it's a greater awareness of my relationship with God and the need for a love that transcends all distinctions: religious, social, gender, sexual orientation and race. As the poet Gwen Harwood put it, "We are a skinful of elements climbing from earth to the fastness of light." Despite my resistance, God has drawn closer to me. One ghost from my childhood that keeps surfacing is the way my sister and I treated our younger sister, Marilyn. A pretty child with creamy, unblemished skin and large blue eyes, she had a natural gift for music and her rendition of "Danny Boy" at Dad's annual St. Patrick's Day bash (after Dad's maudlin performance) would drench the room in tears, the sentimental Irishmen stuffing her purse with nickels and quarters (even dollars). Because she was chubby Shirl and I mercilessly teased her, nicknamed her "Fatty." Oh, the mindless cruelties of children! And when she'd wet her bed we added "stink hole" to our repertoire of insults. "Fatty, Fatty wet her bed," we'd chorus until her face crimsoned, eyes brimmed and she'd run off to her bedroom, sobbing. Gaby, who hated the smell of urine, would punish her by slashing her legs with the maple switch, thrusting her into the dank and smelly basement and throwing off the light. "Bluebeard will eat you for what you've done," she'd taunt through the trap door, and even today when I'm lying alone in bed at night I think I hear my sister's screams.

Weeping Wall

All the monsters were there
under the trap door
next to Mom's peaches and pears.

They slept on the earth floor,
they waved their razor wands
in our faces,
smelled like greasy hair.

All night we heard them
clopping, clopping, clopping
in and out of the black hole
in the stone wall
where the wind came in to shout.

Once I saw them disguised as rats,
grey and furry with needle teeth.

They howled and howled
desperate to get out
like my sister's scream:
"Please don't leave me here alone!"

When they finally rolled the house away
I was amazed to find
all the monsters had gone,
only the stones remained,
huge and brilliant in the sun,
a weeping wall.

CR

ANOTHER SAD DAY IN COURT: AN ELDERLY MAN AND WIFE HAD BUILT UP a sizeable nest egg in Canada with the intention of retiring to their native Jamaica. To sweeten their retirement years they'd invested all their savings in a truck and a fishing boat, hoping to do some hauling and commercial fishing in their off hours, and in anticipation of the arrival of the goods moved to Jamaica. But when the freighter docked at Kingston they were horrified to discover that both the truck and the fishing boat had been destroyed in transit during a storm. Now they were seeking judgment against the carrier for their loss (truck and boat had been inadequately secured), but unfortunately their lawsuit had been commenced several weeks after the expiry of the six-month limitation period. You remember how wrenching and frustrating I found it to have to stand by helplessly and dispense a law I considered morally repugnant; though I racked my brain I could find no loophole in the jurisprudence that would have permitted them to circumvent the prescription period and recover, and with heavy heart I dismissed their motion for summary judgment, but not before telling them I thought the law was an ass and they should appeal my judgment. And when counsel for the carrier shot to his feet to demand costs of $15,000 (to which he'd normally be entitled) my frustration turned bilious. "What are you trying to do, rub salt into the wound?" I snapped. I requested he reconsider his position during recess. After the court reconvened in the afternoon he rose to announce the insurers had rethought their position and had decided in the circumstances to forgo costs, which eased my conscience somewhat and took some of the sting out of what I'd had to do.

These kaddishes are turning into an exercise in self-disclosure: your suicide has cast a wide net and dredged up many inchoate longings of the heart and buried traumas of childhood, especially the unfinished business between Dad and me. One summer morning during the war years I discovered an anvil in Mr. Nelson's coal shed and boosted it onto the red wagon Santa had given me for Christmas, the metal awkward and slippery in my hands, and pulled it all the way across the tracks to Albert's scrapyard. Albert ran his greasy hand along the shiny top and plunked a nickel and dime in my palm. As I told Mom what I'd done I watched the growing alarm on her pale face. When I finished she took a deep breath, grabbed my hand – her palms were cold and clammy – and hauled me down the street to Mr. Nelson's office. The small office reeked of coal dust; I could taste its gritty texture on my tongue. Mom poked my ribs, told me to doff my cap. Mr. Nelson tapped a yellow pencil on the wooden counter, fixed me with his gimlet eyes. I couldn't take my eyes off the creases on his big earlobes, his sagging leathery cheeks, his red porous nose. I felt suspended in a world of giants, weightless as the hollow bones of birds, accused of some terrible deed, and wished with all my might that I was a speck of lint and could blow myself back to my sanctuary-bedroom, invisible, lost in pitch-black darkness. Through my tears I glimpsed Mr. Nelson's stern face, wattles shaking, lips quivering, as he rattled on about my hero father overseas, "fighting Hitler to save the likes of you," how betrayed he'd feel to learn his only son had let him down, was just a common thief. A common thief! The words stung like a swarm of hornets. I looked into Mom's stricken eyes, wanted to shout: "Never again, I promise, I promise."

Missing in Action

He came alone to Canada from Belfast at thirteen.
He joined the army on the 28th of June 1940 when I was six and
he was thirty-one.
He had brown eyes.
He was 5 foot 5, weighed 176 lbs and had a small scar on his left patella.
He had superior intelligence and good teeth.
He refused promotions.
He landed with the Third Canadian Division in Normandy on D-Day.
The Field Medical Card says a sniper's bullet passed through the base of his right ear and mastoid area on the 8th of July 1944 outside Caen – a "gutter" wound the medics called it.
He was shipped back to Canada on the 8th of Feb. 1945.
He felt lost "about the future."
The Medical Board said: "No treatment indicated."
The Repatriation Summary concluded: "He should adjust well to civilian life."

During the remaining twenty-three years of his life we rarely spoke.
He never talked about the war.
He never ate at our table.
He never.paid me a compliment.
I'm still searching for his face.

CR

IN COURT YESTERDAY A POLICE OFFICER TESTIFIED ABOUT A YOUNG WOMAN
who was on a visit to the farm of her fiancé's parents; the couple were having
fun, basking in the Easter weekend sunshine when someone suggested pictures.
The crown introduced a series of photos the couple took that afternoon by
the barn, showing them in various comic poses and smiling broadly. The
fiancé then asked that she take one of him holding his dad's rifle. The last
photo on the roll showed a young man standing on a small incline, rifle
raised, pointing directly at the camera and about to squeeze the trigger. That
image was the last the woman ever saw before the bullet penetrated her brain,
killing her instantly. Unbeknownst to both, the rifle was loaded. That day I
couldn't get the young woman or the idea of how perishable life is out of my
mind.

Sometimes I question these shapeless jottings, wonder if they're leading
anywhere. There doesn't seem to be any finality or closure in sight. Since your
suicide I've tried to bend my mind around the question of cosmic causality,
how you reconcile the monstrous horrors, both natural and man-made, (like
your suicide and the young woman's freakish death), with belief in a God
of justice and mercy. Over the ages, many brilliant and learned minds have
tackled the problem and come up empty-handed, concluded there are no
satisfying answers. The great earthquake of Lisbon in 1755 – All Saint's Day
– prompted Voltaire to attack the unthinking optimism of Christians that
"tout est bien." Dostoevsky's Ivan Karamazov didn't accuse God of failing to save
the innocent; rather, he rejected salvation itself as not worth the "tears of one
tortured child." Voltaire saw only a strand of truth, that the terrible history
of suffering and death is not morally intelligible; Dostoevsky, a convinced
Christian, went further; he believed it would have been more terrible if it were.
In Christian thought, evil is defined as the absence of good and possesses no
essence or reality of its own. I do not see the face of God in your suicide or
the death of the young woman, nor do I draw much consolation from the

idea that your deaths are part of the mysterious course of God's goodness in the world and that they serve some ultimate meaning or purpose. I believe God hates death and misery and the message of Easter is that he entered the cosmos to break down the burden of fallen nature, restore the ancient beauty of the world where neither the emptiness of death nor the scourge of pain have any place – foolishness no doubt to the skeptic and unbeliever. Can it be as Rabbi Heschel says, that God wants to be wrestled with, that the refusal to accept the harshness of his/her ways is a form of prayer? Even possible, dare I say it, that anger and bitterness can lead to a compassion for God, a widening of the circle of love?

Last night I couldn't sleep thinking of you and the young woman, got up at 3 a.m. and turned on the TV. A program on the theme "How do you cope when you've lost a loved one?" was in progress and a middle-aged woman in a striking zebra-striped white jacket was talking about the death of her three children in a car accident. She explained the necessity of going through all the stages of bereavement, including anger at God, but said it was only when she turned over her loss to Jesus that she found peace. "He carried me," she stated. Other callers phoned in to recount similar tragedies, how the grace of God had sustained them through immense suffering, saved them from bitterness, and brought a certain measure of acceptance and peace once again into their lives. None dwelt on the incomprehensibility of God's ways. Reason alone can't justify the ways of God. Perhaps the answer, like these callers found, is humility of spirit, is willingness to trust, trust, trust in the goodness of God and his world, and find meaning through a life of love. Wasn't it Coleridge who said that Christianity is a life, not a doctrine?

CR

IN COURT TODAY A DAUGHTER TESTIFIED ABOUT THE DEATH OF HER PARENTS in an automobile accident – both killed instantly when a drunk driver ran a red light and smashed into the side of their small car. After describing how they had escaped the death camps of Nazi Germany, came to Canada after the war to begin a new life, the woman took me aback when she suddenly turned to me, tears streaming down her cheeks and blurted, "Why, why, why, your Honour?" The anguish in her voice caught me off guard and I had no recourse but to call a recess so that she could regain her composure and continue the testimony. Her words not only flustered me but yanked me back to the unanswered question that has shadowed these kaddishes from the beginning: What does God mean when a good person like you takes their own life? As a wannabe Christian, someone trying to lead the Christian life but often failing miserably, I believe there is no place that is literally "godforsaken." Despite doubts and intimations to the contrary, I cling to the belief in the essential goodness of life that nothing, no matter how horrendous, can destroy. Though we have limited control over the circumstances of our lives, I believe we still retain the power to shape our attitude towards what befalls us, affirm life no matter what happens. So the central question for me becomes not the meaning of your suicide, but the meaning of my life. Despair, stoic resignation, compulsive distraction are not the only choices. As Victor Frankl put it, "Man doesn't merely exist, but always decides what his existence will be, what he will become in the next moment." Though I can't accept that God willed your suicide or suffering (or anyone else's, for that matter), I still believe in human capacity to respond in ways that bear witness to the core reality of creation – love. Though it is not always self-evident, I like to think that your suicide shook us out of our anomie, uncovered portions of humanity in us that had lain dormant and in some ways made us stronger, more caring people. Paradoxically, you could say your death quickened us to life. I say yes, yes to life now and everlasting. In the end it all comes back to "letting go" and trusting, as Julian of Norwich put it, that "all shall be well and all shall be well and all manner of things shall be well."

CR

AFTER MY RULING IN A FAMILY LAW CASE THIS WEEK, THE HUSBAND STOMPED
out of the courtroom, but not before he shot me a dirty look. Not too long
ago a colleague on the bench got a death threat in the mail. In a fractious
society such as ours, I find that more and more people are using the courts as
a theatre for emotional catharsis. One wise old judge said, "With every ruling
you make a permanent enemy and a temporary friend." You never know when
a disgruntled litigant will explode (especially in family cases, where nerves are
rawest) and take out his or her frustrations on the spouse, the judge or some
official. In the U.S. in recent years, several judges have either been killed or
assaulted, and even in Canada "bench bashing" has become commonplace. I
try not to be intimidated, knowing such episodes of vengeance in our country
are rare, but I'm still chary of the disappointed litigant with the murderous
gleam in his eyes.

Your death was such a big discontinuity in my life that I wanted to distance
myself from it. Yes, I know we're all becoming habituated to the flyblown eyes
of children with distended bellies on TV and that death in its many guises
haunts our waking and dreaming hours, yet how often we turn our heads,
go about our daily amusements and obsessions. But each death is personal
and unique and that's the way yours affected me. More than anyone's – my
mother's, my father's, my sister's – your death sundered my heart and every
evening it's the one I see reflected in the mirror. I am constantly reminded of
you every time I hear the name "Niagara." I want to blot that accursed word
from my lexicon. And each day, like this fogbound Friday morning as I drive
to work along the Hanlon, I am reminded that this is the route you took
that sunny Palm Sunday in the New Yorker, your mind fixated on the death
you envisaged as the final solution for the pain you believed your continued
existence was inflicting on me and the children. Such days as this – on the
401 I could barely make out the electric pylons or the white toothy smile
of the Schneider kitchen maid in the abutting fields – remind me, too, of
the darkness that overshadowed your mind and led you to the Falls. Other
reminders abound: last week I was invited to our friends the Fishburns, who
were so kind to us after your death, to watch the movie *The Mission,* and when

the first scene unfolded — a Jesuit roped to a cross plunging over the rim of a high falls — I had to leave the room. Just last weekend, driving to Ruth's apartment along Hog's Back Road in Ottawa, the sight of the swollen yellow Rideau River cascading over huge boulders stiffened my whole body and made me turn my head away. When Dave Stewart rang the other day and I told him I was still writing these kaddishes he fell silent, no doubt dismayed that I was still brooding over you more than two years after your suicide, wondering if perhaps I'd turned morbid and was losing my grip. You can't short-circuit grief, I told him, and assured him that the road to Niagara was the road to sanity, that only by entering fully into the shadow and grief of my own heart could I ever banish the fear of living, find the fresh living waters beneath the rocks.

For the Healing of the Spirit

ca

Querencia, A SPANISH WORD THAT MEANS A LOVED PLACE TO WHICH ONE returns for healing of the spirit, sums up my feelings about Limerick Lake. When we crossed that invisible line at Madoc Friday evenings on the way to the cottage for the weekend or a holiday I could feel my preoccupations and cares drop away like old baggage and I was filled with a lightness of being, for I knew we were entering a realm where we could stretch our souls, forget the bustle of the world and re-create ourselves. Remember the roller-coaster rides on the bumpy St. Ola road, the contests to see who could hold their breath longest as we rolled through the hamlet and how we'd honk to announce to our neighbours at the lake that we were back in the promised land. My mind brims with happy recollections: the scent of cedar and pine resin, the sweet clang of cold spring water on the tongue, clouds sauntering across the belly of the lake, a heron sculling across the skyline above the marsh, cicadas spinning gauzes of sound in the evergreens, the shouts of children down at the water, cloud shadows shifting like a dark veil down the green hills and over the lake, the lake on windy days, bigger than Lake Ontario and more dangerous, the whitecaps leaping in line, spindrift blowing, the trips to the open field with the children to pick hawkweed, black-eyed Susans, wild roses, yarwood, phlox, yellow rocket and milkweeds – how we loved to pry open the seedpods and let the tiny silvery parachutes float away. And the dragonflies at evening, small helicopter gunships, their motors whirring, picking off flies and mosquitoes, and the rose, yellow and scarlet evening skies, the clouds taking on different shapes and hues, every sunset different; reading or playing cards or listening to music on the CBC on the side verandah, the yodel of loons, the croaking of frogs in the bay. And sitting in front of the blazing hearth at night, and later, after the children were asleep, making love in the bunkie – those were beautiful days and enchanted nights, when we winged from blossom to blossom and death was not even a speck on the horizon, that I'll remember all my days. My zen was the swinging boughs of pines; having slipped outside the thought stream I was able to make peace with my monkey-mind, stop building the cold house of my own devising – the narrow house of self, and enter, however fleetingly, the virginal timelessness of the stars.

Spirit House

Like water
through the bottom
of an old pail

or sunlight
through a torn
black coat

it catches you
by surprise,
the heart stalls,

you step out
of your body,
break into wings,

whirl
above the tips
of evergreens

till you ache
to touch
the bright, descending roof,

those nights
at Limerick Lake
when stars come out.

I'VE BEEN ALONE IN THIS BIG HOUSE FOR ALMOST A WEEK, FREE TO DAYDREAM to my heart's desire. This evening Marilyn dropped in to pick up one of your nudes – the painting you thought you'd ruined with the beige paper collage; she wants to hang it in her living room. "The house is so quiet and tidy," she observed. Naturally it's quiet and tidy, I reflected after she left; nothing is touched by human hands anymore; no one's here except me, floating around like a wraith amidst the dustprints and jangling hangers. Yes, I still make our bed every morning – you used to joke that it looked as if it made itself – and at dusk I stand in the sunroom and watch the black whirl of Canada geese honking over the house as they circle back to the waterfowl park. This place used to be like Grand Central Station, as you liked to put it, with seven kids streaking in and out, the slap of bare feet on hardwood floors every morning, the thrumming of never-ending showers (we were always running out of hot water, remember?), the asthmatic breathing of the rowing machine in the basement, Belle yelping, children bickering, your heavy clomp in the kitchen – I can still hear the pop of the toaster, the fridge door bang and the loud clack of cupboard doors, for you were rough with things, they were your enemy, the instruments of your enslavement – but most of all it's your ringing voice and hearty laughter on the phone I hear. Could I have ever imagined I'd miss the voice of Madonna from Joy's stereo blasting my eardrums at full volume? Now everything's different; our house is like an old abandoned Hollywood sound stage, full of old dreams and fading memories; sometimes I swear I can even hear the tinkling of falling dust. The wall clock in the foyer no longer ticks (I forget to wind it), the phone rarely rings, and when the front door chimes it's usually the paper boy to tell me I owe him money. Even your cherished plants are brown at the edges, droopy and moribund. The only sounds are the hum of the fridge, the splattering on the bathroom skylight on rainy nights, the rumble in the ductworks as the gas furnace kicks in and the joists creaking when the wind plays hide-and-seek in the attic. Occasionally the clap of a door in the middle of the night curdles my blood and makes me think you're still around and trying to tell me something. Sometimes I even imagine I hear your ghostly mouth breathing. As silence settles like snow over the house I lie awake and hear the thump, thump of my heart against the pillow and memories on little cat's feet creep into consciousness. Unlike you I'm a mediocre caretaker of people and things. This morning hoarfrost silvered the grass and the leaves of the harlequin maple scrunched into balls. A fly buzzed at the kitchen window, no doubt trying to escape into the great outdoors – a prisoner like me with nowhere to go. I took pity on her, raised the sash window and let her out. Our family has no listening skills. Nicole says; we jump from subject to subject, never finish a conversation. I feel that "unfinishedness" in my bones. Yes, I'm a work-in-progress in an unfinished house.

Fly

During the morning recess
the judge gazed from
his chambers
to the bleak November sky
above the Niagara mountain.

The two men had picked her up
on Jarvis Street,
drove to a field north
of the city;
afterward, the Crown said,
they slit her throat.

Observing the fly
on the windowpane trapped inside
the judge grabbed a newspaper
cocked his arm,
          then froze,
shocked at the violence
within him.

CR

Spent five days with Bruce, Mira's boyfriend, opening the cottage. The cottage is no longer the unqualified pleasure it used to be; now it triggers so many souvenirs of you and our happy times together as a family that I sometimes find it oppressive to be here. This year the lakefront is thick with saplings; Bruce, a graduate forestry engineer, named the trees for me: poplar, birch, maple, larch, spruce, balsam, red and white pine. The towering red pine next to the cottage — your favourite — looks sickly, lower branches bare, black and brittle, but Bruce says it'll probably live for years, survive us all. Remember the heated debates every spring over what trees to cut? I liked the wild natural look, the sensation of being soaked in greenness; you wanted to see more of the lake, create vistas, let in more light, and every year you'd badger me to chop down more trees. The argument never ended and if Norm or Doris or any of our other neighbours were in the vicinity they'd get conscripted reluctantly into taking sides. Most, being forest-tamers, wanted to curb nature's random and unpredictable ways and voted with you. When Bruce told me he preferred the wild look you can imagine how pleased I was: an ally at last. Sleeping in our bed rekindles memories of our cuddling on summer nights with the sky full of stars, only the plash of the waves on the shore and the sigh of the wind in the pines to mar the silence. While I read, Bruce spent most of his time (when we were not doing chores together) writing an interminable letter to your daughter Mira, and we both agreed that she is very special. One afternoon Bruce started to rummage in the bin where we keep the old toys and got me interested. It was like fishing in the past — Frisbees; crushed badminton racquets; an orange beach ball; wood building blocks; a scruffy tennis ball; a ping-pong bat made in Taiwan; a Barbie doll case; the Amazing Spiderman puzzle; a Tomi plastic clock with white buttons you pressed to make a bear, a rabbit or a lion pop out of a small aperture on its face; a section of a two-by-four that one of the girls covered with a brown flowered fabric to make a bed with pillows; etc. — relics and mementos of our bygone summers in a paradise that we thought would last forever. How frustrating to look at this detritus of our past, even old photos of you, and not be able to convey to strangers the depth of our feelings and what you meant to us. Mere words, no matter how artful, cannot bridge the gap, for all grief is private and ultimately incommunicable. Bruce found a coverless book, *This Is Your Life, Charlie Brown,* on which Mira had scribbled her name in blue ink, pencil and green crayon on the front page. "Look," he announced, "it's Mira's," as though he'd just discovered her hiding at the bottom of the bin. He also retrieved a Holly Hobbie doll with stiff red hair and brown smudges for eyes that twirled on top of a music box (Bruce identified the tune as "Music Box Dancer") and asked if it belonged to Mira and when I told him I thought it belonged to our redhead, Marilyn, he seemed disappointed.

The Yearning

This spring for the first time in thirty
years buds didn't appear on the paper

birch in the crevice of the rock by the shore.
Last summer it quaked like a young bride

in the breeze, swallows nested in the thick
dazzle of its green hair. Every April

it's worn the same hard appearance of death,
the empty spaces like the terrible longing

between people, but that has never stopped its
soft, fluent growth, the green-tipped nubbins,

then the pale yellow petals unfolding from
every twig. "The buds are always late,"

I say, touching a bare branch. My daughter
Ruth thinks I'm in denial. "Give up, Dad,

they're not coming back," she says. I kneel
on the rock, numbstruck, unwilling to disbelieve,

wondering how long I'll have to wait.

CR

THE SUBCONSCIOUS STIRS GROGGILY AND RUBS ITS EYES THIS MORNING.
Sometimes I feel like a grand inquisitor; not a day passes that I don't probe
the festering sore of your suicide. Mira says her memory of you is fading away
into a vast fuzzy space and that saddens me. I want you back to embrace, to
kiss, to tell you how much your absence hurts us. I want you back to atone
for all my failures, my insensitivity to your needs. You disappeared like a thief
in the night, no adieus, no note, no body, no closure – vanished without a
footprint as though you'd never walked on the earth, leaving behind a heap
of unfinished business for all of us. Yes, we had valid reason to be angry. My
heart sinks at the thought I'll never see you again. People with no religious
beliefs don't fret about the afterlife: the prospect of *nada* or pure extinction
doesn't upset them unduly; they've written off all hope of ever meeting loved
ones again as self-serving delusion, an ego trip. I'm not reconciled to the
tombstone facts of life, the idea that there is no life beyond this life. You
were always better than me at handling the jagged edges of reality. All my
life I've been an adept at finding refuge in the mind and imagination. How
often in exasperation did you not say that I had an uncanny ability to deny
what I found too hurtful to acknowledge? Did I turn a blind eye to the
clues that might have prevented your suicide? Is the scared boy inside me still
kicking and fighting for his life? Nicole challenges me all the time to drop my

defences. "You're a successful and powerful man," she constantly reminds me. "You don't need them anymore." The other day I got a wedding thank-you note from Paul and Gabriella that lifted my spirits; Paul wrote that after your suicide I became the lightning rod for the family's wrath. "We always want to hurt the one we love," he said, and wanted me to know how grateful he and his sisters were for the example we gave as parents.

Yesterday I finally got around to cleaning out the rest of your things from the bathroom cupboards: a pink puff encrusted with white powder; Johnson's foot soap, which promises to soak away foot misery; your black shower cap; two half-filled prescription containers; corn cushions; Dr. Scholl's lambswool for the toes; two bottles of Algicon; a prescription for heartburn and stomach acid (which surprised me as I was unaware you had such problems); two bottles of Natural Styling perm lotion and neutralizer; a Beauty Salon, "all you need for beautiful skin and nails"; etc. I gathered everything up in a green plastic bag and tossed it in the garbage. Next I'll have to tackle your dresses and hats in the closet; every time I see them they revive painful associations. Yes, Mira helped me to see: you must fade into a memory if we are to live our lives, we must learn to let you go, give you your freedom to be dead and accept our freedom to be alive.

Vestiges

"Get rid of everything,"
friends said
after the memorial service
where we hung your portrait
in the sanctuary
to keep your memory warm.
O how we tried,
ransacking closets and drawers,
hauling boxes of dresses, blouses,
coats, sweaters, shoes
to the Sally Ann,

stuffing dark green garbage bags
with leftovers of a lifetime,
hoping to forget forever
our failure
to love you back
to life.

But like flotsam
from a drowned wreck
particles of you
keep washing up on shore;
yesterday
I opened a bathroom
drawer to find:
brown bobby pin,
pink puff encrusted with powder,
three corn cushions,
black shower cap,
three old prescription bottles
– grains of grief,
sifting into nooks
and dreams,
burying you
over and over.

CR

I ENTER THE DREAM CIRCLE AND THE DREAMS UNFOLD.

1

I search for the wedding
ring: under the bed, the closet, the cabinet
in the washroom — even the rumpled bedclothes —
but it's nowhere to be found. I can't even
remember what it looks like. When the nurse
comes in we go through the dresser drawers
together: an old nightgown (the top torn),
a pair of soiled white gloves, one onyx earring,
a broken rosary, her Bulova watch still ticking,
a brush with three loops of red hair, a journal,
some entries torn out, but no ring.
I wonder if someone has stolen it.

2

I see her coming down the centre aisle
of the church; she's smiling and in a rush as
usual, dressed in yellows, duns, russet
reds, the colours of autumn, her
favourite season. I wave but she
pretends not to notice. Suddenly it
strikes me that I've been the victim of
a black joke, that she faked everything,
and knew all long that sooner or later
I'd find out.

3

I have a speaking engagement at Niagara Falls.
The city is beautiful, a wide main street with
19th-century architecture and a postcard view
of the Falls in the distance. I try to leave the city
but get snarled in a traffic jam. I get as far as the 401
when a parade of marching strikers slows down traffic.
Mary materializes out of nowhere and we talk about
our plans for the future. She seems interested and I
grow hopeful, as though I was being given a second
chance.
"Then, you're not going to the Falls," I say, thinking
she's changed her mind.
"Yes, I am," she replies, calm and resolute.
"Why, Mary, why? Please don't."
"There's nothing you can do about it," she says.

4

Smoke engulfs the motel. The children
are inside but it's too late, heat
singes my skin, flames shimmy
up the walls. She bolts towards the
entrance — I grab her sleeve but she breaks
free, dives into the tumbling inferno. The last
I see of her, she's running across a window,
hair on fire, a child in her arms.

CR

LIKE THE CELLS OF OUR BODY EVERYTHING CHANGES, INCLUDING THE COTTAGE. I've cleared some of the hemlock, cedars and small brush to improve the view of the lake, built a large floating dock, installed a wall furnace, bought a new boat, and this year replaced the shingles with a new metal insulated roof. When Marilyn, little Mira and I got to the cottage last week the workmen were still hammering on the roof and the interior of the cottage was sprinkled with dust and bits and pieces of grey and black shingle that had fallen through the cracks of the roof boards. Sheets of white Styrofoam covered with blue plastic, piles of two-by-four spruce and chipboard, aluminum ladders, stacks of metal roofing cluttered the ground and I had to park down the driveway and lug Mira and groceries to the cottage through damp air teeming with mosquitoes. The screech of circular saws, pounding of hammers, and rattle of aluminum ladders scraped our ears, and Marilyn looked disappointed as she'd counted on four or five days of peace and sunshine and birdsong. But once the workmen left we set to work and vacuumed the entire cottage and it turned out to be a pleasant week. Every day we swam in the cool satiny lake. Oh, how you would have loved your granddaughter, who bears an uncanny resemblance to you as a child and reminds me of the children when they were young. She made friends with a couple of nervy chipmunks with miniscule hands for feet and dark brown stripes down their tan backs who helped themselves to peanuts in the shell from her palm and stuffed so many in their mouths their cheeks expanded like storage bins. Gord Kelly came up for the day and we talked about loss, how difficult it is to accept that we will never see you or his daughter Denise again, that the seeds of love could take root, only to be torn up and never come to fruition. One evening before turning in I went into the bedroom off the kitchen to wish Marilyn goodnight to find her in tears. "What's wrong?" I asked. "I just can't help it," she said, "just being in the cottage and remembering all the fun times we had makes me sad." She pointed to your floppy leather hat (that made you look so hippie-ish) and your tattered orange housecoat that you wore every morning when you sipped coffee in the sun on the back porch. Sometimes she imagines she hears your loud high-spirited laughter as you bustle about the kitchen preparing sandwiches for a picnic or glimpses you on the sofa, a glass of sherry in your hand, bathed in the coppery rays of the setting sun. Dispossessed of our bodies, we soon become dispossessed of our memories in the minds of the living. Who will remember Mac or Teetaw, my mom and dad, or my sister Shirley in a few years when memories fade? Who will remember you when we're gone? Who will deliver me from the toxin of forgetfulness that makes us all invisible? Is love a divine trick, a leap of vanity? Are these kaddishes my way of making time stand still, stopping the flow of the Lethean waters? A freeze-frame of our life? De Mello writes that our natural state is to be happy — a happiness that can survive the loss of loved ones provided we become aware, learn to live the moment fully. Awareness is all.

Lord, help me to remember.

Beloved

I love the smell of woodsmoke,
the smooth skin of stones,
the shape of babies' toes;
I loved
                your clear eyes too
where I could see forever,
their gentle "yes" to all;
I won't accept
        they've fallen
            into
                the
                    deep
                        down
                            blue
beyond my ken.
Love is like death
                only longer.

CR

LAST WEEK AT THE COTTAGE MARGARET, MARILYN'S NEIGHBOUR AND FRIEND who was here with her two boys, said she and her husband barely speak to each other, have very little intimacy. With pre-schoolers, housework, meals, art classes twice a week, etc., and her husband working long backbreaking hours as a stonemason each day and even longer hours in the evenings poring over math and physics texts in preparation for teacher's college, there's never enough time, she said. Her grouse was a hidden cry for help. Without intimacy marriages becomes little more than two strangers cohabiting under the same roof. The times I remember best were our intimate get-togethers in the kitchen before dinner, chatting about the events of the day over a glass of sherry — you filling me in on the minutiae of the children's lives, me telling you about the small dramas of the office, even getting a little tipsy sometimes and splitting our sides with laughter and when the children barged in as they often did to ask about dinner they wouldn't wait for an answer for they knew we were having fun and loved to see us happy together. Yes, I regret that we didn't spend more quality time together like that. Maybe if we had you might have been able to withstand the onslaught of loneliness. And I remember, too, those warm and lucid summer mornings at the cottage when the lake, smooth and clear as glass, held a mirror to the green hills and blue sky and the mist still burning off the surface under the blindingly white sun as we canoed along the quiet shoreline, the other cottagers still in bed, the only sound the drips from our raised paddles and the loons sailing on the rim of the shimmering horizon and smallmouth bass darting across the coppery sun-webbed rocks — oh, how we loved our little Eden in the mornings, immersed in the seamless spaciousness of the moment, the weight of the past fallen away, the anxieties of the future blanked out, each moment a small death and rebirth, never to be repeated again. "This is too much," you'd whisper. "We're so privileged." How I hated to see the dull day roll in and feel the sweaty hand of the noonday sun — the vision lost, the miracle forgotten until the redeeming night returned with its trillion candles and brought the shining moment back.

Early summer morning at the lake. The children are asleep. You and I are sitting on the small back stoop to catch the sun, the only warm spot at the cottage at this hour. We're sipping coffee, the mugs are warm in our hands. We hear the clack of Doris's screen door; she's an early riser, but the mosquitoes and blackflies are still in bed. The air is limpid and fresh; I can almost taste greenness on my tongue. Sunlight catches the night's cobwebs under the eaves, transfiguring them into delicate necklaces of light. Dew sparkles in the long grass, stillness hugs the earth like a soft cloth. A monarch flits among the black-eyed Susans and blueweed looking for a place to land; a chipmunk pauses on the deck, stares at us for a moment with alert, beady eyes, and then scurries away under the cottage. Only the faint hum of a passenger jet overhead, the chirp of a chickadee and the gauzy sound of cicadas breaks the silence. I feel peaceful and loving, touch you on the cheek; you look at me and smile. "I'm so thankful for the gift of life, Jim," you say.

℞

JUNG SAYS DREAMS ARE THE DOOR TO THE SUBCONSCIOUS AND HEALTHY, but when I wake exhausted after a troubling dream I sometimes wonder. Obviously there's lots of life in my basement, an assortment of ghosts who like to tramp around in different disguises while I sleep. Monday the sky was overcast and it rained, not heavily, but in gusts. When I reached the 401 the eastern sun tinted the water beads on the windshield pale gold and a ribbon of starlings sheered off above the highway as if yanked by a long string. For the first time I noticed the McDonald's arches at the far side of a field — a field I passed every day — south of the Schneider neon; why hadn't I seen the yellow monstrosity before? Tuesday on the Hanlon the fiery hoop of the sun rolled over the tops of the woods and barns and raced me all the way to the 401, the tassels of the tall cornstalks burned in the morning sun and of course there were the customary night casualties splattered on the highway: the brownish red smear of a groundhog on the shoulder, a squirrel flattened on the asphalt, its tail sticking up like a black flag; and at Wellington County Road 34, just before the 401 a yellow school bus, smashed and smoking, leaned up against a light standard, and a little farther south a cream-coloured Chrysler, its crumpled nose in the ditch, front doors ajar, and nearby a black predator tow truck waiting for a man on the shoulder to stop taking photos of the wreckage before pouncing. As I approached Milton, mist hung in alternating dark and light bands on the flank of the escarpment and for some inexplicable reason, like an elegy I never stop revising, Dad edged his way into my consciousness again.

Flying Home Through the Dark

Once Dad got a bee in his bonnet:
the time was ripe for my two sisters

and me to learn a lesson or two about
farming. He was taking us back, he

said, to the old homestead north of
Bobcaygeon to visit Mom and Pop,

the elderly Presbyterian couple he
went to work for when his widowed

mother shipped him off to Canada
at thirteen (there was no future for

him on the mean streets of Belfast,
she'd decided). "Mom and Pop will

be glad to meet you," he mumbled
over the twist of rutted roads

north of Lindsay in Pat O'Hara's
Ford jalopy, my sisters and me

bouncing on the prickly fabric of the
back seat, Dad and Pat up front

taking turns snorting from
a bottle of Johnny Walker,

Dad waxing more eloquent with each
passing mile about the virtues of the

simple life. "You grow up fast on a
farm," he said as he reminisced about

Pete and Bess, the team of family Belgians,
the belled and furrowed fields, milking

the herd by hand, bucking hay in the barn, and
in an eye's blink (or so it seemed),

there we were in the barn,
slivers of sunlight slicing through

the gloom, wind whistling
between the chinks, hay dust

itching up our nostrils and I'm looking
at Dad high up the hayloft ladder, almost

invisible ("I'll show you how it's done,"
he'd said), Pop's warning "Take it easy,

Sam," caroming off the cavernous walls,
when suddenly he slips and falls, comes

crashing down hitting the floorboards hard,
the good white shirt Mom had bought

especially for the occasion stained
and torn. That evening, the wheezy hulk

on the side of the highway, stalled, Dad and
Pat in the back seat, passed out, my two

sisters hunkered in the corner, I climbed
behind the wheel (a chip off the old daredevil

himself, Dad would later brag) my feet
barely touching the floor, my first

blind lesson, flying home through the dark.

The Grace of God Is the Glue

&

267

SOMETIMES IT'S GOOD TO SHIFT THE MIND INTO NEUTRAL, STOP THE BUZZ, let senses, feelings, thoughts flow untrammelled through the brain. Last Friday on the drive to court in Owen Sound I did it: no radio, just the onrushing landscape and the blips that strayed onto my mental radar screen. Before leaving Guelph the new girl at MacDonald's with long blond hair and braces overcharged me a second day in a row. After, she smiled sheepishly and apologized. "You'd better watch out," I chided her, half in jest, "someone might turn you in." Waiting for a light change at the Hanlon a crow flapped in front of the van, so close its wings almost grazed the windshield and uh-oh, I said to myself as the clumsy creature flew away, bad luck for sure. On the Hanlon the two tall silver stacks of a tractor cab spewed plumes of dark oily smoke into the air and for some strange morbid reason Bergen-Belsen sprang to mind and every puff became a Jew. As I drove north across old rural Ontario – Fergus, Arthur, Kennilworth, Mount Forest, Durham, Dornock, Williamsford, Chatsworth (home of Nellie McClung) – no one was astir, only the white glare of headlights pointing south, people like beige moths returning to their beige jobs in the cities, and recollections of rural Thailand (where I'd visited our daughter Mira) popped into my head; how at this early hour the dusty roads were already clogged with animals, buses, pedestrians, workers, etc., most heading for the rice paddies and a day of back-breaking labour in the scorching sun where temperatures sometimes reached 140 degrees Celsius by noon, how instead of black-clad peasants with straw conical hats bent double over flat empty fields, the rolling hills of Ontario were dotted with huge barns, massive red and green farm machinery, and cows and sheep, horses, gulls, etc., munching and pecking the dark brown earth. Overhead, turkey buzzards wheeled in the solid grey sky. As I passed the Highlander restaurant in Fergus I experienced a jab of nostalgia – remember we lunched there once after buying an antique pine dry sink at the local market? Almost anywhere I travel it's the same: someone or something triggers memories of you and our life together.

Last evening as we reminisced around the dinner table, Ruth recalled the time Paul said something that infuriated you and you slapped him on the cheek hard, then stalked away but not before you took another swipe at him but missed, smacking your hand against the wall instead. You paid for your hot temper that time, remember, had to wear a sling for a week. But the children also recalled your countless acts of caring and generosity: the time Belle chewed off the ear of Ruth's beloved stuffed monkey and how the next day you went out and bought some beige terrycloth and sewed the ear back on (a little outsized, as it turned out), small, ordinary acts, but expressions of love that made the children feel cherished. How often did I not exhort you to set aside time each day after the children were in school to do some artwork in the basement studio, but with your supermom complex you rarely got around to it. One of the highlights of your artistic life was the week you spent at Trosly-Breuil sketching for our book *L'Arche Journal*, an account of our family's year at L'Arche, published by Griffin House in 1973. You came back with a batch of beautiful sketches and you always said that that week was one of the happiest times of your life. Alas, such opportunities were few. Duties devoured all your spare time (you would have argued you had no spare time). Unlike me, you were never selfish enough to give priority to your own needs and in hindsight maybe that was a mistake. You confused serving with loving and eventually became isolated from the essence of yourself. You were a poor guardian of your solitude. And if, as the poet Rilke says, the highest task for two people in a relationship is to stand guard over the solitude of the other, be a sanctuary for the other's growth, then I failed you, too. Later, when the children left home to attend university and the nest started to empty and you tried to rekindle your interest in art it was never the same and you felt lost and adrift. At the end, when the Black Dog closed in, your religion proved a frail cudgel to ward off the furies who accused you of denying a vital part of your soul to please others. Did you come to believe your life was a waste?

Last night I had one of those conflictual dreams that never seem to end. I don't remember all the details except that when I woke up and fell asleep again the conflict pursued me and I couldn't shake it off. One detail sticks in my memory: all my teeth loosened at the same time – their roots unhinged like leaves in October – and began to crumble in my mouth, filling it with gritty bits of enamel that made it impossible for me to speak properly: all my words came out garbled. Though I didn't know why this was happening I hesitated to spit out the pieces lest I never recover them again. In desperation I finally willed myself awake to discover, with great comfort, that it was only a dream. Since you left I've often felt that my life has broken into a thousand pieces and that I will never glue them back together again.

CR

LAST EVENING I WATCHED A BRITISH DOCUMENTARY ON VISION TV: "THERE but for the Grace of God," the story of three men and a woman who were saddled with guilt in their personal lives. The woman, who had had a rigid religious upbringing, couldn't forgive herself for having killed a young girl who darted out in front of her car. Though blameless, she remained steeped in guilt, convinced God was out to punish her. That she had a daughter about the same age as the victim only sharpened her feelings of anguish and regret. A young man, a machinist whose failure to use a safety shield led to the death of a co-worker – the victim had persuaded him the shield could be dispensed with – could only purge his conscience by returning to the job site and working at the same machine. A social worker who neglected to follow up on her suspicion that one of her charges was at risk – the five-year-old boy was subsequently tortured and murdered by his sadistic foster parent – tried to exorcize her feelings of culpability by teaching others about child abuse. In the fourth case, a professional comedian with a paralyzed wife failed to check her bath – an oversight that had never happened before in their fifteen years together – and she accidentally drowned. After a long struggle he finally learned to forgive himself and wrote a book about their life together. After your suicide a wild pack of "if only"s assailed me. If only I had stayed home that weekend instead of traipsing off to visit friends; if only I'd been more sensitive to your condition; if only I'd been more emotionally present during our marriage; if only I'd been a better person – a long indictment pointing to one devastating conclusion: if I'd acted differently you might be alive today. "Life breaks us all and afterward many are strong in the broken places," Hemingway wrote; I feel like one of the others for my spirit is still riven with guilt. But I know that I can't live with the "if only"s forever. When Gaby took care of us during the war I could never measure up to her standards. No matter how well I did at school – if I got 98 per cent in math, Gaby would shrug her thin, bony shoulders and inform me that her nephew in Quebec always got perfect – I developed an inferiority complex and came to believe that anything less than perfection was unacceptable. Like the woman in the documentary, why can't I shake this false guilt, admit my fallibility and forgive myself? Perhaps I'm looking for a place of unclouded perfection, a cloud-cuckoo-land that doesn't exist. As I type these words I'm reminded that it was me who willingly got up in the small hours during the infancy of our two youngest when they needed a bottle or change of diapers so that you could get an unbroken night's rest – not much, granted, to brag about yet a breakthrough nonetheless from our familiar roles. Sometimes I think my self-scrutiny is too harsh, that I should become a better wife to myself, kinder and more forgiving, ease up a little, learn to laugh gently at my foibles and shortcomings, accept myself as God accepts me. As I am. When blame is problematic, why do we continue to lash ourselves with those accursed words "if only"?

CR

ON THE WAY TO COURT THIS MORNING THE SUN FIRST APPEARED AS GOLDEN semi-circle above the tree line; next time I glanced up the sky had turned pearly and the sun had become a silvery hazy ball. Kelso Lake had a cold forbidding look. The water has been lowered for winter, exposing the bleached rocks; the blue windsurfers and green canoes have been stored away, the sandy beach bleak and deserted. When I entered my chambers two delightful surprises awaited me: the hibiscus Adele gave me four months ago that I'd thought was dying had given birth overnight to a single bloom – dark core, five finely veined red petals and cone of yellow pollen crowned with five red-tipped spokes. I never know when the hibiscus will bloom and when it happens it catches me off guard, takes my breath away – a resurrection. When Adele was here a couple of weeks ago she was amazed it was still alive. "You're lucky," she told me. "These plants don't usually live more than two or three months." The second surprise occurred when I looked out my office window: a big glossy crow was perched on the top of yellowing foliage of a maple pointing his sleek head this way and that like a princeling in a castle surveying his kingdom.

Nature like sweet warm rain softens my soul.

Winter Prayer

When we arrive the lake
is muffled in glass; overnight

earth finds a new language; pine
boughs breathe white words,

mica shavings carol in the air;
black-hooded chickadees spin and

whirl on invisible threads from
cedars to Palma's feeder, gorging

on oilseed. Rodrique says they
stay all winter, sheltering from

the cold in the angles of the limbs.
I gaze at the stars shivering

in their deep blue caves. How long
O Lord before your sun's reborn,

my frozen heart is thawed?

○3

MORNINGS HAVE AN ILLUSORY QUALITY; THE LIFE I SEE, HEAR, SMELL, TASTE, touch sometimes seems surreal, a prolongation of a dream and death is the dream master casting a make-believe aura over the beauty and commonplaces that parade before me: the jogger in the red outfit, long blond hair tossing in the wind; street lamps shutting their orange eyes after an all-night vigil; election signs proliferating like dandelions everywhere; shifting skyscapes; the balding irascible storeowner at the 24-hour convenience store where I buy my *Globe* and coffee most mornings, who whistles cheerful ditties all day but never ceases to grumble about business and the unfairness of life – all appear like stage scenery in some Neverland drama; and always the sun, the metaphor of the extraordinary, in its various costumes, strutting overhead. If I could peek behind the props what would I see? Angels crouching behind a rock, birds of paradise carolling in the sun? Or perhaps just an abyss, black and unfathomable? You tried to make sense of this death-mystery by being a person for others and asking Jesus to help you, but it didn't work; you lost your bearings and without them your grip on life. Like death the highway intimidates us: as I approached the 401 off the Hanlon this morning I noticed that the traffic was stalled in the westbound lane. When I got to the bottom of the ramp I spotted the trouble: a yellow tractor-trailer, smoke billowing from its engine, lay on its side beneath the underpass, the driver, a man with dark curly hair, slumped behind the wheel, evidently trapped, and a little farther away on the shoulder a sedan, its front end crumpled like blue foil. A police officer stood in the centre of the highway waving the curious onlookers on. Most of us refuse to believe we'll fall victim to one of life's dirty tricks or that false guilt can dog our every step. Andre Dubus, in *Broken Vessels*, writes about the time his daughter Madeline lost the end of her index finger when she poked her hand into the sprocket of an exercise bike her sister Candice was peddling. Candice blamed herself for the mishap and he tried to convince her it wasn't her fault, that false guilt can corrode the soul, that she shouldn't feel guilty. When will I learn to forgive myself for all the missed connections in my life; my absences for the final journeys of you, my father, my sister?

ଓ

ON THE HANLON THIS MORNING A RENT APPEARED IN THE GREY SKY, revealing a swath of pale blue and an arrowhead of nine Canada geese pointing south; rose and gold tinged the horizon where the sun was hiding. I had the bizarre sensation of driving upside down, a fly on the ceiling, that the substantial world was not the cold yellowing earth below, but the shifting skyscape above. After the party for Adele's 30th birthday last night – a warm, happy event – I felt alone in the empty house – a big letdown. I felt your absence keenly, but I'm still angry at you for turning our lives upside down, casting a cloud of sadness over us. If you had known the sharp debris your suicide would leave behind would you have done it, I wonder? At moments like this the insulation of time comes unstuck and your absence surges back like a powerful gale blowing shards of Catholic guilt before it. But today I kept busy: paid bills, did laundry, watched the constitutional debate in French and went to bed early. In the morning I noticed the red and yellow geraniums on the deck were frost-browned and at the edges along the roadside the wildflowers withered and drooping, reminders that I would soon have to put away the garden furniture. Our annual Thanksgiving dinner at the cottage with the neighbours, a tradition you started, is cancelled this year because of the growing number of people involved. Instead we'll have a get-together beforehand for drinks and then each family will hold their own private celebration – a realistic decision, I think, but yet another reminder that nothing stays the same.

Flux

Under the melting snow
a red tricycle takes shape,

apple blossoms, lighter
than the blue silk sky,

stream before my eyes;
seasons come and go,

but no matter how gently
I touch the rose the petals

will fall, the soft circle
round the fire will break and

leaf by leaf the darkening
trees grow cold;

the long goodbyes never
seem to cease, nothing

stays the same or whole.

CR

THERE'S ALWAYS SOMETHING ON THE HIGHWAY TO JAR MY PEACE OF soul. On the way to court this morning a black Ford pickup gunned past me and honked after I'd turned onto the Hanlon; the driver, a bearded young man wearing a black baseball cap, gave me the finger. I guess he didn't like the way I made the turn. Though I had nothing to feel guilty about (the turn was proper) he got my dander up, but when I tried to dispense the finger back I was too slow off the mark and didn't catch his eye. I find it troubling and humiliating that I, a judge, a reputed paragon of good sense and self-control (not to mention pillar of law and order) can't always rein in my own temper, can allow road rage to gain the upper hand. One step forward, two steps back seems to be the pattern, and despite my earnest efforts to change I constantly fall into the same trap. Which proves the old Adam is still alive and well. Why do I feel so intensely? Perhaps weakness isn't such a bad thing. How else can we trample our towering pride underfoot unless we recognize our radical vulnerability and need for God? You labelled me a benevolent dictator and maybe because I was benevolent, at least most of the time, I couldn't comprehend the dictator part. My outbursts, though blustery, were always short-lived and quickly repented. Like the time I exploded at Paul, who'd left our brand-new Sportspal canoe at the dock overnight (I had specifically instructed him to pull it onshore), and a storm blew up overnight and battered it against the dock, punching holes and denting the thin-gauged aluminum hull. "You blithering idiot!" I yelled, and when he, pale and shaky, slunk off to find asylum in some corner of the cottage you jumped to his defence. "Don't be so hard on the boy," you flared, "it's only a goddam boat." Afterward I felt bad, found him and apologized. Remember the rainy night I let Paul, who had just gotten his temporary license, drive the Olds station wagon home from Toronto – the fancy one with all the bells and whistles? The pavement was slick and treacherous and though I'd warned him to slow down he slammed into the van ahead with a decal on the back window: PROUD TO BE MOHAWK. While the van was barely scratched, the impact crumpled the front end of the Olds, but it was still drivable. That evening, I'm proud to say, I kept human under stress and didn't chew him out for his stupidity for I could see he was upset and shaking and I didn't want to add to his misery. The driver of the van, a swarthy man in his 30s with a long ponytail, spoke to us. "It's a bad night, these things happen," he said gently. And when we were about to leave and he noticed the keys in my hand he approached me and whispered, "Let your boy drive home." I was impressed. Paul drove home that night and I never mentioned the accident again. I realized I'd just met a wise man.

CR

I READ SOMEWHERE THAT WE MAKE A BEELINE FOR THE PLACE OF OUR pain, end up writing about the thing we least want to write about. Is this where these maunderings are leading? Nicole keeps chipping away at the soft joints in the invisible wall around my heart, hoping I'll discover why I often take flight when the going gets tough. This morning the Hanlon was a long, straight tunnel that led the eye to a semi-circle of light at the end; the faint yellow and pinkish clouds reminded me of water and for a moment I imagined the Falls lit up at night – an eerie feeling, especially as I knew that this was the same route you took that Palm Sunday. The wind had stripped bare the line of maples outside my window at work: a wide river of yellow leaves made a papery rustle on the asphalt in the parking lot. Since your death I've become acutely aware of the life-and-death cycle of the seasons. After a visit to the hospital that last week, Adele said you looked different, "post-traumatic," a "shell" of your former self were her words and I had strongly disagreed, arguing that you were on the mend, looking better. Were you just a great actress or was this another instance of my need to shape the world to my heart's desire? To escape the lightning of Simcoe Street I'd hunker down in some corner of the imagination to wait out the storm. I remember the crushing feeling of helplessness and panic. Is that when I turned into a roadrunner, began to lean on God, the ultimate security blanket? Maybe my reaction in the hospital was an unbearable reminder of those days when the tenement was a tattered tent on a desolate hill and I could feel the chill of the universe in my bones.

Stolen Days

Stealing out the side door,
I'd hike to Jackson's Creek,
skip pebbles on the pond, wade
in muddy feet, clutch
at minnows darting past.

I'd dive from the yellow rocks,
under the tall oak I'd lie, counting
acorns in the grass.
I'd gaze at ropes of cloud
across the sky.

At sun fall I'd walk the gleaming rails,
peek inside the mail slot, wait
till it was late,
sneak upstairs and close
my lids like stones, listen
to the sleepers, wondering
when they'd wake.

☙

YESTERDAY THE VAN SUDDENLY SPUTTERED TO A HALT ON THE EASTBOUND ramp leading into Milton. When I lifted the hood, steam billowed in my face from the oil-splattered engine and a malodorous burnt smell filled my nostrils.

I had to hitch a ride to a nearby garage and phone Brian, my mechanic, for a tow. Later he rang the office: "I've got bad news for you, Jim," he said. "The motor's fucked." And then the bomb: "It'll cost three to four grand to fix." As if I needed another setback! In a civil trial that morning a husband testified about a freak accident: he was following a 1980 Omni, his wife beside him in the front seat, when the clutch assembly of the Omni suddenly exploded, sending a small piece of metal through his windshield into his wife's skull. Now his wife was permanently brain-damaged, confined to a wheelchair, unable to speak, he said, tears streaming down his face. Another random inexplicable tragedy that reminded me again that I wasn't alone, that sooner or later bad things happen to everyone; it helped get my own problems into perspective. In the afternoon I phoned Brian, told him I'd decided to tow the van back to Guelph and get it repaired by a friend of Paul's, who specialized in Mazdas. I was pleased how calm and collected I remained; since your suicide I don't sweat trivia as much as I used to; somehow your death has made my everyday reverses seem like pinpricks, not worth getting too excited about. How I wish some of that calm would spill over to the children.

This evening I watched part of the Sue Rodriguez appeal before the Supreme Court on CBC *Newsworld*. She was seeking to have the law against assisted suicides struck down as contrary to section 7 of the Charter, wanting the right to control her own body and the time and circumstance of her death, and because she was too physically disabled to terminate her own life argued that the law – neither suicide nor attempted suicide are unlawful – discriminated against her. Since your suicide I have great empathy for people like Sue who've lost all hope and want to die. Without the support of loved ones (even with it, sometimes) life must be bleak and unbearable. A person should have the right to refuse defibrillations, intubation, ventilation equipment, syringes loaded with medications and all the other modern paraphernalia that often amount to a cruel prolongation of physical life when there is no reasonable hope of a meaningful one. The incurably ill should be allowed to die naturally without such artificial supports. How I regret that I allowed my own mother to suffer so much her last days! But I also believe that a law that would enlist doctors and others to assist in the killing of the sick would establish a dangerous precedent. If such a law had been on the books when you fell ill and decided to take your own life and you had been totally disabled, I could have taken you to Niagara and pushed you into the Falls. Armed with an exonerating letter from you, I might have argued with a clear conscience and perhaps legal impunity that you needed assistance, that I was only acting as an angel of mercy to save you from unspeakable agony. The very thought makes me shudder.

CR

TWO EVENINGS AGO I SAW MEL GIBSON'S MOVIE *The Man Without a Face*, THE story of an unhappy teenager who meets a lonely schoolteacher – half the man's face was disfigured in a car accident that took the life of one of his students – and how both learn trust and self-respect. In a fit of pique the teenager's half-sister blurts out the family's dark secret: how his alcoholic father, one of his mother's many husbands, died by his own hand in a mental institution, and the revelation crushes him; his faith in adults and the world is almost destroyed and it's only through his involvement with the teacher – himself wounded and still guilt-ridden over the death of his passenger – that his trust in himself and others is restored. The children loved and trusted you, I loved and trusted you, your many friends loved and trusted you, but when you jumped into the Falls that Palm Sunday you dealt us all a grievous blow; you rejected us and left us with feelings of sorrow, betrayal and anger. Pain made time stand still and we were struck numb, like people must feel when an earthquakes cracks the crust of the earth or the air turns hot and black before a twister. The children were devastated. Paul, who had had previous bouts of depression and knew its tentacles, and the others as well must have wondered if there wasn't some rogue gene running through the family that would make them all vulnerable.

A few months after you took your life I got a call late one Saturday evening from the Guelph General Hospital informing me that Joy was in Emergency, unconscious. As I drove to the hospital that night I couldn't quell my anxieties; horrible thoughts ransacked my brain: Was she on drugs? Did she overdose? Would she die? and I felt a mounting anger towards you for I knew that whatever had happened was somehow connected to your suicide. At the hospital a tall smiley-faced nurse, clipboard in hand, approached me. "Are you Joy's father?" she grinned and when I nodded (my tongue was frozen) she smiled and told me that Joy had regained consciousness and that she was going to be okay. "It looks like she had too much to drink," she said. I was so relieved I felt like hugging her on the spot. As she was coming to, the nurse told me, Joy kept mumbling, "Please don't tell my dad." Then the nurse led me into a makeshift ward, drew aside the grey plastic curtain and there was Joy on a gurney, looking wan and groggy. "Please take me home," she said, eyelids half shut. "I don't like it here." I wasn't angry, just happy she was out of danger but sad, too, because of all the things that had happened to change our lives. I filled out some forms, thanked the nurse and drove home. Next morning a young police officer appeared at the door; he wanted to ask Joy some questions and I had to coax her to come down in her pink nightgown to talk to him. Looking ashamed and chastened she responded to the officer's questions in a thin hesitant voice. When I mentioned your suicide the officer became flustered, snapped his black notebook shut, put his peaked cap back on and as he backed out the front door almost apologetically thanked us for our co-operation and that was the end of the visit.

Frederick Buechner, in his childhood memoir, *Sacred Journey*, tells about his father who believed, like you, that he was a failure and had to do away with himself for the sake of the family. It took Buechner years to acknowledge openly the suicide – his dad's successful younger brother had also taken his own life – and it was only his deep delight in living and a sense of God breaking through Time to speak to him that saved him from being sucked into the whirlpool of sadness and despair. I, too, pray for those moments of insight when the river slows and deepens and out of the dark depths timelessness breaks through to assure us that all is not lost, that love is stronger than death and that someday God will gather us all together within the circle of his loving care.

The Fire

In the dream he walked across the field
under the palest, silken blue, past

the tall sweet corn, all the way to
the big pond where he dug a trench, circled

it with rocks, gathered bark, wood shavings
twigs, coniferous seed cones, dead

wood, branches for fuel; then, as dusk
descended and fireflies came out he

built a pyre that lit up pond and sky, and
wife, child, mother, father, sister, grand-

parents, relatives, old friends, none dead,
none absent, joined him at the fire,

dark faces polished with love, no one
speaking, as though everyone was seeing

each other for the first time, shriven and
accepted as they'd always dreamed, eyes

picked clean by the long patience of death.

CR

A THUNDERCLAP STARTLED ME AWAKE THIS MORNING; AMID RUMBLINGS that sounded like the moving of big tractors, rain pelted the skylight and cold moist air gusted through the open bathroom window. By the time I backed out of the driveway the rain had stopped and the street had taken on a pinky sheen; a freshness braced the air as though the city had just brushed its teeth with Aquafresh. On the Stone Road the sun glowed, an orange ball on the hazy horizon, and when I reached the Hasty Market the ball was three quarters hidden and later, on the Hanlon, it had completely vanished behind a screen of cloud. At the Schneider sign on the 401 a white Chrysler LeBaron swept past me and the driver tossed a Styrofoam cup out the window and as I watched it skip and whipsaw across the pavement my blood level rose. Leaning on the horn I fantasized that I was a cop pulling the driver over to give him a piece of my mind: "It's idiots like you who are giving the planet a bad name," the cop in me shouted, imagining the intimidated look on the driver's face, his grovelling response. "Honest, officer, I don't know what got into me, I promise I'll never to do it again." It was a day of petty vexations. Earlier, when I'd gone to McDonald's for an Egg McMuffin I found the door locked – it was 6:29 a.m. and I could see the attendants inside lazing about in no rush to open. When Ruth came home a few weeks ago she flew into a rage, accused Paul, Joy and me of neglecting Kody, not taking her on regular walks (true), not loving her enough (untrue). "You're a bunch of lazy bums!" she yelled. Then she added: "If anything happens to Kody I think I'll kill myself," which sent a chill through me. "Look," she said later, "I've only been in the house a few minutes and she's happier already." Since your suicide Ruth's focused her love on Kody; the dog for her has become the symbol of unconditional love and loyalty. Last evening around ten while I was undoing Kody's chain fastener she broke loose again and streaked out of the yard into the woods. For an hour I searched everywhere, but no Kody. Wayne, my neighbour, noticed my distress, looped his arm around me, told me to go to bed, not to worry, Kody would show up in the morning, he said. "If it was my dog there'd be no problem," I replied, "but its Ruth's and the last thing this family needs is another death." When Paul got home and saw me pacing back and forth in the front hall, badmouthing the dog, he laughed, bundled himself in a green wool blanket and told me to go to bed, promised he'd find the dog. As I waited nervously in bed upstairs, flipping through Natalie Goldberg's *Writing down the Bones,* my mind ran riot with the worst-case scenario: Kody killed, run over by a truck, Ruth getting the news and cracking up. And then another drawn-out bereavement. So when the front door opened and I heard Paul's voice say, "I don't know what we're going to do, Dad," my heart sank. I heard him clumping up the stairs and a few seconds later my bedroom flew open and there he was, still wrapped in the green blanket, grinning as Kody yapped and hopped out. Now I knew how a condemned man must feel when he gets a last-minute reprieve. "Thank God," I sighed and, emotionally drained, fell back on my bed hoping at last to get a good night's sleep before the big corporate fraud trial tomorrow.

CR

WHEN I WAKENED THIS MORNING JUST BEFORE 6:00 A SOLITARY ROBIN WAS singing on the back lawn and as the windows filled with milky-blue light I could smell, almost taste, the greenness in the breeze. On the 401 the silver backs of the big rigs loomed ahead of me in the heavy slow traffic. Anxious drivers raced past only to stop a few yards ahead; why all this hustle when there's nowhere to go? And how many times have I not done it myself? Is there something in human nature that wants to leapfrog ahead, even when progress is illusory? Or are we all just wired and made jittery by the prospect of another dull day in a dull job in the city? Semi-darkness still clung to the eastern flank of the escarpment; hydro lines looped like strings of pearls through the dark greenwood and Kelso Hill appeared snow-bare except for a patch near the top. Everywhere the green grows bolder, shedding its shy spring look, and a bar of eye-scorching light burned on Kelso Lake. Last night I instinctively slept on my side of the bed, but I could still feel your presence-absence beside me. Your shadow clings to the walls of the house. At the cottage I'll lie in bed and listen to the pitter-patter of the rain on the new metal roof, normally a peaceful and soothing sound, but sometimes it will be like thunder hammering nails into my skull. Nicole's a beautiful and sensitive person, feels your presence, too, and tells me that if we ever decided to live together she'd want to change the furniture and start from scratch, a new beginning. Last Friday we saw the movie *Shirley Valentine* and you would have understood the message: that no one can postpone their life, the unlived life shrivels and embitters, comes back to haunt us. The challenge is how to live compassionately and yet be true to ourselves. Our efforts to love you back to life failed. You were trapped within yourself, inaccessible, paranoid, bent on a self-destruction we were powerless to stop. Unlike Jesus our human love wasn't strong enough to penetrate your private emotional hell and save you.

Last night I dreamt we were talking together in the kitchen of our house on College Street and you accused me of having a date with Nicole in Toronto. At first I felt guilty but then the bulb lit up: "But you're dead," I said. "You ditched me and the kids and have no right to complain" and began to feel resentful myself. The other day when Pat LeSage showed me a photo of a woman in a dark-blue shirt and paisley skirt at one of our judge's functions I got gooseflesh. "That's Mary," I cried, only to have Pat inform me it was someone else. Your presence-absence manifests itself in different ways with the children, too. Adele's hunger for reasons; Ruth's carping about my ignorance of practical needs (before she left for Ireland she phoned about health coverage: "Mom would have thought of that," she needled, and I had to assure her she was covered under my policy); Joy's mood swings, tears of anguish over your betrayal and my inability to fill your shoes, feelings always lurking beneath the surface of her beautiful smile; Marilyn's cheery bravado that hides deep caverns of sorrow; Paul, who loved you so much and thinks of you constantly, as he tries to master his own ghosts; and Mira in faraway

Thailand who couldn't get you out of her mind last Holy Week and fell into the doldrums: yes, your presence-absence shadows us all and you are very much alive.

CR

IN HIS JOURNALS THOMAS MERTON QUOTES RAINER MARIA RILKE IN "1st Duino Elegy": "Were you not forever distracted by expectation, as if everything were announcing to you some coming beloved?" Is this the genesis of the restiveness that Nicole discerns in me, claims I should have rooted out of my system years ago? That I'm faithful to her (as I was to you) doesn't count in her eyes. "It's not what you do, but what you think and feel," she says. The other evening at the Bookshelf Café cinema when two women, both strangers, sat next to us in our row she claimed she could feel my libidinous energy flowing away from her towards them. Nicole is super-sensitive and perceptive; I do not lightly discount her intuitions, which are often close to the mark. Am I distracted by the illusory expectation of some fulfillment? The coming of a beloved? Or is it the Beloved, the One of whom Augustine wrote in his Confessions, the One who alone can fill the empty spaces of my heart? And how much did my restiveness contribute to your own insecurity, I ask myself. Ah, the loneliness of life without God! Henry James said that a writer must become transparent, be willing to embarrass himself. These kaddishes mirror my character, flaws and contradictions, sometimes make me feel naked and vulnerable. But I believe they also contain sparks of truth and flashes of genuine feeling and I'm emboldened to continue. Is Nicole, who tries to see me through the clear lens of honesty (though she sometimes misinterprets what she sees), really an angel in disguise, beckoning me to look behind the mask, confront my inner demons? If I could view her arresting ideas in this light maybe I wouldn't react so defensively.

Lord give me the courage to accept myself as I am, warts and all, and not be discouraged by my mistakes, flaws and contradictions, trusting always in your grace, knowing that my weakness is your strength. Amen.

CR

AFTER LAST NIGHT'S RAIN WOODLAND GLEN GLISTENED THIS MORNING AND the air sparkled with freshness. The sky was pale grey and a mist blurred houses, trees, street lights. On the eastern horizon the sun floated into view, thin and papery, so insubstantial I would have missed it had my eyes not been peeled. Someone has said that a cynic is not merely one who reads bitter lessons from the past but one who is prematurely disappointed in the future. Every day in court I see life in the raw, litigants stripped to essentials, unadorned and naked, and it takes an effort to remain human. After a lifetime in the law I've grown skeptical and wary of language. Words can be argued one way, slanted another, depending on who's using them, moulded like putty for any agenda, no matter how unreasonable or false. Words can even cause wars. But too often in these kaddishes I've painted the hard face of the law and failed to mention some of the good things than happen in court. Like the acrimonious fight among siblings last week over a father's will, stoked by old grudges dating back to childhood, when the parties (at my urging, I'm glad to say) got together in a witness room and discussed their grievances. After much finger-wagging and copious tears they were finally able to let go of the past and reach a settlement. Courts exist not for lawyers or judges but the people, and on such days you leave the courtroom levitating on air, knowing you've helped someone. Traditionally the judiciary has been a bastion of male domination. The appointment of many competent women to the bench in recent years (you would have applauded the influx of feminine energy) has softened the stern face of the law and given it a more sensitive and compassionate dimension.

The other day one of my colleagues reminded me — I'd been letting off steam again about the rancour in family disputes — that it's only the hardcore cases that reach us, that 90 per cent of the disputes are settled more or less amicably without trial. I must recall her words next time I get too dejected about human nature. I don't want cynicism, the occupational hazard of judges, or your suicide to jade my outlook. Before I start a new case, particularly one involving custody of children, I'll often say a prayer, ask God to keep me sensitive and alert to the goodness of others — a next-to-impossible task sometimes; I have to constantly remind myself that people are greater and better than they appear in the distorted mirror of the courtroom. This morning I presided over the bail hearing of a young woman accused of trafficking in cocaine who requested that she be permitted to live with her mother until trial. She wore a white blouse with fancy lacework on the wide lapels with faded jeans and had straight black hair with a blond streak down the middle that fell all the way to her emaciated shoulders. I observed her sunken cheekbones and the way her lips parted as though her mouth was parched. Describing what it was like to stop drugs cold turkey she said, "You ache all over, even your bones ache and your insides feel scooped out." I felt sorry for her wasted life, but refused her request because I was almost positive she'd go back to her addiction (she admitted she still had a powerful attraction) and start selling again. Oddly, after I made my decision I thought I detected a look of relief on her face and the faces of her mother and dad. No noble thoughts here. The life of the junkie signifies hell and survival, nothing else.

Black and White

My old aunt hated drugs,
believed they would be the ruination
of youth, and wanted every drug
trafficker nailed to the cross.

At least that's the way she felt before
I took her to court that Monday morning
for the sentencing of an eighteen-year-
old who had pleaded guilty to selling hash
in the washroom of the high school.
"I'd lock him up and throw away
the key," she said.

But later when she saw the broken
faces of the mother and father
(he was an only child) and heard the boy
testify in a choking voice how he got
hooked (a pusher at the local pool hall had
introduced him to pot when he was fourteen),
that he had to sell to feed his coke
habit, and that he hated himself for all the
pain he had caused his mom and dad, she
changed her mind.

At the morning break, she came to my
chambers unannounced, jaw set,
and pleaded with me to give the boy a break.
"Remember, he's a victim too," she said, as
I ushered her out of the office.

CR

THE SKY WAS OVERCAST THIS MORNING, BUT BY THE TIME I REACHED THE 401
— I'd missed the Schneider sign, daydreaming again — the clouds had begun to
break up and pockets of brightness and blue peeped through the grey. For a
moment I had the illusion I was part of a Jack Chambers 401 landscape — how

uncannily life imitates art. Mornings for me always herald new beginnings. I waken to wonder, a deepening awe before the beauty of creation, what D.H. Lawrence called the sixth sense. Without it I am a dead man walking. Near Milton the grey clouds scattered even more and their purple underbellies looked frayed and freighted with rain. The sun briefly appeared over the escarpment to cast a shine on the asphalt and roofs of cars and trucks; instead of a blue mass the crowns of trees lit up like green lanterns. Last evening the forecaster predicted another rotten summer; Pinatuba – incomparably worse than Mount St. Helen's – has spewed millions of tons of volcanic ash into the stratosphere that continue to block the rays of the sun, reducing the mean world temperature by .5 per cent. How fragile our tiny planet! How precarious our hold on life!

After the barbecue on Sunday Adele mentioned the guilt we all experience over your suicide and it's true. She recounted a dream in which you fell headlong down an infinite staircase as she stood by, paralyzed, unable to help. One of my recurring frustrations is the inability of people to drop their masks and talk to each other heart to heart. We're technological giants but emotional pygmies. And then there's always the misunderstandings that arise from the use of that clumsy instrument, language. Sometimes we can't express in words what's deepest inside and even when we try our words betray us. While I'm still bedevilled by guilt over your death I'm determined to put an end to the "if only" monster; such a mentality assumes a power and control over life and death that we don't possess and is therefore a denial of our humanity. And an end, too, to my hand-wringing, so futile and wasteful, over the children and their future. The great truth I have to remind myself of again and again is that God loves us unconditionally as we are and that we have to learn to love not only others, but also ourselves, the hardest task of all. I pray every day for the grace to accept myself as I am.

Our marriage had sharply defined roles; I the breadwinner (Adele would say I held the reins of power), you the homemaker, but I'm not persuaded our relationship was essentially a power struggle. In hindsight, I wish I'd been less stereotypical as husband and father, pitched in more with the cooking, household chores, shopping and yes, even the yard work. But though our roles bifurcated too widely, sometimes when you and I made love our feelings and bodies melded and we sang together, however fleetingly, as one, almost as though the Creator had slipped between our skins to join us in the cosmic dance of the universe, and as the little deaths of our lovemaking floated us down a shining tunnel we were enfolded in the seamless garment of love.

CR

IN THE PARKING LOT OF THE CHURCH OF OUR LADY YESTERDAY I OBSERVED a young mother with a jovial expression on her face just like yours; she was dressed in a navy-blue suit, rose-coloured high heels, a white wide-brimmed hat with a rose band and was carrying a rose handbag. The sight of her three daughters in white dresses jostling round her just as our girls used to do with you made me nostalgic. The fog of grief still hangs over my life and shining experiences are a thing of the past.

Last evening Paul and I watched a documentary on the Nazi concentration camps; the scenes of corpses, all bone and skin, piled up like cordwood, turned my stomach. "Makes you disgusted with humanity," I said to Paul, but Paul made no reply. Sometimes I think I must be a covert atheist; though I want to believe, lately I've been struggling with the concept of a caring God and benign universe. And the institutional Church doesn't help. Pedophile priests, patriarchal hierarchy, anemic and uninspiring homilies, sexist attitudes, lack of community – the list goes on and on but I feel powerless to do anything about it. Sometimes I'm an erupting volcano inside and like the wife of Lot want to scream, "Curse God and die!" Father Peladeau told me that it was okay to be mad at God, that it's a desperate attempt to control the order of things, since God seems to have let us down, that even a certain amount of self-pity is natural and legitimate. If it wasn't for my faith in God, however battered, and my need to question life and wring some meaning from your death I wonder if I'd ever show up at church. Dietrich Bonhoeffer, theologian and martyr of the confessing church, whom the Nazis hanged from the gallows with piano wire at Flossenberg for plotting to assassinate Hitler, described Jesus as a man for others. You tried so courageously to be a good Christian, took a seamless garment approach to your pro-life activity, opposed both capital punishment and abortion, euthanasia, embraced the cause of AIDS, peace and social justice, etc., and in your personal life walked the talk, preparing meals and serving tables at the drop-in centre faithfully every Saturday morning. For the most part the clients were dignified and courteous, you said, but a few were rude and demanding, like the woman who told you to "fuck off" after you served her soup. Did you find meaning among these poor and often drug-ravaged faces? Or was your desire to serve others just a flight from your feelings of meaninglessness? Sometime I like to think that God called you home because you were too earnest for this sin-sore world.

Last evening *National Geographic* had a program about a remarkable exotic insect in Thailand (a distant cousin of the firefly) that emits a chemical glow in three rapid bursts every three seconds, as though all the insects were wired invisibly together; in the film the Thais gathered on the banks of a river to marvel at the million synchronized green lights blinking in the dark, a phenomenon that baffles scientists to this day. These natural mysteries dazzle my mind and make me realize how much more we have to learn about nature, including the greatest riddle of all – death. My beloved, these musings must appear puerile to you as you bask (as I want to believe) in the perpetual light of God's presence or whatever definition you prefer for God: "the one who is," "the beyond in the midst," "someone present in the quick of being," but it's all I have to offer. Man is born broken, wrote Eugene O'Neill; "he lives by mending; the grace of God is the glue."

Lord, pour out your glue on my brokenness, help me to accept what befalls me and give me the grace to live in peace and love. Amen.

CR

ALONG THE 401 THIS MORNING BIG RAINDROPS SPLATTER THE WINDSHIELD and as I approach Milton the Niagara Escarpment, a whale on the skyline, appears mauve. The trees are spokes of lime green, the first buds of spring breaking through the mauve, and the sky's blue finger pokes between the gaps. Only a few small patches of dirty snow remain on Kelso ski hill, and green is starting to cover the debris and deadfall of winter. I can almost smell the greenness. Green is the colour of hope, and goodness knows I need a greening of the heart. On the front page of the *Globe* this morning a young bride, features contorted with sorrow, stares at the casket of her husband, killed by a Serbian sniper. Your suicide beat the breath out of me – for a while I could barely walk, a stricken animal, curled up in pain, licking its wounds, totally useless. I spilt my guts out to Father Peladeau, the psychologist at the Jesuit College – what a spectacle I made, blubbering like an infant. Thank God he was accustomed to such scenes and had plenty of Kleenex handy. With the round kindly face of a Buddha, he sat in his electric wheelchair listening patiently as I tortured myself with regrets, babbled on about how much I missed you. I became acutely aware that life in a wheelchair isn't easy; every move has to be plotted with care. I'd enter his small cluttered book-lined study first and take a designated chair and then he'd laboriously manoeuvre the wheelchair so we could face one another other, a complicated piece of business. On the second visit he loaned me a copy of *As Bread Is Broken* – "the only copy I have," he said – a book about God's unconditional love for us, how that love envelops us like our skin and though I felt numb-dead our sessions together brought me a certain peace. He told me about his battle with muscular dystrophy, his brushes with death, his fondness for food, the theatre and sightseeing. He revealed that after your death he'd visited the Falls and spent two hours contemplating that wonder and praying for you. "I'm not afraid of death," he told me, a radiant look in his smiley blue eyes, and I believed him. We were becoming fast friends – even made a tentative date to dine together – when I learned in early autumn that he'd died of cardiac arrest.

Nineteen-ninety, your death year, was a year of many deaths. First, Uncle Tom of cancer – you and I paid him a farewell visit in Peterborough in May, remember; then after your suicide Alex and Anita, the children of our cottage friends, burned to death in a fiery crash on the 401 when a rig laden with steel rods crossed the median into their lane; next, my old Cursillo buddy Jim Redmond, sudden death on the golf course; Ed, my brother-in-law, another heart victim; then my bull-necked barber, Tony, to galloping cancer; finally, later in the fall, after two unsuccessful operations I had to have Belle, our dog of fourteen years, put down. Yes, it was a year of death and I reeled from gravesite to gravesite as though in a vast death camp, a reluctant witness to the passing of good people, wondering where God was in all this.

CR

WHAT DOES GOD MEAN WHEN A GOOD WOMAN COMMITS SUICIDE? THAT'S the question I've been wrestling with on and off since your death, but God stays mute and my question keeps echoing back from a dark wall. Oh, how the romantic in me would like to believe your suicide was a kind of gracious somersault into paradise – a gesture beyond our addled and flat ways of thinking, a clean and dazzling break with the world leaving family and friends both sorrowful and awestruck. Such a notion would be in keeping with your artistic soul – you never did things by halves – but it would still leave my question unanswered. All the logical answers put one in a double bind: either God is indifferent and cruel or there's no God and we're all adrift in total absurdity. Or a third possibility: God sees and cares, but for some inscrutable reason – respect for our free will? – elects to stay aloof. None of these scenarios appeal to the modern mind, which sees all suffering as wasteful and meaningless, a result of a cold and random universe. For non-believers,

C.S. Lewis's statement that suffering is "God's megaphone to rouse a deaf world" is errant nonsense. But despite doubts I still believe that the story of Good Friday and Easter Sunday, Jesus' death and resurrection, contains the seed of an answer. Belief for me is a verb, not something you have or don't have, and has more to do with relationships than head-over-heart intellectual assent or theological language. The Greek root for belief means "to give one's heart to," and it is often from in the crucible of the anguished heart that the seeds of love and faith take root. Victor Frankl, the psychotherapist, a prisoner at Auschwitz who found meaning in life through suffering, showed that even in the most brutal conditions we have a choice in our response to what comes our way. While I'm convinced God does not send us suffering – God is a label we too readily stick on our troubles – he allows it to happen as part of our human condition. He does not (barring a miracle) change the shattering events of our life but walks with us through our brokenness – Jesus participated fully in our humanity – to comfort, to help us rediscover hope, courage and direction in our lives, widening our hearts to become more human and compassionate people. In her book *Blessings*, Mary Craig writes, "Jesus's self-offering love is the only force strong enough to overcome death." So maybe I'm asking the wrong question; maybe the question is not why, but what next? How to tap into the fresh springs beneath the desert where we're marooned, not to wallow in self-pity and self-recriminations but make room in our lives for the widened heart. Anyway, you were beautiful in death as you were in life.

CR

MORNINGS ARE GETTING DARKER AND COOLER AND I CAN FEEL AUTUMN in my bones. When I left for court the sun was still hidden, my neighbour's locust a black silhouette against the lightening sky, the street lights in the subdivision just winking out. Off on the southern horizon a dark bank of cloud was expanding like a malign tumour into the rosy brightness and just before I pulled onto the Hanlon after getting my *Globe* and coffee I observed a blonde female jogger in rose tights and pink sweatshirt emerging from the darkness along the shoulder. On the 401 the Schneider sign said 7.04 and wished everyone a Happy Oktoberfest, and the sun appeared at last, a ragged fire casting an orange glow on the asphalt and vehicle. Last night I woke up with a jolt and realized I'd soon be 61, that my life was running out. I stood naked before the bedroom mirror and pinched myself to see if I was still alive. I scoured my body for signs of aging; yes, my light-brown hair is peppered with grey and thinning, the bags under my eyes hang like coins, and yes, the raw animal vigour of youth is gone, but my face seemed relatively intact: no grooves on the upper lips, no wrinkles to speak of around the eye sockets, jawline still visible and apart from a tiny roll around the midriff I wasn't in too bad shape. In fact, in my imagination I pictured myself as a young buck with many good years ahead. Is there a part of us, a separate existence that transcends bone and muscle, that wants to live forever? Yet the premonition of death was so strong I knew my feelings were wrong.

A few months after your suicide I read about Christiane Brusselmans, a renowned catechist, who took her own life in Belgium. She was about your age, a remarkable scholar and person of faith, known for her force and determination, who suffered for years from secret depression and a profound sense of failure. What does God mean when good people commit suicide? How little we know of the dense and mysterious circuitry of the mind. Her life had an uncanny parallel with yours and made me think of the shadow lurking in all of us, how easily the dark forces can overwhelm and smother our spirits. After court today I chatted with a lawyer I've known for a long time who told me that after years of faithful practice he no longer goes to church and has begun to doubt everything. This is causing trouble with his wife, a staunch Catholic, he said, who is also suffering because her two daughters have chosen to live common-law. I shared with him the story of your suicide and my own anger at God, but also how, whatever its origin, and God's sometimes intellectually indefensible ways faith still sustained me and permitted me to carry on in the face of hopeless feelings, how I wait on God each morning (not too patiently, alas) and ask him/her to see me through the day. Contemplating loss is always searing. Often it is only when some reversal or terrifying change yanks us out of the safe trenches of our lives that we are most open to God's grace. Your story is the one I've been given, not necessarily the one I would have chosen. These kaddishes are my prayers, unfolding bit by bit like evidence in court. The jury is still out.

Prayer

Help me to be always hopeful
    Gardener of the spirit
Who knows that without darkness
Nothing comes to birth
As without light
Nothing flowers
(Kali)

In Silence It Is Safe to Go

&

Sanctuary

There was a time in my life when I was always
planning escape. Tumultuous summer nights

I'd hide in the upstairs closet to lock out the
lust sounds, the argument sounds, the skeins

of blue smoke unravelling from below. Friday
evenings in winter I'd steal to the "Y" to watch

the free flicks, trudge home in oily jackboots
beneath the burning ice of stars. Sunday

afternoons I'd take my books and hide at Columbus
Hall down the street where every Saturday night

Del Crowe and his swinging Debonairs held sway,
try to concentrate amidst the whirl of ghostly

dancers swishing past my eyes, till shadows
bled and walls flared red with dying sun and the round

face of the clock above the bandstand hummed
in silence it was safe to go

CR

THESE KADDISHES ARE MIRRORS; A TIME MUST COME WHEN THEY TURN INTO
windows. I think this is happening slowly and that's why it's important I
continue to write even when I'm not in the mood. Last weekend I drove to

Peterborough with Nicole to see my old friend Patrick. Though he hasn't had
a drop since Thanksgiving, Patrick's down-at-heel and has lost 20 pounds.
The three of us drove to Jackson's Park, my favourite childhood haunt; it was
nippy, the sky was overcast and a few snowflakes fell. We sauntered along the
footpath beside the creek strewn with last year's orangey pine needles, past
the steep hill where I used to ski (once I couldn't stop, crossed the road at the
bottom and sailed into the icy creek, splintering both skis) to the old concrete
bridge where they dammed the creek for a swimming hole. The dam is gone
now, along with some of the limestone shelves along the shoreline where we
picnicked; otherwise, little has changed: the same amber creek burbles over
the slippery rocks, the same wind sings in the cedars. As I write this kaddish I
hold in my hand a black-and-white snapshot of Mom and me standing on a
flat rock, the swimming hole behind us thronged with kids. I'm a tow-headed
boy in a droopy bathing suit and Mom is wearing a white blouse and a long
tight skirt that makes her tummy protrude. Mom has a cross look, the same
disgruntled expression she always wore whenever someone took her picture,
and I'm shadowing my eyes with my hand, squinting at the camera, grinning,
no doubt proud of myself because I'd just convinced her that I knew how
to swim when all along I was paddling along the bottom, just pretending.
To my disgust I noticed that the sides of the logs and outcroppings were
frowsy with yellow scum; was the pollution always there, but veiled by the
lens of nostalgia? Below the bridge the creek spilled over a foot-high ledge – a
miniature waterfall that made me think of you and Niagara, and eerily there
were two pieces of driftwood in the configuration of a cross in the middle.
Since your suicide any waterfall, normally a delight for the eye, triggers painful
associations. After, we went to the big pond with the green pagoda where I
loved to net tadpoles and spear bullfrogs in the tall reeds at the shallow end.
A glaze of ice covered the surface of the pond with open water along the
edges, and a boy about twelve, a Blue Jays baseball cap perched on his head
backwards, was breaking off pieces and chucking them on the pond where
they shattered like panes of glass. At the pagoda Patrick and I looked for
our carved initials in the wood railings that might have marked our youthful

passage but found nothing. But some things didn't change: the smell of resin in the air, the breeze sighing through the cedar and pine boughs and the orange creek murmuring through the woods. "Listen to the music," Nicole exclaimed. Enfolded by bittersweet memories and the beauty of nature we locked arms and strolled back to the van.

Later that afternoon Nicole and I visited Simcoe Street. The historic Grand Trunk station on Bethune where we waited for Dad's homecoming after the war and Moldaver's scrapyard across the street, two landmarks of my childhood, have disappeared, as well as the York Trading block next to the tenement, and the old red-brick fire hall has been demolished to make room for the sprawling new city library. Ironically, the terrace where we'd eked out a pinched existence for years is now a nest of financial consultants dedicated to making your money grow, and its flaky brick façade has taken on a modern trendy look. Instead of our wood door with its two narrow vertical windows and brass mail slot there's now an impressive wide glass entrance. Gone, too, was the old woodshed at the back with its rusty tin roof that drummed in the rain and fired my imagination and the rickety board fence and scrawny solitary maple in the dirt yard I loved to climb – replaced by asphalt and a nondescript concrete block appendage. Downtown was different, too: George, the main street, had had a major facelift and the only way I recognized any of the old storefronts was to look up at the cornices, soffits and roofs. The Regent, New Centre and Capital theatres, which nourished so much of my fantasy life had vanished without a trace. The site of the Empress Hotel, where Dad and Mom worked for decades, had been converted into an uninspiring boxy edifice that serves as a retirement home, and the terrace on Water Street where they rented after they got married, a shopping mall. Only the nineteenth-century town hall with its four white clock faces and the Otonabee River remained unchanged. From the window of the Holiday Inn I watched the river flow past the cluster of small islands on the far side and under the CPR trestle bridge, moving slowly and majestically as though time were its ally. How few traces we leave. Even the stones and buildings we relied on for a sense of permanence have betrayed us; only the sluggish river under the dark grey November sky keeps its course. How circumscribed and miniscule, too, the trajectories of my parents' lives, walking everywhere (they never owned a car and had no need for public transportation), measuring out their days and dreams within the radius of a few city blocks. If their lifetime journeyings could ever be plotted on a screen what a crammed and confined world it would be.

After the war Dad brought home a large oil painting, a scene from the Rockies, which some journeyman artist had dashed off for the hotel bar. The bar was undergoing renovations and the new owners had decided it didn't suit the fresh decor. Dad hung it in the hallway upstairs next to my bedroom. I loved to trace my fingers over the hard dry ridges of paint, the details of snow-capped mountains, bark, cattails and lake, marvelling at the skill of the unknown artist. I was hungry for beauty and to my callow eyes that banal bar painting was a revelation, a touchstone of beauty revealing for the first time the transformative power of art – a glimpse of a more beautiful world, a window to the future.

ଔ

LAST NIGHT ANOTHER DREAM ABOUT DAD. I WAS IN A MOVIE THEATRE WITH my sister Marilyn watching a comedy and suddenly she said, "Look, there's Dad." And sure enough when I glanced at the big silver screen there he was, a little younger and slimmer than I remembered, but still recognizable – the same high cheekbones, disarming smile, small brown eyes and blustery "hail-fellow – well-met" manner, clearly one of the stars of the film. In a trice the scene shifted and we were at a post-film cast party when he swaggered in, his old cock-of-the-north self, and started ogling the women and holding forth on the art of acting, scarcely acknowledging the presence of me or my sister. I remember thinking how proud I was of him, that he was now a somebody, finally found his niche in life; but later when I realized that it couldn't be, that he'd died in 1968, I was profoundly disappointed. In another dream a week or so ago a judge friend introduced me to his father, a successful businessman with silver close-cropped hair who looked almost as young as my friend. They bantered like buddies, laughed at each other's jokes, and the affection between them was almost palpable. Observing their rapport made me realize, with a stab of envy, what I'd missed by the absence of a father-son relationship and the shame I'd felt over our shabby tenement and my parents' addiction to alcohol. I remember when anyone offered to drive me home I'd invariably ask to be dropped off a block from the house, citing the same lame excuse every time that I just remembered I had to meet someone or run an errand. And before our marriage don't you recall my nervousness over your first visit to meet my family – I rented a room for you up the street at the YWCA, afraid that you'd be repelled by the gimcrack furniture, the worn linoleum, and the tasteless pictures and decor, not to mention my greatest fear of all, the drinking. I needn't have worried: you were as charming and outgoing as ever and if anything bothered you, you didn't show it. Thanks to you, too (and my growing confidence) I was able to gradually overcome my false shame and accept my family as they were, flaws and virtues alike.

Depression is widespread – the common cold of psychiatry, someone described it – a place of helplessness and hopelessness, and given the trauma Dad must have experienced being shipped to a strange country at thirteen to shift for himself alone, I wonder today if his romance with the bottle wasn't an attempt to escape its clutches. Mom had always dreamed of owning a decent home and when I was articled in Peterborough I finally convinced her the time had come to leave Simcoe Street forever. One day, househunting together, we found what we thought the perfect place: a large apartment near the downtown with central heating, burnished hardwood floors and a lovely mahogany fireplace surmounted by a bevelled mirror; when the landlord offered it to us at an affordable rent we were beside ourselves with joy. After shaking hands on the deal we reluctantly accepted his offer to drive us home (it was pouring), and just as we coasted to a stop at the front door of the tenement Dad hoved into view from the fire hall lane, a bottle of rye in the crook of his arm, lurched up the sidewalk, and after much mumbling and fumbling, unlocked the front door and let himself in. We sat in the car, frozen, mute with embarrassment. We weren't in the house fifteen minutes before the phone rang. It was the landlord. "I'm terribly sorry," he said, "but when I got home my wife reminded me that I'd already committed the apartment to someone else." After apologizing again for the misunderstanding he hung up. Mom's pale stricken face said it all: another dream crumbled into dust. Drink has been the Achilles heel of many a good person, like the lawyer who was once the town's leading advocate, who frequently dropped by the house to pass the time and quaff a few. He was the tall, regal-looking man I told you about who once set me on his knee and predicted I'd become a lawyer someday, just like him. Years later Mom read in the *Star* that the police found his semi-naked body in a rooming house in a Cabbagetown flop house, dead two weeks, an empty bottle of Four Aces, a cheap red wine, on the bed beside him. These kaddishes attempt to say the unsayable, fill the losses and voids of my life by drawing from deep wells of yearning and regrets, and yet Dad refuses to lie down, stay buried, which leads me to ask myself: Have I spent my whole life looking for love and validation, especially from men? Reflecting on Dad's life after all these years I grieve not only the absence of a father but the good man inside who rarely came out, buried himself inside the yawning silence of the house and left no key or clue for me to find his hiding place.

The Casual Intimacy of Strangers

My bluff, blarney-tongued dreamer of a father
hustles all day at the old Empress, greeting
travellers at the revolving glass doors with his
winsome grin and hearty handshake, totes
baggage up the curving oak staircase to the
darkly varnished rooms, cracking wise and
trotting out the latest jokes along the way;
"a good fella" the chuckling salesmen say,

basking in his fluent bonhomie, always
pleasant and keen to please. "He'll even fetch
bootleg beer to ease their tedium," Mom says.

Yet we've hardly spoken for months. As I grow
older our worlds rift far between us, as though
I never cross the essential topography of his life.
Sometimes I wonder what it would be like to meet
him for the first time, a stranger, feel the clasp
of his hand in mine, hear him say just once:
"If there's anything you need, just ask."

☞

BEFORE YOUR MEMORIAL SERVICE I STRUGGLED TO PEN A FEW REMARKS,
which I intended to read at the service, but as the day approached I realized
my grief was too strong, I was too distraught to even read what I'd written,
and so I asked our good friend Gord Kelly, who knew and loved you, to speak
for me.

Dear friends:

For our wonderful children, Adele, Paul, Marilyn,
Mira, Ruth and Joy and for myself I thank you for your
presence at this memorial Mass for our beloved Mary. I
speak today, not the language of law, but the language
of love. Believe me when I tell you that our spirits have
been lifted high on the sea of your prayers, and the
love of God has been poured forth into our hearts to
overflowing. How can we thank adequately the many

compassionate and competent hands that have reached out in love to touch and heal us.

How sad, but how true, that often we see the love of God more clearly through tears than in sunlight. Yes, we are joined together in sorrow, but most of all we are joined together to celebrate the life of a uniquely beautiful person. For it is how we live, not how we die, that is important.

Though she cared little for gold, Mary was one of life's true millionaires. Though she shunned status, Mary was clothed in the rich robes of a child of God. Though she was a stranger to power, Mary possessed the gift of touching hearts. St. John tells us that God is love and that he who loves is begotten of God and knows God. Our beloved thought of others constantly; our beloved gave to others unstintingly; our beloved cared for others daily.

Sadly, she came to believe that her existence on this earth was hurtful to me and the children and thus her death on Passion Sunday became a sacrifice for others. Because she loved greatly, Mary knew God and now shines forever in his light. How fitting to celebrate her passage this Easter Monday, the day of the empty tomb.

It may seem unfair that death, always so rude and unexpected, should claim the best and most beautiful among us. To this mystery there is no human answer. But Jesus showed us that love is stronger than death. And Scripture tells us:

Many waters cannot quench love
Neither can floods drown it.

I see now clearly that God was mysteriously leading our beloved in ways deeper than the deepest ocean.

My dear friends, I believe that the road that stretches before each of us is a challenge to our hearts, long before it tests the strength of our legs.

Our destiny is to run to the edge of the world and beyond, off into the darkness:

assured for all our blindness,

secure for all our helplessness,

strong for all our weakness,

gaily in love for the pressure on our hearts.

Our beloved leapt into the arms of that Tremendous Lover who pursues each of us with unerring steps to lead us into living waters. How appropriate the words from the book of Solomon:

The voice of my beloved:

behold he comes,

leaping upon the mountains,

bounding over the hills.

My beloved is like a gazelle,

or a young stag.

Behold, there he stands

behind the wall

gazing at the windows

looking through the lattice.

My beloved speaks and says to me,

arise my love, my fair one,

and come away,

for lo, the winter is past,

the rain is over and gone,

the flowers appear on the earth,

the time of singing has come
and the voice of the turtle dove
is heard in the land.

Yes, we are joined together in sorrow but most of
all we are joined together in gratitude and thanksgiving
for the gift of a life fully lived. Mary, good mother, may
your life teach us to be tender and caring; Mary, my
bride, my friend, my heart, pray for us and watch over
us so that we too may go forth with renewed hearts, to
build a more human and loving world.

Cushioned by loving family and friends and touched by the grace of
God our spirits were indeed lifted high. We had yet to feel the full hammer's
weight of your absence.

ℂℤ

SOMEONE DESCRIBED SUICIDE AS RAGE TURNED INWARD. YESTERDAY THE *Star*
carried the story of a young woman from Ajax – I'm looking at her lovely
smile as I write – whose body was found at Niagara near the dock of the *Maid
of the Mist* a few hours after the police had discovered her abandoned car in a
hotel parking lot. She'd told her family she was going shopping and intended
to pick up some Chinese food for supper and watch TV that evening. How
complex and fragile we are! Do you remember the middle-aged woman I
once defended, accused of stealing Nivea cream from a drugstore? Married
to a successful doctor and well known for her charitable work (you knew
and liked her for her warm, hospitable heart), she had no logical explanation
for her act. According to the police she never used the product and had lots

of money in her purse. "I just saw the jar on the shelf and slipped it into my handbag," she confessed. "People like her unconsciously signal distress, loneliness or lack of love in their lives," the psychiatrist testified. "Shoplifting is often a cry for help." Do you remember how sad you were when I related the story? "She must have been terribly lonely," you said and began to cry. How many cries for help did we miss?

Jung uses alchemy, the medieval quest to turn base metals into gold, as a metaphor for the transformation of the human heart. How do we transmute the base metal of suffering – loss, disappointment, pierced heart, death, etc., into gold? Your suicide pried me loose from my ordinary complacent self and threw me into a new place that commanded my unblinking attention, not a comfort zone but just the opposite: a scary and unfamiliar place of pain and self-doubt. It shattered the walls of my egoism, helped let in light, began to stitch me back into the fabric of life. I understand more fully what the Buddha meant by the first of the four-fold truths – that life is suffering – and the awareness of that truth has given me the freedom to reach out to others. The choice is stark: like Jung's alchemist we can change our suffering into gold or let it sink us in the swamp of self-pity. These kaddishes give me the solitude and quiet to hear the soft whisperings of the Spirit, help me to make sense of the alphabet of my life that swirls around the cold hard rock of your suicide.

> "Praise, praise," I croak. "Praise God for all that's holy, cold and dark. Praise him for all we lose, for all the river of the years bears off. Praise him for stillness in the wake of pain. Praise him for emptiness. And as you race to spill into the sea praise him for dying and the peace of death."
>
> *Godric*, Frederick Buechner

CR

WHAT MADE YOUR SUICIDE SO DISTURBING AND HARD TO ACCEPT WAS YOUR belief in the sanctity of life. You hated war with a passion, could justly be described as a pacifist. You were a strong advocate for the weak and disabled, for a fairer distribution of global wealth. All your life you opposed abortion and the death penalty equally, an opposition rooted in Christian teaching about the sanctity of all life, born or unborn. You also had a personal reason for opposing abortion. While you admired your birth mother for her courage in giving you the gift of life it distressed you to think that had she been living in our present culture of "free choice" you might never have been born. When Jesus entered the world, the gospel tells us, God affirmed Him as his beloved child. The passage down the birth canal into life is traumatic, but the trauma is soon forgotten in the tender, caring and welcoming arms of the mother. No such loving arms awaited you. You were never swaddled, nursed, sung to by your mother who from the moment you were born rejected you, refused to hold or even see you. You never heard those beautiful words: "Welcome to the universe, you are my beloved daughter." Was your suicide, I wonder, connected in some obscure way with this lack of original blessing? We live in the centre of a hurtsome universe, and who at some time or another hasn't yearned for the comfort of absence or non-being? Clearly, suicide presents itself as a perfect remedy for all pain – physical, spiritual, psychological – at least to the person intending to take their own life. And yet while depression and pain may make suicide understandable, even forgivable, there is still something ingrained in us that says life is God's to give and God's to take away and when nature's order is disrupted our sense of timing is offended, for as Thomas Lynch says we equate nature's intentions with God's intentions and would prefer to let nature take its course. I draw solace from my conviction that suicide is a cancer of the mind and that the pain of mental or physical illness can destroy hope. I believe that you lived the last days of your life in a spiritual and mental coma, that you reached the stage where there was nothing left: no trees, no flowers,

no stars, no moon, no sun, only total darkness and the fatalistic conviction
that you were a millstone around the neck of others, especially those closest to
you and from that perspective the taking of your own life was your last brave
act of the heart.

Lost Feather

Remember that August morning at the lake,
the sparrow on the deck knocked silly
by the windowpane,
a brown fluff
unable to fly or walk,

how the children found the shoebox,
tore up strips of newspaper for a bed,
and you, who always taught
Jesus never forgets his smallest ones,
placed the lost feather at its side;
"Every feather counted," you said.

Then loyal to family lore
you fed the bird a drop of whisky.
"He'll fly again."

And next morning the sparrow
had raised his bones and fled,
resurrected.

Then what went wrong my darling wife
that Palm Sunday afternoon?
Did he not offer you a drop
before you fell?

CR

TODAY I SUMMONED ENOUGH COURAGE TO TAKE DOWN FROM THE SHELF
in our closet and open the cardboard box crammed with the hundreds of
Mass cards, cards, letters of condolence and other tributes we got in the days
following your suicide and riffle through them. Here's a random sampling:

"I always enjoyed Mary's company and she always made
me feel very comfortable and at ease."

An acquaintance

"In my mind, I see a lively, smiling happy woman who
had a life of love, laughter and joy."

A friend

"I always respected Mrs. Clarke. She was always a hero to
me. Always helping and caring… She inspired me to do
a little volunteer work at the drop-in centre…"

A young friend

"I always found her so easy to talk to. With some people
you find an instant rapport and for me she was one of
these."

An agnostic friend

"I thought of Mary with her contagious laugh, her big
feet and cigarettes with lipstick on the butts. She lived
life to the fullest…"

Another young friend

"It's very hard to believe I won't hear Mary's laughter or
discuss ideas and thoughts again... She was closer to me
and knew more about me than my own sister..."

Another agnostic friend

Many, both friends and acquaintances, used the same expression, that
"she was one of my favourite people." Several women said they considered
you their best friend, a couple of whom I knew you only befriended out of
kindness.

"We are left with the memory of a beautiful, caring
person, full of life, who gave her everything..."

A friend

"I myself many times reached the point of desperately
wanting death... But I suspect that her choice was, at the
deepest level, a radical choice for life... something in her
must have rejected whatever hell she was facing and she
turned away from it towards something else."

A young friend

"Mary had many gifts: her love, her faith, her hospitality,
and her concern for others... I'm grateful for the privilege
of my visit with her that last week at the hospital. It was
a time of laugher and friendship..."

A priest friend

"I can't get it out of my mind that Mary was at the foot
of my bed and I was basking in her sunshine only two
weeks ago. I always basked in her light whenever I was in her
presence... She leaves an awful void in a great many lives."

*A close friend we visited in the hospital two weeks before your
death*

And here's a note I wrote to myself at the time.

> "Some impress with their physical beauty, others with
> their power and talent. Mary wasn't a recognized talent or
> famous; nor did she have power or money. But what she
> had in abundance was humanity, an empathy for others
> and her big-hearted soul. She was a good person, a giver,
> someone who lived mostly for others. We remember
> her ready smile, infectious laughter, her feelings for the
> underdog, her devotion to her children and God and her
> simplicity of heart. She may not have been a saint in the
> canonical sense, but she had the wide heart of a saint.
> She saw through the glass clearly, perhaps too clearly."

These are some of the images and voices that emerge, the face you showed
the world reflected back in scores of cards, letters and tributes. Nowhere
do the sirens that lured you to your doom appear. Was it because you, the
peerless actor, hid them so well? Or was everyone, especially those closest to
you, just too blind? Or both?

CR

I'M ENCOURAGED BY HENRI NOUWEN'S WORDS THAT WE MUST TRUST OUR
stories, believe that they deserve to be told and that the better we tell them
the better we will want to live them. Merton said it was his vocation to
remain a witness to the nobility of the private person, its primacy over the
group. I disagree with those who say religion's a cop-out, a form of denial.
While religion may be a refuge for some people afraid of going to hell, I
cling to the old adage that spirituality is for people who have already been
there. Each of us must create our own spiritual map. Rembrandt painted

63 self-portraits – not to save model fees, but to savour the spiritual within himself, plumb his own soul. In revisiting the same themes in these kaddishes, circling round the jagged rock of your suicide, little by little I'm learning to understand not so much the "why" but, as Nouwen put it, to "stand under" the grief, hold it without being in control. And more and more Blake's words that we were put on earth "for a little space that we may learn to bear the beams of love" strikes a chord. We may never adequately understand or define love, but as Gerald May wrote, we are meant to live into life's meaning. Like Michelangelo's sculpture *The Awakening Storm*, which shows a body struggling to emerge from stone, I want to break free from my prison of fear, find the sunlit uplands of wholeness and love. Trapeze artists are not afraid to let go, brave the emptiness of space, trust that someone will be there to catch them. By embracing my shadow side and befriending your death (and all our deaths) I'm slowly learning to face fear and take back my life. We can choose the terminal, snuff out life and spirit, or we can name our deaths, grieve them and let them give us back a blessing. After the tooth and tomb of winter can spring be far off?

Spring Thaw

It has been
a long, hard winter.
The iron lake
is still dreaming

the rumble
of unpacking snow,
the whips
of cracking ice,
tickling water
in the sun.

Silver eyes
open blueward.
The lake is waking up,
elephants are walking.

ॐ

IN ONE OF HIS JOURNALS MERTON DESCRIBES A "DOUBLE BLOOM ON ONE large violet iris" standing out of the green spears of the daylilies outside the door of his hermitage, and how on the tongue of one bloom walked a great black-gold bee, "the largest honeybee I ever saw." His journals are full of such lovingly observed vignettes and I resonate with his gift of rejoicing in the richness of nature, the hidden music of creation, which he found brought him closer to peace and the real root of his existence than all the consolations of *eros*. I believe we loved each other truly madly deeply but I also believe we were created for infinite love and in a different way I've grown to love Nicole. Yet in all relationships how often we deceive ourselves and our loved ones, keep our unacknowledged needs hidden from sight, not only lest we hurt each other but also in the mistaken belief that our nakedness would be too much for them to bear. Hence evasion and denial, strategies I adopted in childhood to keep the harsh world of Simcoe Street at bay and to cover my feelings of abandonment, separation and loss. Nicole is right when she reminds me (as she often does) that Simcoe Street is history and my evasions have outlived their usefulness. And Merton is not far off the mark either when he writes about the difficulty, even the need, for heroism, to keep going "in truth" in a relationship. Who were the demonic voices that lured you to sunder our marriage, the ones you couldn't talk about, that drove you to the Falls? It seems Merton and I have much in common, at least on the level of frailties. How do we look reality in the eye, find the gate of heaven? Can it be done without the grace of God, without the angel of mercy leaning over us?

Last evening Paul and I chatted briefly on the phone about his struggles with the Black Dog. Though harrowing at times, he now sees them as blessings.

"I've learned a lot, Dad," he told me. "They've deepened my understanding of life."

"You mean they've made you more empathetic and compassionate?" I asked.

"Yes, that, and I no longer sweat the small stuff," he said. "My priorities are better."

I admire our son. Suffering had changed him for the better, made him thoughtful and wiser. I'm convinced grace often disguises itself as loss, depression or sudden reversal accompanied by a feeling of aridity that sometimes makes us change our priorities, drop the mirror of narcissism and turn to God. Is there a lesson for the rest of us here? Perhaps in a painful roundabout way your suicide will become the gateway for all our growth.

Undercoat

My son, the teacher, who's helping me paint
the four Victorian-style screen doors I

bought for the cottage, knows my habits better
than myself, spreads papers on the deck where

I'll be working, tells me to leave spindles, gingerbread, the wood around the knobs for him.

"And don't load up your brush," he says. "Remember
less is more." We divide the paint (premium quality

primer — "the best always lasts") and go about our separate
tasks but, not before he chides me to slow down.

"Life's too short," he says. I watch him kneeling by
the bunkie door below, Bach's "Magnificat"

on the radio; he doesn't slap on paint like me; his
strokes are soft and sure, caress the wood; occasionally

he stops, inspects his work, retouches – the epitome
of mindfulness. "Painting's a form of meditation,"

he loves to say. Afterwards he looks at my flecked
face and skin, shows me his clean hands and grins.

ℤ

HAD A REVELATORY DREAM LAST NIGHT. I WAS IN A BIG CITY FOR AN IMPORTANT
meeting at the bank – it was critical to be on time – but during an unguarded
moment thieves stole my van. I spotted a bright orange Volkswagen parked
nearby, keys still in the ignition, and in desperation took it, intending to
return the car after I'd finished my business. But when I entered the bank the
manager confronted me, demanded to know why I'd stolen the Volkswagen.
I started to explain, but he abruptly cut me off. "You're an intelligent man,
Mr. Clarke," he said, looking me sternly in the eye. "You must know it was
wrong." To my dismay he told me he'd have to phone the police. Suddenly
the falsity of my rationalization hit home and I knew I was guilty. What a
struggle to disentangle illusion and reality, resist the evasions of the outer
man. So much to learn, so much unfinished ripening!

Remember in France how saddened we were when we read of Thomas
Merton's accidental death by electrocution in Bangkok on December 10,
1968? You loved his books, considered him a spiritual mentor. Lately, I've
been rereading his work and am struck by our common preoccupations. We

share the zeitgeist of our times — the search for the father. The motherless Merton loved his father Owen, an artist whose bohemian life was punctuated with uprootings and departures. Merton didn't want to share Owen with anyone, especially Evelyn Scott, his father's lover. While his dad pursued his artistic career and personal agenda, Merton was often left in the hands of caregivers, which partially explains his abiding sense of abandonment and lifelong quest for the lost childhood, the "paradisal ground of being," as he called it. He knew little of his father's nomadic life, painted an idealized portrait of him. I, too, hunger to know more of the man I call father. After your death I obtained his military records from the National Archives and often caught myself scanning the contents, trying to catch a glimpse of him, poring over inconsequential details like his English hospital records (after his evacuation from Normandy), dwelling on such details as his sleepless nights, complaints of pain, the various treatments he received, the times he was AWOL, his request to be demoted to private, his superior's notations of his "robust physique, good judgment and leadership" qualities as though these impersonal clinical jottings done in the insanity of war contained the key to the inner man. I even discovered he had brown eyes, not blue as I'd always imagined. Why was this minutiae so important to me? What was I searching for? The other preoccupation Merton and I share is the nature of love. There's nothing like an old fool and after your death my quest for consolation and love led me into the arms of Nicole — fortunately for me, a good person. Merton concludes that the real meaning of love resides in the discovery of the absolute goodness of the loved one, that one only loves when the beloved becomes of absolute value for us. The operations of love, by contrast, sometimes draw a veil over this goodness; the beloved is seen as a desirable object and one begins to love desire instead of the beloved. When I first met you I was smitten by your beauty and goodness, but desire didn't lag far behind, and it took years to move from the blindness of *eros* to commitment, to see you not solely as an object of desire but as someone walking around shining as the sun, an angel in disguise. Perhaps Merton is right: the Beloved is Wisdom itself, the eternal Mother, not someone to be deflowered and exploited, but a warm voice beckoning us to the deeper wisdom of love and joy and communion, a re-entry into the oceanic unity of the womb. And only the wakeful hear that voice. Yes, darling, God has laid his hand on my heart so long immured in ice and I'm still searching for the "hidden wholeness" that I believe you now enjoy in plenitude, the holy longing of the wise.

> ... She gave him a weightless kiss
> through the waiting-room glass
>   and said:
> "Each night I die
>   but it is not
>   goodbye.
> Ice is only rain yielding life again."

Barry Callaghan
"Hogg, The Seven Last Words"

Epilogue: Learning to Love

❦

In the years since Mary's suicide, whenever my old partner and friend Ron Mitchell asked me if I wanted to look at the police file, I always demurred, claimed I wasn't ready. When I finally mustered the courage and read the statement of one of the eyewitnesses — how he observed Mary put her right hand on the rail of the retaining wall, climb up on the ledge with camera in her right hand, drop her shoulder purse to the ground, and then, holding her nose, jump into the river and float backwards towards the Falls, staring at him and appearing very calm, eyes open, blank expression, no struggle or cries, before going over the rim — I was overwhelmed; the old scars were ripped open, and I was left gasping for breath.

Rereading this journal I also noticed that several times I mentioned that my bereavement journey would never be complete until I had gone to the place where she'd chosen to end her life. In May 2004 I finally made the trip.

I retraced her steps, stood with her on the observation platform in Queen Victoria Park before the hypnotic force of the Niagara River, heard the thunder of the cataract, felt the ground quake beneath my feet and tried to blot from my mind all the harrowing images I'd found in the police file.

The sight of the foamy rapids rushing at 32 kilometres per hour over the crest line of the Horseshoe Falls and spilling 600,000 imperial gallons of water per second into the dolomite limestone gorge 173 feet below held me spellbound, filled me with fear and trembling. Amidst the happy and carefree faces of honeymooners and sightseers from many countries I was unable to staunch the flow of tears. I slumped on a bench, bowed my head and prayed.

Not for Mary alone did I pray (I reckoned she didn't need my prayers) but for myself, our children, our friends and countless millions on this troubled planet who each day confront pain and tragedy. I prayed for God's grace and Mary's help so that I could continue my own pilgrimage in peace and love. In the fourteen years since her death I have passed through many trials and my life has been changed forever. But to say I've found closure would be untrue. Though time has softened the sharp edge of pain I now realize that the heart coils around the staff of joy and grief and that our loss will be with us till our last breath. I've concluded that closure is not what it's all about. Our wounds are openings for God's grace.

Surrounded by the white-capped rapids, hearing the muffled roar of the Falls and observing the wheeling mists in the gorge below that sunny spring afternoon I remembered what Mary told me that last week in hospital when the Black Dog howled in her mind. "Remember," she said, clasping my hand, "you've been a good husband and a good father. Never forget it."

She was preparing me for the time when I would stand alone before the children, mouth stopped with grief, heart swollen, the "if"s twisting like a dull blade. And when I glanced up from my bench and saw an immense rainbow arching over the gorge, it was as though someone had tossed a bridge between the living and the dead and her voice again spoke to me:

"I forgive you, husband, father," the voice was saying, "and when you look at the beautiful dark water of my death, forgive me too and learn to love the face you see."

CR

Dream

She waited on the dock for the ferry
to the outer isles, a man beside her —

companion or lover I couldn't say —
with long wise mien, and as sea

roiled and licked its green tongue at
dark clouds I felt fearful

— such a rough and perilous crossing —
till I observed the tender way

he gazed at her, the radiance on
her seamless face, as though

skin, eyes, brimmed with inner light,
a hidden sun, and then I knew

she had returned to her beginnings,
the sun-warmed place of giving and

receiving, and was cherished as she'd
always deserved to be, more

than I could ever love, and all
my sadness turned to joy.

℞

Poetry collections by James Clarke

Silver Mercies (1997)
The Raggedy Parade (1998)
The Ancient Pedigree of Plums (1999)
The Way Everyone Is Inside (2000)
Flying Home Through the Dark (2001)
How to Bribe a Judge (2002)
Forced Passage (2005)

Available through your local bookstore
or through Exile Editions
20 Dale Avenue
Toronto, ON
M4W 1K4
Phone: (416) 969-8877
Fax: (416) 969-9556